TAKE my HAND

by

Audrey Revell

© Copyright 2006 Audrey Revell.
All rights reserved. No part of this publication may be reproduced, stored in a retrieval system, or transmitted, in any form or by any means, electronic, mechanical, photocopying, recording, or otherwise, without the written prior permission of the author.

Note for Librarians: A cataloguing record for this book is available from Library and Archives Canada at www.collectionscanada.ca/amicus/index-e.html
ISBN 1-4120-9410-0

Printed in Victoria, BC, Canada. Printed on paper with minimum 30% recycled fibre.
Trafford's print shop runs on "green energy" from solar, wind and other environmentally-friendly power sources.

Offices in Canada, USA, Ireland and UK

Book sales for North America and international:
Trafford Publishing, 6E–2333 Government St.,
Victoria, BC V8T 4P4 CANADA
phone 250 383 6864 (toll-free 1 888 232 4444)
fax 250 383 6804; email to orders@trafford.com

Book sales in Europe:
Trafford Publishing (UK) Limited, 9 Park End Street, 2nd Floor
Oxford, UK OX1 1HH UNITED KINGDOM
phone 44 (0)1865 722 113 (local rate 0845 230 9601)
facsimile 44 (0)1865 722 868; info.uk@trafford.com

Order online at:
trafford.com/06-1164

10 9 8 7 6 5 4 3

Foreword – Take My Hand
by
Baroness Nicky Chapman – House of Lords - 2005.

****

This book is the story of a disabled person and her family on the journey of life.

The story is of how Jan copes with an ever changing condition and how her family support and encourage her towards independence.

Real life struggles between parents and child are retold in such a clear way; you feel you are there as the events unfold.

Almost inevitably, there are clashes of Jan's needs meeting bureaucratic walls. The lack of medical understanding of her underlying condition, added to the whole family's frustration and distress.

This is a book of humour, sadness, pain, joy, compassion and frustration.

Read it with a box of tissues at your side.

The most beautiful things in the world cannot be seen or touched. They must be felt with the heart.

Helen Keller.

Introduction

This is a book that simply has to be read.

It is the story of a mother's deep love for her child against the harrowing background of a lifetime of struggle against growing disability.

It is a moving story of joy and of family warmth, and of bright achievement tarnished by the coldness and failures of dreary and inefficient bureaucracy.

It is a tale that highlights the shining examples set by caring volunteers, in stark contrast to the paid functionaries of grey, faceless and dismissive authority.

Above all, this book is a searing indictment of a system in which closing ranks is more important than establishing the truth, and in which the concerns of those who are subject to the system are treated with arrogant dismissiveness.

In Take My Hand, Audrey Revell paints a vivid and moving picture of the life and indomitable spirit of her daughter Janis, an exceptionally talented musician and composer despite having lost her sight as a child and progressive deafness. Enduring and overcoming all the difficulties and disappointments of a lifelong fight against the rare and incurable disease Retinitis Pigmentosa, Janis achieved both independence and motherhood in her own right before being tragically sentenced to an ugly, premature death by the insensitivity and overbearing high-handedness of doctors who just would not listen.

This is a true story of love, dedication, shining devotion and black betrayal by the system.

Read it, be moved, and resolve that nothing like this must ever happen again.

Dedications

I dedicate this book to my darling daughter. Your life was not in vain. You taught me something new every day. You were an inspiration to many people. I thank you for all the love, joy, music and laughter that you shared with me through the years. Your rare spirit was only lent but it will never be spent. You showed so much courage in those thirty-four years. Thank you my darling.

To my dear husband who encouraged me when the going got almost too much in writing this book, and to Andrew who withstood so much without complaint over the years, thank you both for your love.

To special friends and family who had no idea how particularly important their love and concern was throughout the whole ordeal. A very special thank you goes to Jackie Hicks of Deafblind UK who came alongside to help me and who put in so much work for the enquiries and managed to cope with my distress during some of the most difficult times. The band of helpers at SENSE who gave so much selfless support throughout.

To those who offered their abilities and knowledge to help Jan to attain so much.

My unswerving love for my very special friend, Ann, who was my Paraclete when I was so desperately low in spirit.

And finally dear Holly. What a gem your mummy left us. I love you so much.
Audrey Revell

CHAPTER ONE

Lunch was over. My husband John and son Andy joined me in the lounge to relax. Spring sunshine streamed through the windows. Appetising smells of roast meat and vegetables hung in the air in the way that is peculiar to Sundays. I needed to relax and gather some strength for our visit to see our daughter, who was in hospital, the next day.

We settled into our chairs but were quickly brought back to alertness by the piercing sound of the phone at John's side. We had been in constant touch with the hospital but this seemed different. John's face became ashen. As he listened, he signalled to us to get our coats. Janis, our daughter, had taken a turn for the worse and the doctor said that we should go to the hospital immediately.

John asked Andrew to dash and ask a neighbour if she could look after our dog, Cluffy. Andy charged out of the house and down the drive, pulling his jacket around his well-built frame as he went. I soon had on my coat and pushed into some shoes left untidily on the floor under the coat-rack. I waited anxiously for John to explain more. He muttered something about 2 hours and replaced the receiver. John tugged his jacket down from the hook. He looked grey and worried. We made straight for the car.

Andy headed back up the drive and fell into his seat panting for breath. We pulled the seat belts around us as John drove off.

The roads were extraordinarily quiet. John drove like never before at almost 100 miles an hour. The journey usually took around 2 hours and we had no time to waste.

We travelled for almost an hour in silence, each of us lost in our thoughts. My mind was trying desperately to deny what was happening, and yet the thought of the finality of the previous months had to be listened to and accepted. Tentatively I raised the subject of organ donation should Janis die. John's reply was immediate.

'No, they are not going to cut her up, she's had too much done to her already. Don't even think about it.'

His hands gripped the wheel, knuckles white from the pressure. We reverted into silence. It was some time before Andy, who had sat quietly behind us, said, 'Dad, Mum is right. Something positive has to come from all of this. I think that should she not pull through then her organs will help others.' John did not reply, and we all remained in silence for the rest of the journey.

The hospital's large car park looked very different at this time of day on a Sunday. It was a late afternoon in May, with a hint of darkness already descending upon us. We hurriedly undid our belts and peeled ourselves from the seats, and made our way towards the huge entrance of this university hospital. John and Andrew were soon ahead of me.

The huge doors at the hospital entrance banged open to each side and the forbidding corridor stretched ahead unfamiliarly quiet. The immense heat and eerie silence of the interior beckoned.

The men were now some way ahead, but my lungs were failing to support my need of oxygen. I gasped in an attempt to draw in more air. I was suddenly without strength and grabbed at the handrail along the corridor wall in an attempt to pull myself along. I tried to call out to John to wait. It was as though I was in a bad dream, my mouth went through the motions but no sound came out. Then, John glanced over his shoulder and called to Andy to come back and help. They stood either side of me taking an arm each as they pulled me along.

The lift lurched into action. I stared at the graffiti-marked doors. The sudden jolt to a halt jarred my body. We all pressed speedily ahead along another corridor, but I still had difficulty keeping up with the others as I was gasping for breath. The eerie silence of the corridors was occasionally broken by distant voices, a clanging bin or squeaking trolley, but we met no one before reaching the ward where Jan had been.

John took me to the sister's office. On this day everything seemed so different and the silence added to the strangeness. The office was empty. John helped me onto a seat, telling me to wait while he went to find out what was happening. I began to shake. My heart was thumping. 'She'll be alright,' I thought. 'She has always been a fighter. She'll do this, I know she will.' But I could not persuade my anxious body at all.

John's face was drained of any colour when he came back into the office alone. 'I think she has gone. Her bed is stripped and the mattress is propped up against the wall.' My body now lost control and shook violently just as the ward sister bustled into the office in a very positive and confident manner.

'Hello, I've just come from upstairs. They've taken Janis up to the Intensive Care Unit. They are preparing to put her onto life support. The doctor will be here with you shortly to explain.' Her voice, although businesslike, was gentle and sympathetic. My tears could not be held back any longer. John asked her, 'Is it possible that you could fetch my wife a cup of tea – make it very sweet, please.' John was always one for caring about me before himself.

'Of course, no problem. Would you all like a cup?' The men nodded and I thanked her. She turned and disappeared down the short corridor. Not one of us spoke. I remained seated and John and Andy stood expectantly waiting for the doctor to arrive.

Our tea arrived all nicely set out on a tray. Cups and saucers, a pot of tea with a milk jug and sugar bowl. It added to my apprehension. 'This isn't the normal way of things,' I thought. Usually we grabbed a drink from the drink machine, in those awful plastic cups that cause great difficulty when they contain hot fluids.

My heart was now banging so hard that it was causing my head to throb painfully. 'At least she is still alive,' I thought, still trying to convince myself that all would be well.

The sister put the tray down and insisted on pouring us each a cup. Her efficient manner gave me a surge of confidence, and the hot sweet tea restored my physical strength a little. I now felt a little more ready for what lay ahead.

I placed the cup and saucer onto the tray just as the doctor rushed across the hallway and into the room. He was an elderly doctor, grey haired and very slimly built. His face was grim as he began, 'I'm very sorry, but your daughter is very ill. We've taken her up to the Intensive Care Unit where she's being sedated so that she can be helped with her breathing. She'll be given a paralysing drug so that the necessary tubes and breathing apparatus can be put into place. She'll be deeply unconscious.' He hesitated before going on. 'I'm afraid there's not much hope. I have to go back up now. When you're ready, sister will take you up.' He turned, and looking at the floor he disappeared in a rush, his crumpled white coat flapping behind him.

I got to my feet. John looked so ill, and Andy was out of the door anxiously ready to see his sister.

The sister brushed past us saying, 'I think it best if I lead the way.' She pressed the button. It seemed an age as we anxiously stood waiting for the lift descend. Then the doors banged open and we all poured in. No one spoke. The atmosphere was tense. There was a sudden lurch as we ascended to the ICU floor. As we stepped out into yet another long and silent corridor I was gripped by the utmost fear, my breath coming in violent spurts. I grabbed John's arm as we followed the sister. Her starched apron swung from side to side across her navy dress and I was aware of the squeak of her rubber-soled shoes on the highly polished tiled floor. Her head was held high and her auburn hair fastened into a neat bun under her cap. Her whole demeanour gave an air of professionalism and confidence that she had everything under control.

We turned into another corridor, and there ahead of us was a huge sign, 'INTENSIVE CARE UNIT. PLEASE WAIT HERE AND RING THE BELL FOR ATTENTION.' The sister stopped and turned to face us. 'Please wait in that room. You'll find some tea and coffee. I must go in and see whether they're ready for you yet,' and turning briskly she went on her way.

We opened the door of the waiting room that bore a brass plate with VISITORS inscribed on it. We entered. I was instantly aware of the shabbiness. There were low green leather seats pushed together into a long row. Some of them were torn. Discarded plastic cups littered the top of the small wooden coffee table in the middle of the room. Well-used magazines lay alongside. In the corner was a small table with a coffee maker and kettle and all the necessary items for drinks. On the windowsill there stood a potted plant that was dusty and wilting from the heat and needing water. A man and a woman sat forward on their seats, their heads hanging over their knees staring at the grubby floor. They glanced up as we entered but quickly returned their stare to the floor. The silence and dismal room added to my apprehension. We were to know every detail of this room in the coming days. We stood, waiting. No one uttered a word.

It seemed an age before the door opened and the sister addressed us. 'They're almost ready for you. I must go now but the sister from ICU will be with you in a moment.' She turned and was gone, and the door slowly returned to its original position.

Another long wait before the door opened again and a tall fair-haired sister called our name. 'Would you like to follow me?'

We followed as she confidently walked to the big black rubber doors. 'Please take a seat there,' she said. Her voice showed no emotion. She pointed to a row of leather-buttoned settee type seats. Her efficient manner prompted us to immediately sit down as she stood in front of us. It is strange, in retrospect, how we automatically do as we are instructed at times like this.

'They've almost finished connecting Janis to the life support system. Have you ever been into an ICU before?' We all muttered 'no'. She continued without pausing for our answers.

'Before we enter we must bathe our hands in the liquid from this dispenser.' She touched the unit at the side of the entrance door and went on, 'It's an alcohol solution, which quickly dries. You must remember to do it every time you go in and when you come out. Now, when you go to see Janis she will be deeply unconscious. There will be many tubes and the machine will be breathing for her. But you can touch her and speak to her as you would normally do; in fact we encourage you to do that.'

I was filled with dread again. We were left alone after she turned to say that she would now go and check to see whether they had finished attending to Jan. She pushed through the ungainly doors. None of us uttered a word.

I stared at the doors as they flapped and finally found their balance and became still once more. The centre of them had been worn a dismal grey with the constant touching of busy hands. People came and went and the doors flapped back and forth. If only doors could talk, what tales these ones could tell. There was a squeaking sound. It was from the wheels of a trolley being pushed by a porter. There was a huge machine placed on the top. He did not move his head but stared straight ahead and pushed on with the job in hand. The trolley banged into the doors and they parted, flying either side of his trolley allowing him to enter, and then flapped clumsily back again.

The sister had returned.

'Right we're ready now. Follow me.' She stopped at the liquid dispenser and watched as we went through the action of cleansing our hands. The liquid was cool and fresh. The action of actually doing something brought slight relief. We followed as her eyes beckoned us forward.

The rubber doors were pushed open. The scene ahead was awesome. Green-covered beds against the navy and light blue uniforms contrasting with white aprons, all the more enhanced by the bright lights shining onto each bed. It seemed so vibrant after the dimness of the corridor. It took me completely by surprise.

We began walking past the beds supporting gravely ill people who in turn were supported by an array of apparatus and machines. The silence was deafening and only emphasised the seriousness of the situation. There were at least two nurses attending each patient, confidently carrying out their medical tasks in such a businesslike manner. Each bed had a workstation at its side, upon which was a very large upright drawing type board with chalk messages dashed across. I later learnt that every detail was recorded – as each medication was administered or action was taken it was doubly entered both here and in the patient's medical record. There was a vast array of dishes, bottles, tubes phials and syringes. An amalgam of equipment. Above each bed were monitors bleeping and pulsating forth their messages. There was so much activity as the nurses watched, injected, marked and monitored and yet everything was so very quiet. Everything I observed intensified the seriousness of what was happening. It was as if it was a really bad nightmare from which I could not waken. We passed a bed in which there was a young man, his head heavily bandaged, and across the front of this was written 'No bone here'. My stomach lurched.

Then we were at Jan's side. I was overcome when I saw our lovely girl with all the tubes and wires coming from her neck, her hands, and from under the covers to a bottle on the floor. She looked so peaceful. Her beautiful face was now plump and her cheeks flushed as though she had been freshly made up. In fact she now looked healthier that she had for many months. I moved towards her. The sister spoke in a very soft tone

'Don't be afraid. You can touch her, you won't cause any problems.' I bent to kiss Jan's face, conscious of the many tubes around her. Her pink tongue was protruding from under the mouthpiece of the breathing apparatus. I wondered whether it was pinched. I kissed her hot flushed cheek. My tears could wait no longer as they coursed down my face and dropped to the floor. I wanted the strength of my love to rouse her to be strong enough, to be powerful enough to bring fresh life into her, to heal and make better. Surely that was my role?

The nurse at the station placed her hand on my shoulder saying, 'It's all been too much for you. But the next 24/48 hours will be crucial. She has pneumonia and we're doing tests to see what antibiotic she should have.' She spoke with such confidence that my heart rose in hope. Pneumonia was no problem these days, especially for someone aged just thirty-four? She would fight this; this was nothing for Jan after what she had been through. The nurses carried out their tasks in a very efficient and confident manner, and even though Jan was deeply unconscious they spoke to her as though she was fully awake, describing just what they were about to do and for what reason. She was treated with the utmost dignity.

. My heart was filled with sorrow and love for Jan, willing her to fight to overcome another obstacle. Then, as I glanced around the ward, dimly lit except for the lamps brightly shining at each patient's bedside station, there was this volume of caring that hit me with such force. I stood in awe: the vision, the colours of the room, the monitors giving out their information and the care of so many dedicated people. Hardly a sound was made. I had read somewhere that in the midst of great sorrow can be profound joy. Tears continued to roll down my cheeks, and I realised I was in the midst of such an experience. Words are inadequate to relay that fleeting moment, a moment that I wanted to hold, to clasp to my heart and to be able to experience whenever I recalled it. As I type this the experience still fills me with some wonder, but no matter; I cannot relive the essence of it in all its power. It was gone and I was drawn back to the awfulness of Jan's situation.

One of the nurses told us that another nurse had been passing Jan's room, in the medical ward, when she noticed how deathly pale she was. She went in and saw that Jan had stopped breathing, and alerted other staff. Jan had then begun breathing on her own. The male nurse in charge of Jan had rung the clinic where she had been a patient for ten months and asked them whether she had ever done this before. He said that the reply was that she had, but she did it on purpose. He was shocked, but this was nothing unusual for us as we had asked them about Jan's facial grimacing long ago and they had said that she was just grinding her teeth. Very often they had told us that Jan was refusing to eat, get up, or try to do things for herself.

Jan's husband, Nick, was out when we had left Peterborough. We had quickly rung his home, but without success. We were anxious to get him immediately, so I now rang our neighbour to tell her what was happening and that we would not be going home but staying at the hospital for as long as we were needed. She told me not to worry about anything and said that she would keep trying Nick's number. We continued to walk back and forth from Jan to the phone. It was about 9 p.m. when, eventually, Nick answered the phone. As I relayed to him what was happening he said that as soon as he had taken Holly, their little girl, to his mother's he would make his way to us.

The hospital now seemed even quieter as the night's darkness wrapped itself around the place. The air hung heavy with overbearing heat. There seemed not an ounce of oxygen to refresh. Outside, the streets were hushed. It was almost midnight as we paced the corridor waiting for Nick's arrival, occasionally going into the waiting room for a coffee or back to Jan, taking turns with Andrew as we had been asked that only two people should be at the bedside at one time. Andrew did not utter one word, but spent a great deal of time with his sister.

An elderly couple was now standing in the corridor, huddled together against a window looking out into the night. There was a quiet sobbing coming from the woman. Her husband had his arm around her. I wanted to know, to ask, but purely from a selfish standpoint. I wanted for them to assure me that all would be well and not to worry, that the people on this ward were miracle workers. To tell me that their tears were tears of joy at hearing that their loved one was getting better. However, we passed by in silence. As we returned, they turned to speak with us. It was their grandson who was very ill. He was the one who had the bandage across his head. They told us he had been skateboarding down a hill and crashed into a concrete post. His brain had swelled so much that they had taken bone away to avoid possible brain damage. 'We're too old for trauma of this kind,' they murmured. I replied something about 'I know and I am so sorry,' and we moved on.

Nick arrived breathless. His face so white, his eyes red from the strain of driving through the night at great speed. 'What's happened?' he gasped. I went through all that we had been told. He sobbed and I tried to comfort him. He had been visiting regularly over the past 10 months but this was just too much. When he had recovered a little I asked him if he was ready to go in to see Jan. I showed him the procedures of hand cleansing and then we went on into the ward. He stood one side of Jan and I the other, each lost in the overwhelming helplessness that engulfed us. We did not speak. He bent and kissed her forehead, and then again, saying, 'This one is from Holly.' Jan's baby was just three years of age. More tears fell from my eyes.

After about 30 minutes we returned to John and Andy to find that a friend had arrived. John had contacted him owing to the hospital accommodation being full. He had come straight across to let us know that the SENSE house had been made available for us. This was close to the hospital and we could stay for as long as we wanted. We knew the house as we had been staying there during Jan's long illness.

Nick and Andy had to be at work the next day. The nurse in charge of Jan had said that the next 24/48 would be crucial as to whether she would recover. I told Andy and Nick that I would keep in touch with them and let them know of any change. Eventually they went back home.

John and I returned again to Jan's side. The staff nurse suggested that we went home and got some sleep. It was now 1.30 a.m. We kissed Jan and very reluctantly walked out of the hospital.

CHAPTER TWO

The streets of this large city were silent. The night sky's blackness wrapped the earth into slumber and muffled its sounds. Traffic lights still flashed their routine colours, and streetlights glowed with a hazy orange halo. It increased the heaviness of my mood. We drove to the house, the silence broken only by the crunch of the car tyres on the gravel drive.

John immediately went into the kitchen and put the kettle on for some tea. I looked over the place, deciding where we would sleep, and then went into the bathroom. No thought process was in operation. An automatic response to unusual circumstances had kicked into play. It was as though I was going through some sort of ritual. I dropped my crumpled clothes to the floor and walked under the hot water of the shower, holding my face up to the water. It painfully pelted against my skin, but it felt good and my heart pleaded for it to wash everything away, all the dreadfulness of the previous hours, days, weeks and months.

Pulling on my clothes I went back downstairs to join John. He was sitting on the settee sipping his hot tea. He did not look up but muttered, 'Tea here for you.' I sat at his side and took the hot cup to my lips and held it there, hoping that the heat would stir me into some sort of emotional response. I sipped. It was benign in its effect.

We made our way into the strange bedroom. Fortunately we had twin beds. I say fortunately because of the fact that I tossed and turned and sleep eluded me. Thoughts tumbled through my mind like unruly children rushing for attention, demanding to be heard, taken notice of, yet all I wanted was for them to be quiet and go away and leave me alone. They disobeyed and continued in their torment.

I am not sure whether sleep came upon me. If it did it was not deep. I tried to find some position that would ease my tense body. There was a hint of daylight, and I could hear the odd car going by, intruding into the night's silence. The stirrings of another week. It was impossible to rest and my tormented mind would not ease. I got up and made another pot of tea that I did not want. I took a cup in to John, who was already up and in the shower.

It was very early, about 5 a.m. I think. Was it too early to ring the hospital? The hesitation went as quickly as it came; I desperately needed to make contact in some way with Jan and so I punched the numbers into action, the pulsing bleep down the wires annoying to my ears. I was put through to the ICU and the sister in charge answered.

'She's the same. We haven't managed to bring her temperature down as yet, but it's still early and the next 36 hours will tell.' I thanked her and said we would be over after breakfast. She replied, 'That will be fine, and do come in at any time.' I clumsily replaced the receiver and sat staring at it in a fixed daze. I felt numb, my body and mind exhausted by the months of anguish and now this critical turn of events.

John came into the lounge. It was a comfortable house tucked away from any others and very quiet. Peaceful, in fact. It was a space for us to come and take refuge. We were so grateful for the use of it. Everything was in place for us, we needed nothing except some clothes, and John, in his usual caring manner, was immediately taking action to deal with the problem.

'I'll go back today. We need some clothes, and I need to see about Cluffy and make other arrangements. Will you be OK? Take a taxi to the hospital or ring someone to take you in?'

'Of course,' I replied. 'But promise me that you'll take great care, your mind is all over the place so your concentration….'

'I'll be OK, don't you worry,' he interjected. 'Just you look after yourself and I'll be back as soon as I can.'

John left without having anything to eat. His face was pained and drawn. His large, six-foot frame now bent. My heart went out to him, I wanted to hold him to me and to try and soothe his pains. He was only months away from undergoing a 5-way heart by-pass operation and I was so concerned for him too. We kissed and hugged, then I waved him off. Half of myself left with him. The house seemed uncomfortably quiet. I tried the TV and sat watching the screen and yet saw nothing as my mind insisted on having its own way.

The morning traffic had become loud and aggressive. It was 8.30 a.m., and the world had reverted to its daily rush. Dashing, hooting cars taking people to earn, to get, to achieve. We were not of that world; we had been thrust into another which was alien and frightening, which held no form or routine for us. Thrown in at the deep end of things yet again and frantically trying to learn how to swim without instructions. We had to learn. This crisis would take all of our strength and fortitude. We had to do whatever was within us to deal with the enormity of it. We had overcome so much in the past in a world that was alien to most people, and we had done a good job I like to think. But this was now a matter of life and death. We meet it extremely rarely, and even less so when it is the life of one's child.

My friend arrived. It was about 10 a.m. She drove me to the hospital. The journey seemed to take so long and it appeared strange to me that Elaine could talk of other things when my entire mind wanted to think about Jan exclusively. I can only guess that she was being kind in attempting to divert my thoughts onto the normal trivia of life. I could not go there. It seemed so frivolous at a time like this. My heart was heavy and my mood low.

How different everything was now as we pulled into the car park. It was crowded. People were rushing about. Ambulances flooded the entrance of the hospital. Ambulance staff were busy lifting and helping their patients. We made our way into the foyer and the bustle was potent. It was almost too much to see all of this lively activity taking place. My child was unconscious, fighting for her life, and I could not entertain any other thoughts. Could anyone see my pain? Every time anyone looked my way it was as though they knew, they sympathised. It was too much and I wanted the doors of the lift to close quickly and scurry me away.

We lurched to a halt and the lift yanked open its doors to reveal the same dismal quiet corridor of the night before. The overhead lights still flickering even though it was broad daylight, and the heat seemed more intense. It was just as quiet and foreboding. We made our way to the ugly black rubber doors and I rang the bell and waited. Quite quickly we were allowed to go in.

Jan had been bed bathed. Her pink tongue was now in a different position and she looked as beautiful as ever. Her cheeks were still flushed with the loveliest bloom. I kissed her and cried. I took her hand and gently spoke to her, telling her how lovely she was and how I missed her and loved her so much. I begged again for her to get well. Then I pressed her hand to my face.

The nurse at her side told me that Jan's temperature was still very high. They had taken a swab from her lungs, for culturing. Now she was receiving large doses of the right antibiotic to deal with the problem. The nurse asked me whether I would like to oil Jan's body.

'Yes please!' I shot back my response and took the bottle of lotion from her as she lifted back the sheets covering Jan's legs. I poured the oil onto my hands and gently began massaging it into Jan's skin. Her body was so hot. I began at her knees and gradually caressed my way down to her feet, where I stopped and looked hard at her uniquely shaped toes. I knew them, every one; they were etched in my heart from the moment she was born. 'She doesn't take after me with my size eights,' the thought came, but was quickly replaced as others came rushing in and I was suddenly transported back to when she was a small baby.

CHAPTER THREE

There was pandemonium around my bed. I had been in labour for far too long and was exhausted. I badly wanted John to be with me, but in those days fathers were not allowed anywhere near delivery rooms.

I had toxaemia, and the doctor had decided to induce the birth slightly early. Very quickly I was in labour, and the pains had been intense for many hours. A very young nurse kept asking me whether I was ready to push. She would leave me for twenty minutes or more, and then come in asking why I wasn't pushing – I was having strong contractions but no desire to push. The nurse's persistent questioning about me not pushing yet soon caused me to wonder whether I should have started pushing a long while ago. I really thought that I was doing something wrong, and so when she came in again I obliged her questioning by saying that I'd push. I pushed for several hours without result, and I knew that concern was growing. Finally I was told to hold my breath and push like never before with the nurses excitedly saying, 'It's coming, she's doing it!' Yet, as I gasped to fill my lungs with air the baby went back inside. The baby was stuck, and the experience was beyond description.

The morning staff had arrived. The senior of the nurses called to the other. They stood with their heads together muttering in the corner of the room and then the senior nurse picked up the phone to ring for someone.

There was a sudden activity and tension in the room, the end of my bed was dropped and two huge poles erected that had straps attached. There was no explanation. Not a word was spoken. I was just too worn out to comprehend what was going on and too tired to ask, I guess. The nurses were lifting my legs up and strapping them to the poles. A doctor arrived dressed in hospital green cap, gown and wellington boots. He was carrying a bucket with instruments in, which he placed at the side of my bed. Although I was exhausted, my mind was desperately trying to grasp all that was happening and I suddenly realised what the instruments were.

I gasped, 'You're not using those on my baby.'

The doctor continued to pull on his rubber gloves saying, 'It's a case of losing your baby or losing your life, or both, if I don't use them.'

I had no choice, and under the instruction that when I had another pain I must push for all I could I obediently did my best. I had to for my child. It seemed there was no time to waste. The pain was horrendous as the doctor inserted the forceps and pulled; I thought my whole inside would come out as my flesh tore. My baby was at last out into the world. As I gasped for breath I heard her cry. It was all over at last, and there was Janis Lorraine, a most beautiful baby weighing in at 7 lbs 4 oz on 17th December 1964.

My pain evaporated as I looked down at the most beautiful face. I was filled with elation that this baby was mine. The love I felt was like nothing I had ever experienced before. It seemed that it was a miracle that we had both survived. I unfolded the cotton sheet they had wrapped around her before placing her in my arms. The doctor was at the foot of my bed repairing the damage. The pain was now forgotten. I looked hard and long at this miracle and caressed her tiny toes. They were just beautiful. Then her fingers and her tiny button nose. She was perfect, with no marks from her traumatic entry into our world. This long-awaited baby, whom we had wanted for over eight years, was finally here.

I was told that she would have to go to a ward for 'at risk' babies. Immediately I asked what was wrong with her, but was assured that it was only a safety precaution owing to her traumatic birth. They would keep a special eye on her for the next two days. Within a short while I was told that Janis was A1 in every way.

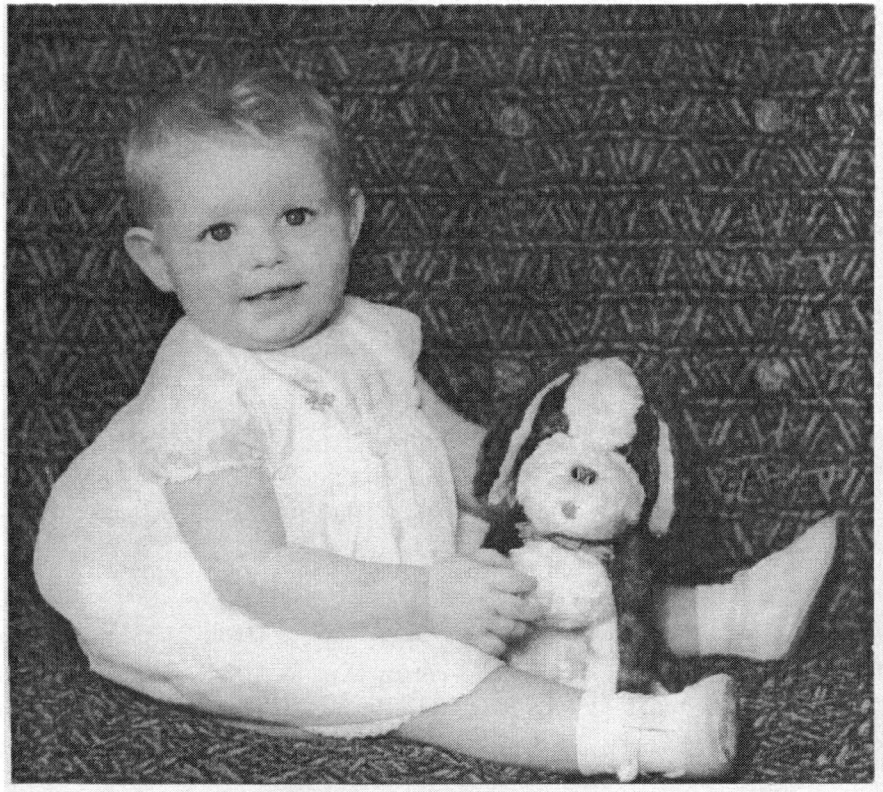

Everyone commented upon what a beautiful baby Janis was, especially her lovely eyes. They were deep set and almost violet in colour, and her dark eyelashes swept almost to her eyebrows. I was so proud of her. She just seemed the absolute perfectly beautiful child. I was on cloud nine and our life was now to change forever. I had no idea that those eyes had anything wrong with them. They were so clear and seeing.

As the months passed, I became aware that Janis was not seeing properly. She did not seem to focus as quickly as I thought she should.

She was such a bright child and spoke many words at ten months old and walked too. However, when she began walking properly I was even more aware that there was something wrong with her sight. She missed steps and tripped, or when going towards a step would tumble down. At first, I thought she was just a clumsy child. Her language quickly developed. She would call out for me not seeing that I was at her side. This was a frequent occurrence. On one occasion she was sitting to the side of me and shouted my name: 'Mummy where are you?' I thought that she needed spectacles.

From the age of six months until she was two years of age I took her several times to our doctor's surgery. Each time I was told that I was worrying unnecessarily and to go home and enjoy my baby. The doctor added that I would cause my baby to become as neurotic as I was if I kept on in this way.

It was when she was about two years of age that I realised that my suspicions were right. She had had some nastier falls and she was very easily startled. I also became more aware of her calling me when I was in the same room. Yet, on other occasions she could follow an insect like an ant with her finger and giggle at the joy of doing so. It was a bemusing situation, to say the least.

During a family reunion at our home, a nephew had been playing ball with her. When he got home he asked my sister Edna, 'Does Audrey realise that Janis can't see properly? I have a mate at university who has a rare syndrome and he has tunnel vision. He can only see directly ahead and I think Jan is the same.' As Edna relayed this to me, over the phone, my heart was racing. I dropped the phone and immediately made my way to see the doctor yet again.

The grubby waiting room was full and stuffy. You didn't have to make an appointment, you just turned up and you had to try to remember who was before you. Often arguments broke out over who should go in next. It was quite some time before I went in with fast-beating heart. I needed to muster up enough courage to get a referral to the eye hospital. The doctor glanced over the top of his half glasses and picked up his pen in readiness to write a prescription before I had uttered a word. Before I reached my seat I blurted out that I wanted to see a specialist and tried to explain why. He belched a huge sigh as he picked up a small red double-decked toy bus. Janis of course, glanced as she heard him and followed the sound of the bus as he pushed it back and forth. Her eyes followed to and fro several times.

'There you are, there is nothing wrong with your baby.'

I was furious and my response took even me by surprise.

'I am not moving from this seat until you give me a letter to see an eye specialist. If I have to I shall sit here 'til the cleaners arrive. I will! I really will!' My voice was now raised and high pitched.

The doctor's eyes widened with sudden surprise. Shock and disbelief poured over his face. I had always been rather timid and shy. He pulled out a drawer and extracted a form, which he quickly scribbled something on and passed to me, saying, 'Fill that in and send it off, goodbye.'

I snatched at the paper and picked Jan up in my arms and walked out with relief. Perhaps at last I could get Jan the spectacles she needed.

Janis was almost two and a half when the appointment arrived. John wished us well, as he left for his job. Neither of us suspected that there was anything seriously wrong. We agreed that he would meet up with us at my brother's home after work. We were having a large family reunion that day.

Edna had offered to come with me to the hospital, and her husband, Andy, was taking us in his car. I was not unduly worried and Jan was her usual happy contented self.

It was a rather daunting picture that met us as we entered the eye department of The Coventry & Warwickshire Hospital. The weather outside was very overcast, wet and dismal, and it seemed to carry over into the large waiting room. There were already many people waiting, sitting in wet coats, some with umbrellas at their side. Most of the people were elderly. What air there was in the room was damp and stale. The windows streamed with condensation. There were not enough seats and so we stood for a while. Jan was quite happy and made no fuss. Quite quickly, a seat became vacant, and after a short wait we were called into a small room. I was asked to place Jan onto my lap facing a screen. Objects were shown and she had to say what they were.

'That's just fine,' said the nurse, finalising her chart and placing it in the folder. 'Now, if you would follow me.'

I picked Jan up into my arms and carried her through the corridor still packed with waiting people. I was asked to sit and wait. The lady next to me said how beautiful my child was. I thanked her and felt so proud. I had given Jan a tube of Smarties I had brought to occupy her. She dipped her little fingers into the tube and extracted them one at a time, raising them to her face to see what colour the sweet was. Then, putting it to my face she would tell me the colour and wait for me to confirm whether she had it right before popping it into her mouth. The wait seemed so long before we were called.

The nurse in the room explained that Jan had to have some drops put into her eyes and that they would sting. She went on to explain that these would enlarge the pupil so that the doctor could see to the back of her eyes. Jan complied with all that had to be done without a tear or struggle. This attitude was to stand her in good stead for the road that lay ahead.

We were told to go and sit outside another door until yet another nurse ushered us in. There was this lady doctor in a white coat. Glancing up from the medical notes in front of her, she asked me what I had noticed to cause my concern. When I had finished telling her, she picked up her ophthalmoscope and began peering into Jan's eyes, asking first for her to look to the right then left, up and then down. She placed the instrument back onto her desk and excitedly said, 'I won't be a moment, just wait there.' She flew out of the room, her loose white coat billowing up into the air behind her.

After a short while she reappeared, followed by three or four other white-coated doctors, turning her head to talk to them as she came towards us. She did not address me but continued in an excited way to discuss Jan with the other doctors, in medical terms of which I had no knowledge.

She continued, 'Look it's incredible. How does she do that?' referring to Jan tipping her remaining Smarties onto the table and picking them up one by one and putting them back into the tube. I remained seated with Jan on my lap but was becoming increasingly worried when I heard "Sunshine Home" and "albinoism" mentioned. They were the only words I could understand, and they alarmed me. I knew that Jan was no way an albino, but Sunshine Homes ran a shiver of fear through my tense body. I was now becoming very annoyed as they continued to talk between themselves and over my head. The loudness of my voice seemed to reverberate as I asked, 'Would somebody please tell me what is going on here?'

The female doctor turned to me and quite calmly said that Janis was going blind. She just burst forth with her diagnosis. Then, obviously seeing the shock on my face she tried to explain that Jan had a very rare eye condition called Retinitis Pigmentosa and that she had it in a very advanced form. She then blurted out that most probably Jan would be completely blind by the age of seven, and that a decision had to be made as to whether she should go into a Sunshine Home for Blind Babies.

I screamed, 'No! Never! No-one is going to take my baby from me!' and picking her up onto my shoulder I almost ran from the room. The doctor handed me a card to take to the reception and said to make an appointment for six months' time.

Edna had been sitting in the waiting room. She jumped to her feet and looked anxiously up at my tear stained face, then at Jan and back to me. She began to ask questions, but I dashed out of the room and into a corridor. Seeing the ladies' toilet I made a beeline for a place to hide to take stock and maybe gather my thoughts. Jan, sensing my distress, was pushing hard against my chest as she tried to gain some space between us to see my face. Edna followed asking, 'Whatever is the matter? Here, let me hold her for you.'

I screamed back, 'No! No one is ever going to take her from me. She's mine. They want to put her in a home.'

'You must be mistaken, you've got things all wrong,' she answered.

'No, I have not. They say it's a rare eye disease and she's going blind,' I sobbed.

'Oh, Audrey, you may have heard wrong, and anyway nowadays they can do wonders.' Edna's face was shocked and ashen at the news.

I managed to control my sobs and we made our way to the reception. The young woman said, 'Can I help you?' as the tears poured down my cheeks again.

I sobbed, 'My baby has Retinitis Pigmentosa and she's going blind.'

I wanted the receptionist to reassure me, to tell me I had made a mistake, but her reaction was one of control and getting the business done as she asked for my appointment card. 'When do you have to come again?' she asked.

'Six months,' I sobbed, still scanning her face for some recognition of the seriousness of the situation. There was none. She just quite calmly handed the card back to me and turned to get on with other work.

We made our way to the car park where Edna's husband waited. I got into the rear seat with Jan. She was still poking down the Smarty tube for the last of her sweets. Edna told Andy what I had been told and we all lapsed into a pregnant silence as we made our way to my brother's house. My head felt as though it would burst. The last thing I wanted was to be amongst a crowd of people, but there was no way out. I rested against the seat, my mind unable to comprehend what I had been told.

As we turned into the drive my heart began pounding. My face was red raw from crying. Jan was so anxious to get out to see her aunts, uncles and cousins, and she was out of the car and into the house like a shot. Who would think that there was anything at all wrong with her as she ran into the house?

The family was gathered in the lounge. How could I face all of them? I took a deep breath as I hung up my coat and called Jan so that I could take off her hat and coat too. She ran to me excitedly, pulling her arms out of the coat and trying to tug at her hat chord at the same time. I slipped into the room. My brother Frank looked up and immediately asked how we had got on. I had no control over my emotions as more tears cursed down my face and my body shook from the sobs that I couldn't hold back. I could not reply, so Edna blurted out that I had been told that Jan was going blind.

Frank's wife spoke in a very firm manner: 'Nonsense, they have to be wrong.'

I sobbed, 'There's no mistake and there's nothing they can do to halt the disease.'

'They must be able to do something. They do marvellous things these days,' she replied. Suddenly the room became very quiet. Jan joined her cousins in play as though nothing untoward had happened at all. Edna went into the kitchen with others to get tea. I knew that they were talking about what had happened at the hospital. It all added to my lack of control over the situation.

The tea was brought into the room, and one by one people began to fill their plates from the buffet. I could not eat. I wanted John with me. He was strong and he would know what to do, but he was working late and the time dragged. Eventually, I heard his car turn into the drive and my heart leapt. I was shaking.

'Audrey, let John have his meal before you say anything to him,' Edna offered in a sympathetic tone.

John came straight to me and kissed me, then took Jan into his arms and kissed her, speaking his usual greeting: 'And how is my little sweetheart today?'

He put her back down and asked, 'How did it go? What did they say at the hospital? Does she need glasses?'

'Eat your meal John, and then we will talk,' I tried to persuade him, fighting back my tears.

He picked up his knife and fork to start but again asked, 'Well, come on, tell me all the news.'

'John, I have some bad news. Jan doesn't require glasses, she...' I couldn't go on without the tears spurting again.

'Whatever is it?' he asked, without tasting any of his food.

The voice didn't seem to come from me as I replied, 'She's going blind.'

'No, no, never!' I nodded; he looked at the others. 'Come on, we're going,' and sweeping Jan up onto his shoulder he signalled to me to collect everything. His eyes were now red from suppressed tears.

I can't remember leaving the house nor saying goodbye to anyone. It is all a blur. I do remember going to my mother's house. She had not been well enough to join the family gathering, and I wanted her to say that the doctors were wrong. She had had nine children and she would know, surely?

John put his foot down as we sped the short drive and I rushed in to see Mum.

'Whatever are you doing here? I thought you'd be at Frank's house with all of the others.' She looked into my face. 'You've been crying. What is it?'

'Oh, Mum, they say that Jan is going blind.'

I was not prepared for her reply.

'I knew it! I just knew it. I've had my suspicions for some time,' she said as she reached for a cigarette.

'No, Mum please tell me that it's not true. There must be some mistake,' I sobbed.

John was deathly white and silent except to say, 'Come on love, let's go home. It's time Jan was in bed.'

Taken just after she was diagnosed

CHAPTER 4

How does any parent assimilate news that their child has a serious health problem? Even the common childhood complaints cause us so much concern. We want to protect our children from all harm, but now John and I had this prognosis to come to terms with. How would it develop and what affect would it have? There were so many unanswered questions, but the prevailing emotion for both John and me at that time was one of shock and disbelief. Could it really be possible that those beautiful deep blue eyes were beginning to fail? Try as I might to envisage our daughter as a blind child, it was incomprehensible.

John managed to return to his job, but how he coped I will never know. He always looked so pale. His job was one of precision in the motor industry. He worked long arduous hours and the toll began to show.

I was a full-time mum at this point, but nonetheless I wanted someone to talk to, someone who could offer me some hope or comfort of some sort. The days were lonely and the dark nights were beginning to set in. I knew I was sinking into another depression. I had had a very bad post-natal depression, and my fear was that I would sink right down again.

When I was around 3 months pregnant I had worked in the maternity unit of the Coventry & Warwick Hospital, on the reception desk. One night, one of the ambulance drivers came to say that he was dropping someone off in my road, and did I want a lift. I accepted gladly as it was always difficult to catch buses at that time of night.

I climbed into the ambulance and took a seat opposite a young mother who had the most gorgeous baby on her lap. She had white-blonde hair and a lightly tanned skin and the most beautiful eyes. I commented to her mother on the loveliness of the child. I was not prepared for the reply.

'She's deaf and blind,' the mother said. I clutched at my stomach and felt physically sick. She went on to tell me that whilst she was pregnant she had stopped to speak to a little boy playing in the street. She asked him why he was not at school, and he replied that he had German measles. She thought no more about it until after the birth of her baby, when she was told that her daughter was Rubella handicapped. Just that one chance meeting had damaged her baby. The child was not only deaf and blind, but had severe brain damage and other problems.

As I attempted to continue in conversation, I discovered that she was my next-door-but-one neighbour. I did not know her because we were new to the area.

We did not meet again for some months. Often I would think about her baby. I saw her once or twice in the garden in her pram, and occasionally I would stop for a quick chat with her mother, Margaret, but nothing more.

Who could help John and me in our dilemma? On a miserable November's day I suddenly had the urge to go and see Margaret. Surely she would know what I was to do? I dashed round and knocked on the door. She opened it and I was shocked at her curt manner. She said that she had friends in and it was inconvenient, said goodbye and closed the door. The next morning she came round to my house and apologized, saying she had not meant to appear rude, and asked me what I had wanted. She did not have any words of comfort really, but suggested that she would ask the vicar of her church to come to see me. I was not a member of the church but the thought crossed my mind that maybe he could ask God to stop the disease. Perform some miracle and everything would be all right? Such was my state of mind.

The elderly, crusty old vicar called at our house. He entered and asked me a few questions and then said he would pray. He placed his hand on Jan's head and said a very few words, then turned to me with his hand held out to shake mine and finished with, 'And may God bless you my child.' Was this supposed to help me? If so then he was badly mistaken because the serious intonation of his voice caused me to become more depressed. My spirit was in agony.

John and I were ready to sell our house to find a cure. I had read an article in a newspaper about a woman in Russia who claimed to have cured people of this disease with specialist bee stings applied to the back of the head and neck. The following night it was on TV, and the programme showed a man who had been unable to see, now driving his car. This was the miracle we needed. We would have to raise a lot of money, not only for the travel and hotel expenses but for the woman's fees too.

Shortly after this I had to go for my usual eye check. The optician asked me the usual questions as to what problems, if any, I was having. I didn't even relate to myself. I blurted out that my baby had Retinitis Pigmentosa. He asked where I had taken her. He then asked whether I would be prepared to go privately to a doctor who specialised in the condition. Of course I jumped at the chance. He said he would take the necessary steps to make contact.

A couple of weeks passed before we received a letter from the doctor, a Mr. Austin, offering us a consultation. This was to be in Birmingham at his private address. We had hope in our hearts for the first time in months and set off for the meeting feeling optimistic.

Mr. Austin's house was very grand. We rang the bell. Eventually a light came on in the hall and then the heavy oak door slowly opened. He was a large man with a kindly face and his welcome was warm. Quickly, he was down to business and began examining Jan's eyes.

After a while, he turned to John and me and in a very gentle voice said,

'I am sorry, there is nothing anyone can do. The only thing I can offer you is to get you to see a Professor Crewes at the Birmingham Eye Hospital. He is an excellent research fellow, and if ever there is a breakthrough he will have your daughter's name at the front of the queue. But I must impress on you that there is no treatment or cure at present. Please listen and take to heart what I am telling you. I want you to promise me that you will not go across the world looking for proclaimed cures because you will be throwing your money away.'

His sympathy and compassion only added to the seriousness of the situation. John put his hand into his jacket and took out his wallet, but Mr. Austin told him to put it away, as there was no fee.

We returned home in silence, numb from the confirmation of our worst fears. But who knew what could happen. We were going to see one of the finest people in retinal research and any day a cure might be achieved.

How would we ever be able to accept this? It was the cruellest blow any parent could have, or so I thought at the time. I barely slept that night and was exhausted.

CHAPTER 5

Janis was coming up to her third birthday. She could already read the first of the Janet & John books I had borrowed from the library. She was a very bright child, full of energy and curiosity and a delight to teach. Questions arose at every event of the day. She would often tire me with her unrelenting inquiries. Little did I know how extraordinarily important this would be for her in later years. Of course, she was oblivious to all that was going on regarding her eyesight, and the fact that she was still able to do so much and read such fine print was baffling.

Eventually an appointment to see Mr. Crewes arrived and eagerly we set off to Birmingham. Our hopes had not been completely diminished, as we had put our faith in this man.

He was charming, and a quiet gentle man. We followed him as he took Jan from department to department to carry out many tests. After about an hour and a half he turned to his PA and asked her whether she would take Jan to see the rabbits (we later learnt that these were used for research). He ushered us into his private office. His attitude and body language told me that it was to be serious news. In fact he had great difficulty in beginning the conversation. Very slowly and gently he gradually explained to us that in his opinion Jan would be totally blind by the age of seven. He followed this with a lot of information about the disease.

It was a genetic problem. In a way he gave us some hope, he enlarged on the retinal research that was taking place in the hospital and all over the world and said that if ever there was a breakthrough, Jan would be at the top of his list.

He then continued, 'There are special homes called Sunshine Homes for children with little or no sight.' He saw my reaction to this, and before I could say anything he added, 'But because I can see that you are both very capable of doing the right thing for Janis and that she is a very happy child in a good home, I hesitate to refer her. I am, therefore, going to say that she will be better off staying with you at present.'

He went on to ask whether we would permit Janis to return at some point to stay in the hospital, quickly adding that there would be a special room laid on for both of us. He explained that he wanted to perform specific tests, that these would be intensive and there would be many. One of the tests would be to insert into the eye a type of contact lens which had electrodes attached. He could then take complex pictures of the retina. Sometimes this is possible with a local anaesthetic and if possible he would do that, but as Jan was so young he thought it highly likely he would need to put her to sleep. I looked at John.

Mr. Crewes then said that perhaps we should think about it. He stressed that it was all a matter of research in the hope of finding a cure for RP. For my part, I did not have to think about it. I immediately said that I thought it an excellent idea, and John nodded his consent. Mr. Crewes added that he would be grateful if I would record anything that might throw any light on the problem, and to find out more about a distant relative who had gone blind as a child. Maybe the RP was in the family and this was a throwback. He said that both John and I carried a recessive gene. Because we both wanted another child I asked him about the chances of this happening again. He asked whether we would like to see a geneticist and we both agreed. It was to be arranged. He then stood, shook our hands, and said that we would have a letter shortly regarding Jan's tests.

Quite soon after our visit, the letter arrived. I had tried to prepare Jan for what was ahead, and she was her usual happy, unconcerned self. I had also determined that the visit should be made as good an experience as possible, so I packed lots of treats and some food for the rabbits. I had promised Jan that she could go and visit them again.

As soon as we had settled in, we were taken to various departments for tests. Over the next few days all manner of things were done to Jan and so many times she had drops applied to her eyes, but it made no difference to her. She always seemed so happy, and enjoyed the amount of attention that all of this brought. The nurses allowed her to walk round the ward with them when they gave out the tablets to other patients, and Jan would be given the little pot to take to the patient, under the nurses' supervision of course. She was so happy doing this and any other little job that they would allow her to do. The patients just loved her. She was a very friendly tactile girl and accepted the many cuddles with joy.

Jan would get excited at phone call time, and every night she would ask, 'Daddy have you got my wumberwella yet?' She had been wanting a small umbrella for some time and John had said he would try to get one. He looked everywhere but could not find one small enough. So he decided to buy her a nurse's outfit as a surprise, and brought it in on the last day.

That day she was taken to the theatre and put to sleep. It was supposed to be a very short examination to enable Mr. Crewes to place special contact lenses into her eyes and then take pictures of the retina. However, time passed by and I became concerned. I was told not to worry, but I so wanted John to be there. It was his early finishing day and he was due at the hospital as we had an appointment to see a geneticist. How glad I was when he arrived. I hurriedly explained that Jan had been away longer than I anticipated and John was quick to reassure me that everything would be OK.

We went to another department for the chat with the geneticist, who asked many questions. The result of this was to be told that it was probable that any other children we had might have the same problem as Jan, and he put the chances down to only one in four not being affected. But his next remark shocked us. He suggested that we put Jan into a home and got on with our lives, continuing, 'In parts of India, if a handicapped child is born it is taken to the mountain and left there to die.' We were incredibly shocked by such insensitivity and could not comment, but returned to the ward, my heart so heavy with sadness.

Quite soon afterwards, Jan was brought from theatre and transferred into her bed. She was still asleep. John sat on one side of the bed and I on the other, taking hold of a hand each. The nurse told us that she seemed to have taken the anaesthetic deeply, but suggested that we kept talking to her and patting her face. I cried as I looked onto her tiny-featured face, her eyes all sticky from the ointment they had used. Her long eyelashes were stuck together. I prayed so hard, pleading with God that this might turn out to be the miracle that we wanted. 'Please God, I will do anything you ask, but please, please, when she opens her eyes tell me they will be free from any problem.'

The tears now dropped and John reached across to take my hand. A lady patient was passing the bed and she said, 'They break your arms at this age but they break your heart when they are older.' Little did she know how prophetic her words were.

Eventually, Jan rallied round and immediately asked her daddy if he had her wumbwella. He apologized but took out the bag that contained the nurse's uniform. It was not long before she wanted to put it on and show the doctors and nurses.

On the way back home I just sobbed and sobbed. It was a release of all the anxiety that I had pushed down during the week. My throat had felt as though it would burst from the pent up emotions, and so I allowed the tears full reign out of sight of Jan. She was in her seat at the back of the car playing with a toy. I kept turning to see whether she was interested in what was happening on the road and sure enough she kept turning to watch the other traffic. How could it be that in just four years she would be blind? Moreover, how would it happen, and what would the affect be on her? My tears would not stop. Exhausted, we arrived home to continue our usual roles as before, but our lives had been changed forever.

CHAPTER 6

John returned to work and I had a part time job. We decided to place Jan into a crèche rather than for her to go to my mother's place as before. We wanted her to be able to cope and interact with lots of children, and cope she did. She loved the company of the other children and her limited sight did not impinge on her enjoyment nor cause any problems.

It was some time before we had a visit from a social worker, and even then it did not help a great deal. She talked about special schools, and said that eventually Jan would have to go away from home. The thought filled me with dread, and I knew that for as long as I could I would send her to the local primary school with other sighted children. The social worker continued telling us about the options that we needed to consider, but I did not want to think about my baby having to be brought up by someone in an institution. I remember trying very hard not to assimilate the information, until she went on to tell us of a school for the partially sighted that was very close to our home. She said that it was the best of its type and that they only took very bright children. She had already commented on how bright Jan was, and said she could see no reason why she should not be accepted, but that there was a waiting list. On leaving, she again asked us to think about what she had said and left us her phone number in case we wanted to get in touch.

We pondered on what the social worker had told us. It suddenly struck me that it was a full-time boarding school with only monthly exeats, and I knew that every Saturday the children were allowed to visit the tuck shop at the end of our road. No way would I be able to tolerate knowing that my child was so near, and yet I could not contact her or she me. Supposing that I saw her at the shop and could not make contact? That would be unbearable. John and I debated the situation and decided to sell our home and move a few miles away.

Our longing for another child was pressing in on us and we talked through the options we had. Eventually we decided that we could not risk bringing another child into the world with the possibility of it having RP. It was not an easy decision. We talked about adoption, which was the other option open to us. John longed for a son. After several weeks of debating we applied to Warwickshire County Council, and quite quickly we were asked to attend a meeting.

This meeting was really to sort out the people who were determined to adopt a child no matter what was stacked up against them. There were many hurdles to overcome, and the investigations would be awesome. The social worker went on to say that because we insisted on a newborn baby it would reduce our chances, as most couples wanted a blue-eyed new-born baby and there just were not enough to go around. If we were to opt for an older child, then we might have more success. But we had made up our minds and Janis had said that she wanted a baby brother. The forms were all filled in and the ball was set in motion. However, we were advised not to build up our hopes just yet.

Quite soon we had a house visit from the same man we had seen at Warwick. His questioning was very probing and he wanted to know so much about us, down to how much money we had and were we in any debt. This was only the first of many visits. Not only did he inquire of us, but interviewed local tradespeople and our best friends who lived across the road.

No wonder they stressed how difficult it was to adopt a child. It was not just a case of John and me enjoying the delight of a sexual union to bring about a baby. Adopting a child was fraught with anxiety and doubt; doubts about whether we would be considered good enough, capable even. Then Mr. Oakley, the social worker, had mentioned that not all mothers would want their child to come to us. I was startled at this suggestion but he went on to explain that there would be concern as to whether the adopted child would fit in and whether too much attention would have to be given to Jan. At the time, we thought that we had enough time for both of them and we most certainly had enough love.

After several months, a letter arrived to say that we had passed the assessment and that we had been placed on the waiting list for a baby boy. We had been told that the baby would be closely matched to both John and me, as far as was possible. Suddenly my maternal instincts kicked in and I began buying things for the new baby and choosing names. However, the wait seemed endless. Some neighbours had just had their baby through the same agency, and some other friends were waiting too. They had only been waiting about eighteen months before a baby was placed with them.

Gradually, and over a few months, Jan's impending blindness began to register but we were determined that she would have as much chance as anyone and I began to recognize that she needed extra help in seeing the things that most of us take for granted. It made not one iota of difference to her, and she found it very amusing when, sitting upon my lap to watch TV, I would bring my fingers in to the side of her eyes to see whether her tunnel vision had reduced. She thought I was playing games, and as soon as she saw my hand she would try to snatch it and this caused her to laugh. So I decided that I would treat it as a game. Sadly, over the next year, I realized that the length of time before Jan saw my fingers was becoming longer, meaning that her tunnel vision had closed down even further.

I also became aware of the dangers she faced. I now had to tell her when there was a curb to step down or up. She had some nasty accidents. One occasion was when she had been jumping on the end of my bed as I cleaned the room. She had her dummy in her mouth and she did not see the end of the bed as she bounced up and down. As she fell, her chin hit the floor and the hard piece of the dummy pushed one of her front teeth back up into the roof of her mouth. There was so much blood.

She was an adventurous child and there was no way that I could impose too many restrictions, so I decided that she should be allowed to do most of the things other children did. It was nothing unusual to find her climbing the scaffolding that was around houses still being built, and up trees with the neighbourhood kids. On one occasion she was playing chase around our home with her best friend Claire, and she ran into the corner of a wall and gashed her head. Blood dripped off the end of her long ponytail. I am not good where there is blood to deal with. I am OK on myself, but not on my children, and so I shouted to Claire to run next door and fetch my neighbour. She in turn, after looking at the gash, fetched her husband. We all piled into his car to go to hospital.

Even at this stage, Jan was still her happy self and into asking so many questions about the hospital and doctors. My neighbour went in with her when they stitched her head, as I was, I have to admit, too upset and felt faint. I was brought to my senses with a jolt when a doctor came out, looking very solemn, to tell me they were going to admit Jan. When I asked what the problem was he replied, 'We are very concerned because she is not seeing properly.'

I was so relieved, and when I commented, 'Oh that!' he looked very puzzled, especially when I added, 'Is that all? I know she can't see properly, she's going blind.'

It must have been such a shock for the doctor, but I was now growing accustomed to the fact that this was a part of our life and I suppose I talked of it as an everyday thing. Jan was not admitted, and she was full of information about what the doctor had done and how she had to come back to have the stitches taken out.

I was working part-time in a doctor's practice around this time. One Saturday morning I took Jan into work with me, with the permission of the senior doctor, as John had to go into work too. Jan was her usual inquisitive self and sat at a typewriter typing out a letter. As soon as the patients had left I began sorting through medical records to be filed, at which the doctor came in and asked whether Janis would like to go with him, as he had to visit an old lady. I was surprised, but he went on to explain that she was a lovely lady and had a beautiful garden, and he would love to take Jan along to meet her and show her the garden. Off they went, Jan clinging to his large hand. She looked so tiny next to his 6'4" frame. Smiling to myself and feeling that Jan was in very good hands, I got on with my work.

They had been gone for a couple of hours when suddenly I heard this very loud noise coming along the corridor. It was awful. The doctor came in with Jan still clasped to his hand and he was grinning. He had taken Jan to see the patient and allowed her to explore the garden. Then he had called at the Saturday market and showed Jan around the toy stall. Between them it was decided that he buy her a trumpet, of all things. And now she was blasting away full pelt. What a quiet weekend we had!

One other particular thing that stuck in my mind about this doctor was when he asked me about Janis going blind. He asked me what the disease was, and when I told him that she had Retinitis Pigmentosa his face became very serious and he said, 'I am so sorry.' I did not question him but I had a gut feeling that I had not been told all that there was to know about the disease. It was an uncomfortable feeling, and I did not want to explore his remark for fear of learning even worse things. I was to discover the reason behind his comment as the years went by.

As Jan's birthday was near to Christmas we always tried to buy her a big present halfway through the year. She was coming up to her fourth birthday and we decided she should have the bicycle she had been asking about. Boy, was she excited when we took her into town to choose it! John attached stabilizers at the back wheels and took her down to the footpath at the front of our house. He held the back of the saddle but she shot off along the footpath with John running after her in the hope of stalling her before she reached the edge of the kerb. There was no need, as she peddled like mad and pulled up sharp when she reached the end of the footpath. Within days, her two little friends had bicycles too and they would all three race along together until they reached the kerb and then spin round and race back. Everyone was amazed at how Jan coped. It was no good holding her back, she was determined and her strong will was to hold her in good stead for later years. She never ever had an accident on that bike.

CHAPTER 7

The time came when Jan was to begin school at the local primary at the top of our road in Nuneaton. We took her along for an interview with the head, and I took along the books that Jan was now reading and some of the things she had written. The head was very impressed, confirming that she was, indeed, a very bright child. She had no hesitation in accepting her, and Jan looked forward with her usual enthusiasm to the day when she was to begin.

There were no first day tears on Jan's part, but the day seemed endless for me. When I returned to pick her up she was full of chatter and so excited.

The head had agreed that the staff should continue letting Jan mix with the other children and doing everything that they did. One day, I decided to carry her bike into the playground so that she could ride it home. When she came out she got onto her bike and rode it like mad around the playground. The head was at the door and was amazed at how she managed to ride, and especially at such speed. But quite soon after this I was to learn that Jan was not being allowed to play outside at playtime and was kept in with another child who had a heart condition. The two of them became very good friends. However, Jan was miserable about the new ruling. Upon enquiring into this I was told that there had been some nasty collisions and the school was not prepared to take the risk of a serious accident happening.

One day I went to collect Jan and she was in tears. Thinking that something terrible had happened I asked her what the matter was. All I could gather was that she had missed someone coming to school. 'Who was it?' I asked.

'It was Jesus.' I was taken aback but she then went on to explain. 'My teacher said we had to put our hands together and close our eyes. Well I did that and she said 'Thank you Jesus for bringing our milk'. But when I opened my eyes he had gone so I never saw him.' Her little body was wracked with sobs. It was difficult to explain what the teacher meant, but I did my best. She was still very disappointed. However, I picked up on her desire to know more about Jesus and read Bible stories to her.

One evening whilst I was reading to her in her bedroom she asked me whether I could see Jesus. When I said that I couldn't, she suddenly became very excited and her face shone as she replied, 'But I can see him. I can see Him all around me.' I cried tears she could not see. Her beautiful little face shone with happiness. Who was I to deny this fact? Her interest continued and I brought more stories to read to her.

It became obvious that Jan's field of vision was closing down and I shared my fears with someone who had a very ill child. We had met at a lingerie party and I discovered that her baby had been given a death sentence. We commiserated over our misfortunes. Gaynor suggested that I take Jan to a healer, saying how marvellous she was. Of course, John and I snatched at any hope and quickly made the necessary appointment.

Two days later we were off to see this miraculous person who had supposedly healed so many people. As we sat in the lounge of the large house in Coventry I saw, through the patio doors, a man pulling himself along some rails at the back of the house and into the back room. The woman noticed my reaction, saying, 'It's my husband and he has an illness that is the work of the devil. There is nothing I can do to help. Look at this mark on my forehead it is the sign of Christ.'

It all seemed very spooky to me, but we continued as she beckoned us to sit. She told us of many illnesses she had cured. Then she took Jan onto her lap and looked at her eyes and said, 'There is nothing too bad here that I cannot deal with.' My heart leapt at the hope given. She proceeded to place her hands on Jan's eyes and then told her to 'look over there, and over there, and here'. Then the woman turned to John and me, saying, 'She is better already. Now I'm going to give you a hanky to take home with you. This is a blessed cloth. I want you to place it on her eyes every night while she sleeps.'

That night I crept back up to Jan's room. She was fast asleep. I took the hanky and placed it on her eyes and then I prayed like never before as my hot tears dropped onto her bedcovers. I pleaded with God to do his work and heal her.

Each day I tested in my usual way, but nothing. Then, one morning I noticed that Jan's right eye had turned into the corner towards her nose. I rang the "healer" who said it was the healing taking place that had caused the eye to turn inwards. She went on to explain that Jan's eyes were just lazy and the healing had freed the eye up and it had moved into the corner. Now she wanted us to return so that she could fix the other.

We had an appointment to see the professor in Birmingham the following week. As Mr. Crewes examined Jan his face grew very solemn. He examined Jan's eyes yet again, then turning to his P.A. he asked her again to take Jan to see the rabbits. His manner conveyed that he had some seriously bad news for us. He had great difficulty in expressing himself, but very gently he told us that Jan's right eye was now almost without sight and the left was doing all of the work. He went on to say that we needed to think about special education. He said something about white sticks and Jan being a bright child, and that she would overcome her blindness. The information was almost too much to comprehend. My heart was beginning to crack.

Although we had been trying to accept the fact that Jan would eventually go blind, we still secretly held the belief that something would happen to prevent it. The so-called healer had further raised our hopes. How cruel is it for some stranger to tell such untruths? Now we had to not only accept that blindness was quite imminent, but that our beloved daughter would very soon have to leave home and go away to boarding school. I resolved that I would show her and teach her as much as I possibly could before she lost her sight. I knew how vitally important it was to her if she was to recall what things looked like, and that it would stand her in good stead for the rest of her life. It proved to be tremendously important, and Jan had the mind to want as much information as it was possible to give her.

My life had changed dramatically, never again to be normal in the best sense of that word. I quickly realized just how much we take for granted when we can see everything around us. Now I had to try to see things through Jan's eyes. I had been given a special blindfold at the hospital, to wear so that I might have some idea of the limitations imposed upon Jan. There was just a pinprick of light to be seen, and this signified the amount of vision left to her. My mobility was reduced to almost nil. I was so scared as I attempted to walk around a room. How on earth she managed to do all that she did, I could not imagine.

CHAPTER 8

THE CIRCUS COMES TO TOWN.

Just after our visit to Birmingham, I saw in the local paper that Billy Smart's circus was coming to Coventry. I wrote to them, addressing the letter via the newspaper. I explained as best I could about Jan – that her sight was now failing fast. I asked whether they could arrange for her to go backstage to explore whatever was possible. I was pleasantly surprised when a letter arrived, by return, asking me to ring to make arrangements for Jan to go to the circus on the opening day and meet with someone named John-Paul. I rang straight away and spoke with John-Paul who suggested that we go over the next morning. He told us where to meet him and said that he would show us around.

When we arrived, John Paul made such a fuss of Jan. He asked her whether she would like to meet the animals. She jumped at the offer. We went to the marquee. John Paul brought buns so that Jan could feed the elephants. As we went past some horses, one cocked his tail and let out a huge fart. John and I looked at one another trying to act nonchalantly as if we had heard nothing, but Jan blurted out, 'Mummy, did you hear what that horse just did? Isn't he rude?'

We saw dogs and lions. Jan had always adored animals so this was quite a treat. Then John-Paul took us into the circus ring, lifting Jan up onto the platform of the ring, talking to her as he did so, explaining what happened on there. He held her hand and walked with her slowly all round the ring. He lifted her down, and took her to the trapeze ladder and explained to her all about the events that took place on there. He asked whether she would like to climb a little way. Of course she did. Up and up she went without any fear. My heart was in my mouth, as I hated heights and she was going higher and higher. John-Paul was close behind. When she came down he asked us to follow him back to his caravan. It was huge and luxurious. We went inside and he handed us an envelope explaining that these were tickets for that night's performance in ringside seats. He told Jan that he would be looking for her. He handed her a huge box of chocolates and made her promise to share them with Mummy and Daddy on the night. She nodded clasping the box tightly to her chest.

All through the rest of the day, Jan was very excited. I was too, but I was concerned that she would not be able to see most of what went on.

We arrived at the big tent with apprehension. As we entered the huge marquee we were handed a program by a magnificently dressed clown. He bent low to speak to Jan and taking her hand he led her to the ringside and pointed to where we were to sit. How different it all seemed now with the bright lights and atmosphere, as adults and children chattered excitedly. We had a ringside box seat all to ourselves. Jan's little head was moving all over the huge arena as she attempted to take in all that was around her.

Eventually the music struck up and the loudspeakers announced the first act. The lights dimmed and the spotlights came on. The clowns came tumbling out into the ring and the place was now alive with music, clowns, jugglers, and trapeze artists. Amazingly, as the various artists toured the ring they came to a halt in front of us. It was just a little while before I realised that John-Paul had arranged for the artistes to stop in front of us. Each in turn leaned over the ring in front of Jan. I was overcome by their compassion. Each act and each animal halted for a second or two in the hope that Janis could catch sight of what was unfolding in that ring. Little dogs were brought to a halt. Horses and elephants, it was all just too much. I was choked with happiness and joy. My theory about engaging Jan in as much as possible was beginning to bear fruit. I was elated beyond words. The atmosphere was electric and Jan sat on the edge of her seat transported into their world of colour and magic.

The show over, we made our way towards the exit. There stood the same clown. He called out, 'Janis!'

She stopped. 'It's John-Paul,' she said, her face glowing from the excitement of the evening and recognizing John-Paul's voice.

'Hello again Janis, you did not know it was me?' he said as he bent down so that she could see his face.

'How did you change like that?' she asked.

'Would you like to be like me?' And he very gently pressed his face against her cheek, and then the other, and said, 'There, now you have paint on your face and you can be a clown.'

He took Jan's hand, walked with us to the exit and kissed Jan on her cheek.

'I won't wash my face tonight, I want to show my friends!' she said. We bade him farewell and went on our way with Janis chattering about all that she had seen. She had managed to see a great deal by her account of the night.

The next morning she was out of bed like a shot and wanted to know whether she had the paint on her face. Of course it had rubbed off during the night. She was rather sad, but undeterred she went off to school eager to tell her classmates about the night before.

CHAPTER 9

Janis continued to do very well at school and was a very keen scholar. She was always anxious to get there, but one winter's morning I had overslept. I awoke to an unusual quietness in the streets. I looked out of the window. There had been a terrific snowstorm during the night. The streets were impassable to traffic and there were snowdrifts half way up the front doors of the houses. The world was suffocated and muffled into a winter wonderland. I guess the unusual quietness had lulled me into sleeping longer than usual. Quickly I went into Jan's room and asked her to hurry, telling her, as I attempted to help her dress, about the snow outside. She ran to the window shrieking with delight at the sudden transformation.

'Can we build a snowman, Mummy? Pleeeeeease oh pleeeeeease, Mummy.'

I explained that we were very late and rushed her to get ready and have some breakfast.

'Please let me wear my new red wellies.'

I made for the wellies, and quickly pulling them onto her tiny feet we sped out of the front door, snow falling and drifting like white confetti in the crisp air. We ran as fast as we could. She loved to run. I tried to tread on impacted snow where other people had trodden. I had to guess where the kerbs were, as they were submerged under the white carpet. We laughed happily as we ran, hearing the school bell in the distance.

'Mummy, Mummy!' Jan tugged on my arm.

'Run darling, we're late, can you hear the bell?'

She began to flag and eventually could run no more. She was in fits of laughter.

'What is it?'

'I've been trying to tell you that one of my wellington boots has come off.'

I looked behind. The open plan gardens were lost in the mass of glistening white. There was no wide road separating them, it was all one. The drifts were piled very high in front of the houses. Hanging heavily from the edge of the rooftops were curtains of heavy scalloped snow draping the windows like pelmets as if daring to fall but amazingly holding onto their beauty. There was not another soul in sight. The muffled atmosphere was awesome. Then I saw the red boot lying far away, scarlet red as blood on the driven snow.

I picked Jan up into my arms and hugged her, kissing her cold, flushed cheeks. We gasped in the bitterly cold air. I thought my chest would burst with the overwhelming love I had for her. This was a most magical moment. We both laughed; I turned and carried Jan all the way back, collecting her boot and taking her indoors to dry and warm her feet. It was one of those moments that come out of the blue in the most bizarre circumstances. Again, not to be captured in its intensity but to be remembered for its exquisite love, joy and happiness. It was a very rare and spiritual moment, of nature and a mother's love for her child uniting.

There was more sad news around the corner a few days later. I was asked to go to see the head of the school. When I arrived she seemed to be rather anxious.

'Please come in and close the door.' She beckoned me to take a seat. I had grown to recognize the body language that portended bad news.

'I have some rather sad news for you,' she began. 'Quite recently we have had to let Janis sit right at the very front of the class, in fact at the foot of the blackboard.' My heart was leaping in my chest, anxious but not wanting to hear what she was about to tell me. The head went on:

'Because Janis was not responding to questions in her usual bright way and teachers had commented on how quiet she had been lately, we devised ways of assessing how much she can see. I'm sorry, but I think the time has come for Janis to be assessed for Exhall Grange.'

I tried to remain in control. I had told the head that Exhall was the school we would want Janis to go to if she had to, as we had heard such excellent reports. The head went on to say that in her opinion Janis would sail through the interview and be accepted.

Janis was now six years of age. The prognosis of her being blind by the age of seven loomed ever larger, bringing with it feelings of frustration, impotence and despair for me. There seemed nothing anyone could do to halt this rampaging eye disease. We had, it seemed, done all that was possible and yet it was not enough to maintain even a little sight for Jan.

Steps were taken to arrange an interview at Exhall. It was another anxious time of waiting for the unknown. However, I had to prepare Jan for the huge upheaval that lay ahead. She would have to leave us and her home, no matter whether she passed for Exhall or had to go elsewhere. She would only see us at the end of every month for a weekend, and during the usual school holidays. And so began the story I was to tell her over and over again. If I missed any part of it she would remind me.

I began by telling her of this very special school we had heard about. I told her that we would invent an imaginary place in our garden that had a door, which led to an underground passage. Through this passage we would travel until we came to the school. Here we could peep in and have a look at what was happening. I said that the children were having midnight feasts and all sorts of wonderful goodies were available. There were lots of games, and the children were very happy. I made the atmosphere in the school as appealing to a small child as possible. Jan added to the story day by day. Eventually it became a magical place, which we would visit frequently. Janis loved the adventurous story.

For myself, I have never felt so awful. I was portraying confidence to my child that she would be well looked after. Supposing I betrayed her? Maybe someone would harm her? I was to entrust my child to the care of strangers.

The letter arrived for us to go for an interview.

We had heard that the head of the school, a Mr. Marshall, was a lovely man who had been there for many years and only had the best interests of the children at heart. He lived and breathed Exhall Grange School. As soon as we met him this was apparent without many words being spoken. He introduced himself and made it perfectly clear that there were far more children wanting to go to Exhall than there were places. Because the school had a very high academic achievement record, they only took those children they thought would benefit the most from it. He stressed that from among the many parents present on that day only a chosen few's children would be accepted.

We were given a tour of the school including the different houses around the grounds. I was in no doubt at all that I wanted for Jan to go to this school and my attempts at reassuring her about the school in our story time had not been wasted. Jan was so excited and eager to please in the hope of being accepted.

After our travels around the grounds we were asked to wait in a certain room. Mr. Marshall came in and addressed the group of parents and children. Again he emphasized that many of us would be disappointed. He went on to say that he would have each child separately in a room and he would ask them questions and carry out certain visual tests. It was a long procedure because every child had to be assessed. After every child had been in, we returned to wait for Mr. Marshall to come back into the larger waiting room.

Whilst he was explaining the final details to the gathered parents, Janis asked whether she could go to him. Before I could answer he said, 'Of course you can Janis, come along,' and held out his hand. Jan very carefully went round the group, feeling her way as she went, and eventually got to Mr. Marshall.

He lifted her onto his lap and began by saying, 'Those are pretty ribbons in your hair. What colour are they?'

Quickly she replied, 'They are pale blue with dark blue spots on.'

'And what colour is your sailor's dress then?'

'It's white and navy blue.'

I knew that she was thrilled that he was asking so many questions. It was a game we played at home. I would set up quizzes for her to answer.

Then Mr. Marshal looked directly at John and me and asked, 'Why do you permit Janis to do so much by touch. From my observations, she is more than capable of using her sight.' This comment was balm to my troubled heart.

Mr. Marshall concluded the interview by saying that we would all receive a letter in a few days' time.

The news that Mr. Marshal thought Jan's eyes not to be as bad as we thought had cheered us up considerably, and so we decided to go to my brother Frank's home. He was eager to know how we had got on. When I told him about Mr. Marshall's comment he told Jan that if she could find it without feeling her way she could have the money that was on the mantelpiece. Surprisingly she did not hesitate but made her way directly to the shelf and picked up the money. Frank said he thought we had allowed her to feel more than look. I was not convinced, but was overjoyed at what we had just seen. I was to learn more about these occurrences later.

Meanwhile, we attempted to get on with life in as normal a fashion as was possible and to encourage Jan as much as we could. Trying to conceal my pain and anguish at losing her to some house-matron to look after was almost too much, but conceal it I did for the benefit of Jan and her ability to adapt to her new situation without too much foreboding.

We had the anticipation of a new baby to balance things a little, but time had dragged on and we were now two years down the line. Both John and I would come on and off the boil as we waited for news. We had several phone calls from the social worker to keep us informed, but no baby was available for us.

John was coming up to the cut off point as far as ages go for adoption. He is eight years older than I am and therefore I was OK, but a phone call from Mr. Oakley came to tell us that because of John's age the inquiries and investigations were to be looked into again. It was not an easy ride at all. It just felt as though things were stacked against us, but we lived in hope that all would be well in the end. This was all part of the inquiries. However, eventually we had a call to say that all of them were satisfactorily and we were still on line for having a baby boy. But when? That was the big question. Not only had we been preparing Jan for her new school, but also for the coming of her little brother.

The tremendously long wait for the adoption and now for Jan's acceptance into Exhall grange seemed an eternity. On a day when I had for once forgotten about Exhall Grange, the letter plopped onto the hall carpet causing my heart to palpitate. Tearing at the envelope I unfolded the letter. Jan had been accepted, and she was to begin in the autumn after the school holidays. That school holiday was very special, and we packed as much enjoyment as we possibly could into it. We travelled all over, and went to stay at our holiday caravan on the coast as frequently as John's job would allow.

One of our outings was a day trip to the Cotswolds to the beautiful village of Bourton-on-the-Water. There was a village fete taking place, and many stalls and events. It was a gloriously sunny day with clear blue skies, and so peaceful.

We had visited the birdhouse, and on the way out stopped to buy a huge softy ice cream for Jan. We continued to walk around the village green. Jan held her daddy's hand, holding the ice cream in her other. Soon there were tears and Jan tried to speak to us between her sobs. 'My ice cream, it's all gone.'

When we looked, expecting to find the huge mound of ice cream on the ground, we discovered that it had arrived on the backside of a ginormous man who had been bending over to bowl in a "bowl for the pig" competition. John and I laughed at the comedy of the situation. The man muttered something about, 'You should look where you're going'. Jan had held the ice cream outside of her field of vision, only to discover at the next lick that it had disappeared. We quickly replaced it with another and continued to enjoy the rest of the uneventful day.

That summer went by so very quickly, the preparations of school uniform had been done and name tabs sewn inside all of her garments. Tears fell as I stitched, thinking that another person was to launder the clothes and get her ready for school in the mornings. The wait was heart wrenching and filled with apprehension. It appeared that I had done a good job in preparing Jan for what lay ahead, but I guess nothing could prepare me for the day when she would be taken away.

We were told that parents often appreciate a car being laid on so that the child can leave from home. I thought this to be the best for all concerned.

On the day that Jan was to leave us she was full of high spirits. At last, she was going to live at the school that I had familiarised her with as best I could. I was a useless wreck and busied myself around the home. John offered to go to the shops and took Jan with him. When they returned I heard the sound of excited laughter. I could not see Jan behind the enormous bunch of flowers that John had bought. Jan came to me holding her daddy's hand and the flowers in the other with John supporting them.

'These are for you, Mummy. They are because you're the bestest mummy in the whole world.'

Hot tears flooded my face as I bent to kiss her. This is one time when I was glad that she could not see my tears. 'They are so lovely darling. I'll pop into the kitchen and put them in water.' I closed the kitchen door and howled and howled.

Eventually, the large car drew up outside our home and a very kindly looking man came to our door. He introduced himself, bending to speak to Jan first. She was so pleased to see him that she took his hand and was almost out of the door before him.

'I think that Mummy and Daddy want to kiss you goodbye,' he offered as she reached up on tiptoe and we bent and kissed her and hugged her. They drove away chatting happily.

The driver had promised that he would ring and let us know how she had got on. It seemed such an age before the phone rang in the late afternoon.

'Mrs. Revell?'

'Yes,' my voice shaking.

'Janis is fine. She went off quite happily to be dressed in her summer uniform dress and came back to show me how she looked. She is a very happy child and you have nothing to worry about at all.'

'Thank you.' I returned his goodbye, my voice now breaking with emotion.

The house was silent.

CHAPTER 10

To see the children passing our home to go to school was almost too much to bear. Mothers talking to one another and children happily running back and forth. I had had mine for such a short while and now she was elsewhere. The days were long and terribly quiet.

Jan had her first monthly weekend at home. The thrill of seeing her lovely face and picking her up in my arms again is beyond description. To smell her again and hold her close. We had a lovely quiet weekend at our home, but Jan was quite keen to return to school on Sunday night. This brought mixed feelings for me. The school, all of the staff and the residences were second to none. There was a lovely atmosphere about the place, and I admit to pangs of jealousy when Jan ran into her house without any qualms whatsoever, kicking off her shoes in the cloakroom and pulling on her pumps. There were no tears on Jan's part at us leaving.

It was only a matter of about another week before a letter arrived from Exhall Grange. It was quite long, but my eyes quickly picked out that Jan was now unable to see at all. I had to sit down and re-read the contents. Mr. Marshall said that since coming to school Jan had tended to do most things with her hands. The teachers had tried everything, but realised that Jan's sight was now so poor that she must go to a school for blind children. He went on to say that she was an extremely bright child and would do well, passing her eleven plus for the excellent girls college at Chorleywood and then on to university. He had no doubt about that. He finished by saying that it was not normally allowed, but under the circumstances we could visit the school whenever we wanted to. We rang straight away to make arrangements.

It was not a joyful visit, as you will imagine. The woman in reception notified the classroom and Jan was eventually brought to us. I thought she would run into our arms but she stood by the teacher's side. I bent to kiss her and she said, 'Who is it?' The sob reared up and stuck in my throat. I stepped back in shock and looked at her little face with the blue rimmed glasses still perched on her nose, and I remember thinking, 'Whatever have they put those on her for? She can't see anymore.'

After spending a little time with Jan we went to see Mr. Marshall. He said how very sorry he was, and that he was baffled because Jan had stood by his side the day before and had seen some dove pigeons take off. He suggested that Jan could stay at Exhall for a few more weeks and they would introduce her to Braille using large dots to teach her how to recognise the alphabet. Finally he asked us if we would like to join the school on Bonfire Night. We thanked him and said our farewells. It was now a matter of seeing the social worker and making the necessary arrangements for Jan to go to Lickey Grange.

I could not return to my job for several days. Even after I thought I had some control and I went back, it was not long before the tears flowed, especially if anyone showed any expression of sympathy.

Finally the 5th November came, and we were anxious to see Jan again. It was an evening spent with very mixed emotions. Jan seemed no different to the way she had always been: happy, chatty and excitable, except that she now clung tightly to our hands as we stood around the huge bonfire, only releasing them to eat sticky toffee or a hot-dog. We tried to guide her face in the direction of the rockets in the hope that she might just be able to see them, and I believe that she saw something. However, the noise was obviously very frightening for her.

When the time came for us to leave, Jan was still happy to join her housemates and go to her house. We returned to ours in a very downcast mood.

We had heard nothing about the adoption, so this was still hanging in the air, and now we had another anxiety as we waited for the letter telling us to take Jan to Lickey Grange School. We did not have long to wait. The head agreed that Jan should spend the rest of term at Exhall and then go to them for an interview at the beginning of the January term.

It was soon time for us to fetch Jan home from Exhall for the final time. It was a really emotional time for all of us, to say goodbye yet again to some lovely people who had worked their way into our hearts. Jan took it all in her stride. She was excited about Christmas and decorating the tree.

As John set off for home, Jan began playing three blind mice on a penny whistle that she had bought with her pocket money at the tuck shop near to our previous home. John begged of her to stop, making the excuse that he had a bad headache.

'It's OK, Daddy, I know that I'm blind now,' she replied.

Mr. Marshall had suggested that I place an interest board in the hallway of our home. This was to hold many items and he suggested that I change this frequently so that Jan developed a greater sense of touch. Jan was delighted with it, and quite easily named all of the items on the tray. There were things such as a comb, a tube of toothpaste, one of her ceramic whimsies, a cone off a tree, a conker, toothbrush, and so many more things. It did become more difficult to find new things to introduce, but this became a fun thing and very important.

That Christmas we bought her tactile toys, such as play-dough and Lego. We also bought her a very good child's piano and we were amazed when she, without hesitation, began playing tunes on it. She had always loved music but it was evident that she had a gift and we were certainly going to encourage this. We searched the newspapers for a second-hand piano, and were lucky enough to acquire quite a good one for her. We were stunned when she took her place at the keyboard and began playing with both hands. But this was put to the back of our minds until we had her settled once again in another school.

Jan's love of music was evident from a very early age. John found a little record shop tucked in a side street of Nuneaton and he would take Jan along, occasionally, to buy a record. The Jewish lady and her son, who owned it, were lovely. As soon as Janis entered the shop the old lady, who was very frail and could hardly walk, would throw up her hands and speak in her native tongue and then say, 'Janis my darling'. She would then ask her son to bring out the bag of sweets she had for Jan and often she would have a record ready as a gift for her too. Jan adored the little old lady and would give her a big kiss and cuddle every time she visited her. When she came home from school she would always ask whether she could go to see 'her old lady', but she meant it in the nicest way, of course.

CHAPTER 11

The time quickly arrived when we were to travel the forty-five miles to Lickey, as it was called. As we were travelling along Jan piped up, 'Mummy, I wish our house was on wheels.' Once again my heart was in my throat as I choked back the tears.

It was a dreadful winter's day, and the snow was crisp and the roads icy. We entered the drive to the school, at the sign which read "Lickey Grange School for Children with Little or No Sight". My heart began to thump and I was shaking. It was real. My child was to go to a school for the blind.

John pulled up at the huge Edwardian manor house type building. There were children making their way to classes or various places. Handrails led them all over the place, along buildings, walls, and across the grounds. I was shocked at the sight of so many blind children. Several children were in a line holding the shoulder of the child in front as they made their way to wherever they had to go. The force of this brought it home to me that Janis was now one of them.

But she seemed so different from the other children. I was later to learn that Janis had good facial expressions because she had been sighted even though only for seven years. Many of the children had been born blind, and therefore their faces did not show much emotion. Neither did their bodies portray the same body language as children who had developed with sight and learned from experience how to act and behave. Some of the children had developed bad habits such as eye poking, head shaking and rocking movements. It was most traumatic to see this on such a large scale. I later learnt that these were referred to as "blindisms" by some people. Janis had none of these; in fact she still appeared as though she could see. Her rapid eye movements had long since stopped and her eyes were as lovely as ever.

As we waited outside the head's office, a little girl of about the same age as Jan came along. She was feeling her way and hesitated as she bumped into the bench where we were sitting. She said, 'Hello, who's that?'

I replied by telling her my name.

'What are you doing here?' she asked as she gradually came to my side and began exploring my clothes, my handbag and then my shoes. Her fingers delicately travelled over the large buckle and design on the shoe.

'They are nice shoes. Where is your little girl?'

I told her and she went over and had another exploration and then she said something very surprising: 'Can I come to live with you?'

I was very taken aback, but before I could answer a woman came and led us into the head's office, calling to the little girl to go on her way. I told the woman what the little girl had said, and she replied that a lot of the children were left at the school all year, only going home at the major holidays. I later learned that some parents were unable to accept their child's disability and it became easier and easier for them to leave their children at the school with the periods between visits becoming longer until they hardly went home at all. Indeed some of the children went into foster care during the school breaks. My heart was heavy.

We were introduced to the headmaster. He began by telling us about the school and its achievements. He said that Mr. Marshall had already told him that Janis was university material and that in three years time she would sit the eleven plus and would go to the finest school in the country. I was not in tune with his thinking. All I wanted was for my child to be at home and to go to the local school along with her friends.

He invited us to look round the school. One of the amazing things that stood out to me was seeing boys on sledges tearing down a snow-covered hill. When I asked how they managed to stop before hitting the fence at the bottom he replied that they usually stopped when they hit the fence. He told us of some parents asking a boy how he managed to ride a bicycle. The boy replied that you have to cock your leg over the saddle and just pedal. If they fell off, they just got back on again without help unless it was asked for.

I should have realised all of this, because no one ever thought that Jan was partially sighted. She had been involved in all of the kids' activities and nothing ever prevented her from joining in, even though it meant that she had more bumps and cuts than the others. But it was sad to watch Jan gradually losing her friends at home. I had watched as she went to their homes to call for them. No longer able to run down the drive and along the footpath, she would go out of our door and gradually edge her way until she found the raised kerb between our drive and next door's with her feet. She would then use the edge of one foot and kind of shunt along to the end, then stop and turn. Finding the edging stone on the front of the gardens, she would continue in the same way. She knew exactly when she had reached the home she wanted. It pulled at my heart when she returned to say no one wanted to play.

GHOST
by Janis Revell

A little girl came skipping through the wood
Hair wild-flying; face so good
And sweet; her eyes a-light

With the joys of youth's delight.

She came, that dauntless Fillette,
With words I never shall forget.
She said: "My years are few; but oh!
Even my life has one sorrow!"
"What," I asked her, "can this be?"
"Nobody will play with me."

"Little one," I said with a sigh,
"If I was young like you then why...
"I'd skip and run; pick daises sweet,
And kick hard shoes right off my feet."

"But oh!" she said, "the wind has lost
It's way, and life is cruel as frost."
"How," I asked her "can this be?"
"Tis true, no one will play with me."

I felt the years release my youth
And in grim and bitter truth
I held my arms out to Fillette
Dreaming youth was within me yet.

She gave a haunting cry of joy
That still now does my peace destroy.
Then came the wind...One hollow gush
Blew her from me with a rush.

And as she fled, she cried in agony:
"YOU FOOL! Mortals can't play with me!"

The head of Lickey agreed that Jan should start school as soon as possible, and so arrangements were made. I tried to convince myself that I was happier because Jan could now come home at weekends. My heart was not convinced; the crack that had begun on hearing the prognosis when she was two, was slowly getting bigger.

Janis was very quiet on the way home and I could find no words of comfort for her. I have to be honest and say that I was totally introspective. I was oblivious of John and the journey until we pulled up at the front door. However, as soon as we entered the hall Jan made for her interest table and sighed, saying, 'Mummy you haven't changed anything!'

I was surprised at her normality. I immediately set my mind to find something different to place on the tray.

The gloom of the bleak and cold winter added to my heaviness of spirit, but I had to get a new uniform for her new school and begin to prepare Jan for another move, trying all of the time to make it better for her by saying that she would be able to come home every Friday until Sunday tea time.

It was the beginning of January; a dark and dismal day as we drove her to become another child in the blind institution called Lickey Grange. This time, however, Jan was not keen on going to her new school. It was so far from home and I guess that, not being able to see her surroundings at all, it filled her with trepidation. On our journey there she was very engrossed in her inner thoughts and as much as I tried to jog her out of it she relapsed into her own world.

Unlike Exhall Grange, we had to drive her to the school and leave her there. Everything seemed fine until we bent to kiss her goodbye, and then she threw her little arms around me and cried, 'Please Mummy, don't leave me.' My tears dropped onto her blonde head as I attempted to pull her away. The housemistress came and gently pulled Jan, saying, 'She'll be fine when you have gone, you'll see. It's best if you just turn and go.'

We walked through the huge wooden doors but could not leave until we were sure that she was OK. We wandered along the outside of the building and peered into a window. There she was, and sure enough she was happily walking along with the woman who had taken her.

Jan was allowed to ring us once a week, and how we looked forward to hearing from her. She settled in quite well at first and we were quite confident that all would be well.

One of the teachers introduced us to another family from our town. I made friends very quickly with Sandra. We agreed to take it in turns to do the 90-mile round trip on Fridays and again on Sundays, and this arrangement seemed to work very well.

Jan's teachers were very impressed by her intelligence and hunger to learn. Also it was quickly noted that she had a gift for music and so she was given piano lessons as she could now read Braille fluently. She had learnt it in no time at all. The Braille music was more difficult, but she mastered this and soon passed her first grade in Piano with distinction.

Our social worker put me in touch with another young mum who had a three year old girl who had been born blind. She said that she had wanted to meet me. I did not hesitate and we soon became very good friends. I was shocked when I saw her baby for the first time, because she had the most beautiful eyes too and they seemed to perceive so much and yet they did not.

Carol and Sandra, the two other local mothers of blind children, got together with me to have Braille lessons. Every week on a Wednesday evening we would gather with the social worker at my home and learn how to read Braille, not by touch but by sight, and to write it. It was very difficult, but what a joy for me to be able to write letters to Jan and for her to write to me. Although she often told me that I was doing it wrong!

This, and my job, kept my mind from dwelling on Jan's blindness, but whenever anyone said such things as 'you're as blind as a bat', or 'open your eyes', and similar comments referring to sight, it went right through me, bringing unhappy thoughts to mind.

Chapter 12

A BABY BOY?

Jan had been at Lickey for a few months when I had a phone call from Mr. Oakley to tell us he thought there was a possibility of a baby for us. He said not to build up our hopes too much, as it was not absolutely certain yet. He rang a week later to say that the mother had changed her mind. This was to happen again a few weeks later.

It was almost the end of Jan's first term at Lickey and summer was approaching. We had planned to go to our holiday caravan as soon as she came home. I was busy getting things ready when the phone rang.

'Audrey, are you alone?' asked Mr. Oakley.

'Is there a problem?'

'No problem,' he replied, 'We have a beautiful baby boy for you.'

My heart leapt in my breast as though my baby had quickened inside of me. Tears jumped from my eyes as Mr. Oakley went on to explain that it was a sure thing. He went on to tell me that the baby was two weeks old and was with a foster mum. He was feeding well on Carnation milk and was a bonny boy.

'Now phone John, then make yourself a strong cup of coffee and phone me back later. Bye.' He was gone.

With trembling fingers I rang John immediately.

'John, guess what?' He sounded worried as he asked what it was. 'We have a baby boy,' I sobbed.

'Are you sure. Has Mr. Oakley phoned?' I told him it was definite.

'God bless you love, Oh God bless you,' and he too broke down and cried.

'I'll get home as soon as I can. When can we fetch him?'

'I don't know yet. I have to ring Mr. Oakley back.'

'God bless you love, I love you so much,' he repeated through strangled sobs.

I quickly rang Mr. Oakley back to set in motion the date that we would collect our baby. I wanted him immediately, but Mr. Oakley suggested that as Janis was looking forward to her holiday, we leave it until we came back. It was very difficult for me to wait, but I understood why Mr. Oakley was delaying things and we agreed.

A couple of days later a letter arrived telling us about the baby. The letter finished by suggesting we bring a blanket and carry cot 'in case you decide to take Craig home with you'. Craig was the name the mother had given him, but we had decided he was to be called Andrew Paul. Immediately, my mind rejected the idea that we would not want to take the baby home with us.

Jan came home full of excitement about going to the seaside again. I told her that when we came back we would be able to fetch her little brother.

'When can we see him?'

I explained that we had to wait two weeks. I was still shocked that she used the word "see".

We tried to enjoy the holiday and for Jan's sake made it as happy as we could. Our minds were not truly in it. I was into every baby shop buying all manner of babies' requirements. The time dragged by.

Eventually it was the day to collect our son. We entered the vast hallway nervously and gave out our name to the receptionist, who ushered us into a large room with a high ornate ceiling. She said that she would notify Mr. Oakley that we had arrived. In quite a short time the door opened and he came in with another woman we had not met before. Mr. Oakley introduced her and immediately went on to explain a little about the baby's feeding and a little detail about his background. He added that he was a gorgeous baby and very contented. He then asked Jan whether she was ready to fetch her baby brother.

Then he turned to John and me and asked us to wait where we were. He took Jan by the hand and the woman took the carrycot we had brought with us, and they all walked out of the room. Janis had taken to using a white cane, and as she walked away we could hear the tap, tap of the stick on the floor of the large, high, marbled hallway. John and I fell into a strained silence, with him perched on the edge of his seat.

Eventually we heard the tap, tap, tap of the cane and Jan's little voice echoing as she chatted excitedly to Mr. Oakley. My heart was beating so fast I thought it would burst. The door opened and Mr. Oakley lifted the carrycot onto a chair alongside John. Jan immediately stood at the side and said, 'Look at my brother Daddy. Isn't he beautiful?' I bit my lip and tears burnt my eyes.

I managed to stay where I was as John lifted the baby out of the cot. He was bundled up in a lovely shawl (I later learnt that his birth mother had sent this). I stretched my neck hoping that I might just get a peep of him. I knew I must not rush this for Jan's sake. After what seemed like an age Mr. Oakley said, 'Well I think it is time that your Mummy had a little hold of him.' Janis quickly felt her way to me and onto my lap. It suggested that she was a little threatened by the new arrival. I waited and hugged her, and then Mr. Oakley lifted the baby and placed him into Jan's arms with mine holding them both tightly to me. I peered into the bundle that lay before me and saw the most beautiful round peaceful face shining back at me.

My heart leapt with joy. How could I possibly not want to take this bundle of joy home with me? Now the tears began to fall and John was crying too. He handed me his only hanky and we wiped away the tears, as happiness and joy flooded us both.

Mr. Oakley turned to the other woman and said, 'I think it's time we left. We'll be back shortly.'

This was the moment I was waiting for. I slowly and carefully unfolded the shawl as best I could, with John's help. I looked at his little perfectly formed body. All he had on was a tiny vest and nappy. I looked him over from the top of his head to his tiny toes. One of the first things I must do when I got him home was to put oil onto his scalp as he had a covering of cradle cap. I then wanted to bathe him, put him into the clothes that we had bought, feed him and tuck him up. I also wanted for him to open his eyes.

We spent some time just looking and talking between us before Mr. Oakley and the woman returned. Mr. Oakley began by explaining what we must do to register the birth and that we might claim family allowance and tax benefits, which were allowable at that time. Also he explained about the six months we would have to wait until the court hearing. He went on to say that we would be getting a visit from another officer, and explained that this was all normal procedure as an independent person now had to do further investigations. This was purely to confirm that all the right precautions had been taken before the baby had been placed with us. I asked what the chances were of the mother changing her mind. Mr. Oakley said that it was highly unlikely, and if there were to be any problems he would fight hammer and tongs for our case.

I asked Jan to hop down as I lifted Andrew off her lap and suggested she help me tuck him up in his cot. I had placed a record under the pillow before we arrived. It was the music from Jesus Christ Superstar. As Jan tucked him up I said, 'Oh! What's this under here?' and taking her hand I put it onto the record.

'What is it?' she asked. I told her the title and she spun round saying, 'However did he know that I wanted this?' I said how clever it all was.

John placed the carrycot on the back seat and fastened Janis into her seat beside it, asking Jan to look after her new baby brother. I could see her grow with pride as she stretched out her hand to caress Andrew's face. The crack in my heart had begun to heal over a little.

As soon as we arrived home, I took steps to get the bath ready and his new clothes laid out. I asked Jan to help me by telling her where she would find things like the baby talc and his hairbrush. Eventually he was ready, and I placed him in the warm water. His eyes were wide open and his little fists flailing as he obviously enjoyed the warmth of the water on him. He was so beautiful.

Jan helped me to towel him dry and apply the talc. Then she gently brushed his hair and I settled down to give him the bottle that John had been preparing. I sat with the baby in my arms and Jan perched by my side on the arm of the chair. She did not miss a thing and laughed out loud when he filled his nappy. She didn't wait around as I changed it!

The next four weeks were idyllic. Janis was still at home during that time, and she loved coming with me for walks as I pushed the pram along. She did not show much sign of jealousy, or so I thought. She had already been to three schools and she was only 7 years of age. We were soon to find out just how difficult this further change in her life was for her.

When the time arrived for Janis to go back to Lickey Grange, her insecurity really showed. As we started to say our good-byes she screamed like never before, begging of us not to leave her. We had been waiting for almost four years for our baby boy, and his arrival had coincided with Jan's loss of sight and her having to go so far away from home. In her mind I guess it was as though she had made room for this baby boy. I was determined that I would have to do all in my power to address the situation. But the strength of her jealousy was to be more evident on her next visit home.

I was preparing to go to the shops and called to Jan to ask whether she wanted to come with me. John was working on the car in the drive. Jan called back that she wanted to stay and play, so I gave her a kiss and promised not to be long. When I returned, John was still in the drive but met me with, 'I think you'd better prepare yourself for some trouble indoors.'

I asked him what he meant but all he said was for me to go in and find out.

When I entered the lounge I was shocked. There were lipstick marks all over the carpet and a white powder scattered all around the lounge, hall and up the stairs. I could not find Jan. I called her but there was not a sound. As I went up the stairs the powder became denser. I followed the trail into my bedroom where I discovered all of my and John's clothes pulled down from the wardrobe, and the bed completely stripped with the bedding piled on the floor. I was shocked. For a seven-year-old to do all this showed just how angry she was.

I then went into the bathroom, and there in the bath was a pile of dirty linen taken from the basket. It was strewn about and the powder, which I then discovered was cleaning powder, was scattered on top of the clothes. I thought that she might have been into Andrew's bedroom, and I opened the door dreading what I might find in there. Surprisingly, not a thing had been touched. It quickly dawned on me that her unconscious anger was aimed at John and me.

Still there was neither sight nor sound of Jan. I ventured downstairs and looked all around. Then I heard a little squeak. I called her name and listened again. It was coming from behind the settee. I heard a sob. I sat down in an armchair and gently called her name.

'Janis, I missed you when I went for a walk. Are you crying because you really wanted to come too?'

Her crying turned into deep sobs. I called her again, and slowly she crept out of her hiding place and made her way to where I sat, feeling her way along the furniture onto my lap.

'I'm here darling,' I called, so that she could follow my voice. I wrapped my arms around her and held her tight as I kissed her tear-stained face.

'My, you have been busy while I've been out, haven't you? But I guess we need to do some tidying up. Will you help me please?'

As quickly as she could she shot from my lap and asked me to show her what she had to do. We spent the next hour or so putting things back where they belonged and I hoovered through, leaving the lipstick stains for John to remove. Then we cuddled up in front of the TV while Andrew slept. She still enjoyed the children's programs, but now I had to relay and fill in the visual parts audibly. I just reassured her of my love for her and her body relaxed and nestled into mine.

The return to Lickey became more and more distressing for Janis and for us. It was terrible to hear her screams as we left through the great oak doors of this institution. It was a matter of trying to harden ourselves to the fact that we had no choice and this was the best place for her. The staff assured us that as soon as we had left the building she was fine. Academically and musically she was doing exceedingly well, and in 1971 there was no way that a blind child could be integrated into a mainstream school.

Christmas that year was a happy time, and Janis now seemed to be adapting to having Andy in our home. It would soon be necessary to attend court for the finalisation of the adoption. The letter arrived with the due date of the court hearing, and in the meantime Mr. Oakley had been in touch and was very encouraging. However, we still had to prove that we were fit parents. To lose Andy would have been just too much to bear and so the strain began to take its toll on John. He worked long hours and at weekends had the school run to do – a round trip of almost 200 miles. We were becoming irritable with one another. I did not realise that John was undergoing severe exhaustion.

We arrived at court in plenty of time. Jan was with us, and we went into the judge's chambers filled with fear and trepidation. We did not realise that it was to be quite so formal, but the judge arrived in his wig and gown and everyone was told to stand as he entered. He proceeded to question first one and then another of the experts involved in placing the child for adoption. Finally he turned to Janis, saying, 'And what does Janis think of her baby brother?'

She quickly replied, 'I love him, he's mine.'

A chuckle went round the room and the judge said, 'I can see no reason why this child should not be officially placed with Mr. & Mrs. Revell.' Pushing back his chair, he stood up and everyone followed.

I can't remember who came to us to congratulate us, but I do remember clearly how John grasped Andrew to him and then lifting Janis into his other arm he marched out of the room crying like a baby. I tried to keep pace with him. As he strode down the long marbled corridor, a little old lady came up to him and asked, 'Are you OK, love?'

John was now crying so much he could not answer and continued to the car. I trailed behind him. He asked me to unlock the door of the car, and as I did so I asked him to let me have the children. I was shocked as he sobbed out 'No one will ever take these away from me, ever.'

I begged of him to let them go. It was some ten minutes before he gained control of his emotions and set off for home. Although it caused me some concern it seemed to pass over. I thought it was just all so much relief following the months of strain. That is, until the weekend when it was time for Jan to go back to Lickey.

Jan playing her new piano as Andy and I look on.

CHAPTER 13

Sandra and her husband Geoff came to pick John and Janis up. I waved them all goodbye and as was my usual way of coping, out came the polish and hoover. I worked like mad until John returned. I heard the car in the drive and then there was thumping at the front door. John had his key, and I was puzzled. When I opened the door I found John slumped between Sandra and Geoff with his arms around their necks and he kept repeating, 'I'm so sorry love, I really am.' He said that his head hurt a lot.

Sandra and Geoff helped me to get him upstairs and onto the bed. They went into the lounge while I undressed him and put him into bed. I went downstairs and asked them what had happened. They explained that Jan had been crying a lot and begging to come back home. He had left her with a care worker and as he walked to the doors he had almost collapsed. He'd started crying and holding his head.

I immediately rang our GP who was a lovely kind man. He asked me questions and asked whether John had taken the Valium he had prescribed the week before for anxiety. I said that he had. He suggested that he should take another followed by a shot of brandy.

Sandra and Geoff said they would get off home and left me to do what was necessary.

We are not drinkers and neither did we keep drink in the home. However, I knew that a friend across the road would have some. I dashed across and asked her for a tot of brandy, explaining what the doctor had said. Neither of us knew what a tot was, and her husband was not at home. So she proceeded to pour out a good amount of brandy into a glass, I dashed home and told John that he must drink it and he complied without question. He drank the last dregs.

Shortly afterwards, the doorbell went. I was surprised to see Raj our GP, at the door. As he entered he said, 'I was a little concerned about John so I thought I'd just pop round to check on him,' and proceeded up the stairs.

We were met with loud snores. John was well away. The GP asked how much brandy I had given him. When I showed him the glass and pointed to the level of drink he laughed and said, 'It won't do him any harm. Let him sleep the night away and I'll come in again tomorrow just to check him out.'

I thanked Raj for coming round at such a late time of day.

When John did wake in the morning he was still complaining about his head but I was sure that this time it was a hangover. However, he was extremely tearful and continually asking about the children. I was relieved when Raj arrived at lunchtime but rather perplexed as I listened to his questioning. He sat by John's side and asked him who did the decorating.

He commented on the wood cladding on the dining room wall and asked John how much it had cost, had he done it himself and how did he do it? The questions seemed to go on and on.

After about fifteen minutes, Raj got up to leave and as I led him to the door he turned to me and said 'John has had a nervous breakdown, he's crying the tears he has stored up for many years. You must let him cry as much as he wants at this stage. He has been strong for you and now you must be strong for him. He should go into hospital, but between us I think we can help him to recover. When he is up and about I want you to bring him to my surgery twice a week.'

I thanked him and he was gone.

John came down and immediately lay on the sofa in the lounge and turned his face to the back. He was still crying like a baby and there was nothing I could do for him but allow him to cry out his pain.

I went to collect Janis from school on the following Friday and confided in one of the teachers, who had a kindness about her that asked for your confidence. When I explained what had happened she asked whether I would like the school social worker to visit. This was arranged, and the following week the woman came to our home.

John still lay in the same position. The woman introduced herself and asked him whether he could tell her exactly how he was feeling. He turned and sat up to face her. His face was ashen and puffy from crying. He looked so worn out. There were some photographs on the coffee table, taken when we were at the caravan, showing Janis and Andrew in the swimming pool together. John picked them up, and blurted out amid deep sobs, 'You tell me what use these are. She can't see them.' The tears still flowed down his cheeks.

The social worker turned to me and asked whether I could write Braille. When I said that I could she smiled.

'What I suggest is that you Braille up some large labels the size of the photos, describing what the pictures are, and stick them to the back. You'll be surprised how much pleasure Janis will get from this.'

John sat bolt upright, his face pained, he shouted 'And what experience have you? Have you got a child that is blind?'

'No, I haven't,' she replied gently, 'and I don't pretend to know your pain. But my husband is blind and his hobby is photography.'

I was quite taken by her answer and asked her to tell us more about him. She did talk a little but then said she thought John had had enough for one day and after finishing her tea she wished us all the very best.

We had to go to see Raj. I drove the car and we both went into the surgery. Raj asked how the week had passed. John was silent and so I explained that he had been crying on and off.

'Tell me,' Raj began, 'what hobbies does Janis have?'

I explained that she had many but most of them were visual and since she had lost her sight she was not able to take part in them. I explained that she was rapidly learning Braille. Also, that she was leaping ahead with her music.

Raj turned now to John and asked 'John I wonder whether you will help me. I have given a great deal of thought to this problem. There is no riding for the disabled in this area. Would you help me to raise funds and set up a school?'

John looked thoughtful. I had not seen him look peaceful for a long time but this had triggered something in his mind. 'Of course I will. But how will it benefit Janis? She can't see and won't be able to ride.'

Raj placed his hand on John's arm. 'She will. You'll see that she can do it, I promise you.'

Twice a week for the next six weeks we went along to visit Raj. His counsel and the idea of the riding school seemed to have awakened something in John, and gradually I saw him begin to pick up the reigns of life again.

It was now time for Andrew to be christened and all arrangements were in place. The day was planned down to the last detail, but I did not realize how fragile John's emotional state was. Everything went well until the vicar was about to put the water onto Andrew's head. Just before he took Andrew into his arms, he turned and handed Jan a lighted candle. He just held the candle in front of her, saying that this was a light for her and the baby. Of course, there was no response from Janis. John almost snatched the candle from his hand and the tears began to pour down his face yet again. The rest of the day went along as planned, but I was concerned about this fresh bout of crying.

It was time for John to visit Raj for another talking session. As we entered his room and seated ourselves at his side he asked his usual question: 'How has it been John?'

John sat looking at his hands folded in his lap. He was silent and made no move to answer the question. I answered by saying that the christening was a bit too much for him. Raj turned directly to John and asked him to explain, and John proceeded to tell him about the candle.

I was shocked at Raj's response. He raised his voice and said, 'Enough! That is enough John! You are now letting emotional matters get out of hand and the time has come when you must get a grip.'

John's face was white, his eyes large in disbelief at this turn of attitude. Neither of us realized that it was all part of the therapy and it was just what John needed to finalize his grieving process and to help him to get back to his former self. Surprisingly it did just that.

The following Monday, John got ready for work. He was in terrible fear after being away for almost three months. Added to this was the fact that he thought it an unmanly thing for him to have been off work for so long. But Raj had assured him on that score and told him that it takes a good man to cry as he had done. 'It shows you have a good heart John, so don't be ashamed of crying, ever.'

I waved him goodbye as he set off and asked that he ring me when he had a chance. Sure enough, at coffee break he rang and I was so pleased to hear from his tone of voice that he was back to his old self and happy to be back at work. He was still very concerned for the kids and me though, but that is John. He always had our wellbeing at heart before anything else.

Things began to settle down as we began adjusting to being a family of four. I still worked a part-time job at the local GP's surgery in the evenings. It fitted very well with the hours that John worked, so that there was not any problem with baby-sitting.

I loved the work and got on very well with the senior GP, Dr. Banister. He was a very warm friendly man, and he gave me permission to take Jan into surgery on my Saturday morning duty. She loved to come in with me and was intrigued by the typewriter. She had begun lessons at Lickey, as they encouraged typing, not only for pleasure but also for the future in schoolwork and for writing to people or writing down instructions, etc. She would tap away in a proper fashion and later she became a very proficient touch typist.

CHAPTER 14

Jan had been begging me to buy her a pair of red shoes. I took her all over town in the hope of getting her a pair, but without success until I was offered a pair of brown leather shoes which also had a hint of red, a sort of oxblood colour. The shop assistant persuaded Jan that they were red, and by this time I was too tired to argue. As soon as we got home, Jan put on her new shoes and ran round to her friend. She quickly came back in floods of tears.

I was bemused as she sobbed out 'You lied to me. You lied. You said they were red and they aren't.' I tried to explain, but she said that her friend had told her not to be stupid and that her shoes were brown. It was a huge lesson to me, and never, ever again did I try to convince her that something was not exactly what she wanted. It took a little while for her trust to be built up and she would repeatedly ask whether I was sure when I was describing certain things to her. How careful we had to be, and how much do we all take for granted in our everyday lives?

It was imperative that I told her every detail so that she could know what was happening in the world she could no longer see. One day I was in the kitchen making a jelly. The smell of it stirred her imagination.

'What are you doing mummy?'

'I'm make a strawberry jelly'

'How do you do that?'

'Well. I break the jelly into cubes. It's already scored to make it easier for me.'

'What does scored mean?'

I explained and continued, 'Then I put them into the dish and pour on some boiling water until they have dissolved.'

'What colour is it now?'

Her questions went on - 'But how does it get hard again?'

'Well I put it in the fridge and it sets.'

'But why do you have to do that? Why don't we just eat it as it is in the beginning'?

And so the questions and descriptions were endless, and at times my patience did wear thin, but all the time and effort that I put into helping her visualise and know were so very important for a little girl who had an inquiring mind but no sight.

Raj had kept us informed of the progress towards setting up a Riding for The Disabled school in our area, and now the time had arrived for the grand opening. It was all so very exciting and Raj was especially pleased with how quickly it had all happened.

Janis was really excited. She loved animals. I remember when she was about twelve we took her to a farm and whilst there we could hear a horse whinnying. Jan immediately asked what was wrong with it. The farmer explained that it was rather wild, but undeterred Jan asked to be taken to it. The farmer was hesitant but Janis insisted. So, very carefully she was led to this beautiful horse in the field.

The farmer took Jan's hand and reached out so that she could just feel the horse's nose. But within a matter of minutes Janis was creeping closer and closer, talking to the animal all of the time, telling him how lovely he was and how she loved him. Quite soon, she was kissing him on his nose and the farmer said he was amazed because this particular horse did not tolerate people at all and would lash out with his feet if ever anyone approached.

Whenever we visited a farm she wanted to get really close and was a frequent visitor to the animal sanctuary near our home. On one occasion she asked me to meet her at the huge pet centre in Peterborough. When we arrived her friend. who had taken her, led us to the aquarium section. We were amazed to see Jan standing with a huge snake coiled round her neck arms and waist. It was a huge thing and she stood there giggling and insisted we went over to stroke it. She never failed to amaze us.

On the Saturday of the official opening of the Riding for the Disabled school, the Mayor and Mayoress were to attend together with the press. It was a delightful, sunny summer's day, and the crowds had come in great numbers. Janis was shown her horse, a lovely white beauty whose name happened to be Revel. Janis asked whether he had been named after her.

She was soon up into the saddle without any fear whatsoever, and a crowd of young girls was at her side as she gradually moved off. She shouted, 'I want to go faster.' It was a grand experience for us all. My heart was full of thanksgiving for all of the work that had gone into bringing this about. It was evident just how much this would mean to Jan. The horse gave her the freedom to get around which her loss of sight had taken away. Revel was her eyes for the hour or so that she was up on his back.

Jan's inquisitive face showed her delight as the horse began to move. She took to horse riding as she took to most things, with great enthusiasm and a desire not only to learn how to ride and jump the horse but to clean out and brush and look after Revel herself. She had fallen in love with him.

Every Saturday morning without fail we would take her to the school. She looked very good in the saddle, her back upright and her head held high. I was so proud of her. In no time at all she learnt to trot and then canter. Quite soon she wanted to gallop and jump. Even then she was not completely satisfied because she knew that she had someone at her side holding an attached lead rein. 'I want to go on my own, all on my own with no one around me,' was her plea.

Jan meets Revel with her daddy(John in glasses).

Eventually Jan was proficient enough to be let out along country lanes, the only proviso being that she had another horse alongside with a lead rein. She was a little disappointed but agreed to the compromise when I explained that if there was an overhanging branch at her eye level then a nasty accident could occur. It did not matter to her that a car could collide, as her answer was that they could see her, couldn't they? Riding was to become a love of her life.

When Andrew was about five years of age he asked whether he could try horse riding. He had always stood and watched Jan, and had never once shown any enthusiasm for getting on a horse until now. We had a word with the owner of the school and she agreed that it would be a good idea. She suggested that Andrew borrowed a hat just in case he did not take to it, saving us some expense. How true that was. There was great excitement as the two of them got ready to go. I had to stay at home and get on with some jobs that were pressing in on me. I kissed them all goodbye and waved as they drove off.

I was just about to serve lunch when I heard the car pull into the drive. I waited for Andrew to come racing in to tell me all the news. Very slowly, the kitchen door opened. Andy poked his little face round. He was a shocking colour.

'Whatever has happened? Did you have another car-sickness bout?' I asked, as I bent down to look at him more closely.

'No, it wasn't that, it was the horse,' he replied.

'What do you mean?'

'It was all that up and down and round and round. I didn't like it Mummy, and I don't ever want to go again.' The tears were now filling his eyes. I struggled to cover my amusement and assured him that he would not be made to go, and he seemed very relieved.

It was so good that Jan now had many interests to occupy her busy mind. Braille, music and horse-riding. Andy was able to run and play out with his friends and to get on his bike and enjoy all the boys' things outdoors, and so our lives began to become less worrying for the first time in a very long time.

Jan was progressing very well at her academic studies too. Her teachers were always telling us that she was very bright and would go to Chorleywood Grammar School. This was another school for high achievers and we were told that they only took the cream of pupils from the many schools run by the RNIB throughout the country. I tried to prepare Jan for the entrance exam and she showed no sign of apprehension.

Her love of spiritual stories and love of Jesus had begun to grow, and on one of her weekend visits home she told me how she had seen Jesus again. I was taken aback by her comment and asked her to explain.

'Well, I get lost at school, sometimes, and I get very nervous, but I have discovered that if I ask Jesus to help me he comes along and takes me to where I want to go.' It was said with a childlike innocence, and yet my heart was moved. Would the crack in my heart that had begun years before be healed?

Jan wanted to read about Jesus for herself. She was now a fluent reader of Braille but there were no children's books available for her to read. Coincidentally, on a holiday to Butlins around this time Janis entered a talent competition. She wanted to sing a song called "Sitting here so lonely in the moonlight". It was obvious to the audience that she was visually impaired. A lady sitting at the back of me tapped me on the shoulder and began telling me about her daughter, Joy, who was also partially sighted. She asked me whether it would be OK for her to contact Janis. A lovely friendship developed as a result.

Joy was a teacher, and she was so encouraging to Jan when she had to leave home and move schools. She also sent her some lovely gifts, some of which were of a Christian nature. Joy came to stay in our home, and through her I learnt about the Torch Trust for the Blind. It was in its infancy. They transcribed Christian literature into Braille. As soon as Jan heard of this she wanted to know whether she could have her own Bible story books.

We made arrangements to visit the Torch House which was in Hurstpierpoint. As we were having our evening meal, Mr. Heath, who with his wife are the founders, came to speak with us and said hello to Jan. She immediately blurted out, 'I want to read about Jesus.' He was a very gentle man and kindly told her that they had never had an enquiry from someone so young, and therefore, they did not have anything suitable for children. She was not dissuaded but asked whether she could read something. Later, he produced a Christian magazine for older readers and Jan was soon lost in its contents.

Dad Heath, as he was affectionately called, was so impressed he had a photograph taken of Jan as she sat engrossed in the magazine. A few weeks later he asked whether we would give permission for the photograph to be blown up and used at various Christian conferences. The photograph was very large, and I was thrilled to see it on the billboards in the foyer of a conference we attended. Not only this, but at the next committee meeting they discussed the lack of literature for small children. From this came the production of a Braille magazine called Spark. This was eventually circulated to several schools for the visually impaired.

One Friday I had driven to pick Jan up from Lickey. One of the staff was waiting for me and took me into a room. Her face was serious; I recognised the expression and it caused me to be anxious. She quickly explained that it was thought that Janis had a hearing problem.

'No.' My voice seemed loud. 'No, you must be wrong.'

The teacher went on to say that Janis had some lessons from a teacher who was blind. She had been concerned that Jan had not been answering any questions, and knowing how bright she was had become concerned. She asked a sighted member of staff to stand in on a lesson and observe. This teacher had witnessed that Jan was sitting with her head turned to one side in the direction of the teacher straining to hear what was being said. She suggested that I went along the corridor to look for myself as Jan was still in class with the blind teacher. I was shocked when I saw her. She was sitting with her back to the side of her desk and facing a wall with her head tilted towards the front.

I looked at the member of staff and she put her hand on my arm.

'I think that you should make arrangements to have Janis looked at by a hearing specialist.' She suggested that we got a referral letter from our GP for a hospital in London. My heart was thumping. Could it be possible that she could become deaf as well as blind? I struggled to push the thought from my mind. But this was serious stuff and no time must be wasted to get her seen in the hope that something could be done.

Again I had the job of telling John when he came home from work. As was usual, he took control and tried to reassure me that things were OK. I had been testing Jan and she seemed to respond to everything I said or any noise that I made, so what could possibly be wrong? Surely if there was nothing too seriously wrong she would not need to go to a specialist hospital, especially in London?

Another stomach-churning day arrived as we made our way to see the consultant in children's ear problems. The hospital waiting room was most appealing for children, and great lengths had been taken to stock it out and decorate it for the benefit of reducing a child's anxiety. There was a huge beautiful rocking horse. A small child already occupied it.

My attention was drawn to a young couple sitting together. The woman had a small child on her lap and the baby was obviously very disabled; her head was rolling and she was obviously blind. There was no communication between her parents and the man's body language suggested great anxiety. His wife was in tears. The tension between them was palpable. I wanted to go over and hold them or at least talk with them. To encourage or help in whatever way I could. But who was I to do this sort of thing, and was it the right time? I tried to relax into my seat as we waited for Janis to be called into the consulting room.

Once again, Jan was oblivious to all that was going on and was happily building with the Lego blocks provided.

The consultant proceeded to tell us that he would carry out several tests on Janis. We followed him from room to room, and in her usual fashion Janis was happy to do whatever the doctor or nurses asked of her. At the end of a very arduous day the consultant called us into his room. He was smiling. I could not let my hopes rise for fear of having them broken yet again.

'There is nothing wrong with your daughter's ears,' the consultant told us. 'She has some catarrh and I think that this could be causing her some problem, but that should clear and she won't have any further problems.'

Such a feeling of relief engulfed me. John and I both said at the same time, 'Thank God for that.'

The teachers at Lickey were not convinced. For myself, I had begun taking note of the amount of times I had to repeat things to Janis. I had observed from my nieces and nephews that often children would become so engrossed in play that they did not always respond when spoken to, and I tried to convince myself that this was what the problem was.

CHAPTER 15

We had become members of the Baptist church. Jan was very keen on going and loved the music side of things. She also loved the pastor. He was a well-loved man and always made such a fuss of her. The Sunday school teachers were also very good and quickly adapted to the needs of a blind child in their class. Furthermore, they asked us whether it would be possible for Jan to become a member of the Girls Brigade. We had no objection and, of course, in her usual inquiring way, Jan was very happy to have something else to occupy her. She attended all of the marches through the town centre. An officer marched either side of her and anyone watching the procession would never have known that they had a blind child walking with them. Jan absolutely loved the music and the striding along to the sound of the drumbeat. It was all very moving for us to watch. Later, Andy joined the Boy's Brigade and church became a big part of our lives.

Jan's love of music was growing every day and her piano playing was excellent. She flew through her first grades and gained some with distinction. It was because of this that John and I decided to buy an old piano accordion that we saw at a jumble sale. We bought it really out of a sense of fun, and knew that Jan would get some pleasure from it. But we were taken aback when she quite quickly managed to get the straps on to her shoulders with the accordion in front of her small frame and play a tune. The next stage was to take her along to an accordion teacher. Yet again we were shocked at the teacher's response.

'Janis has perfect pitch and is an excellent pupil. However, this instrument does not do her justice and my advice to you is to buy her the very best that you can afford.'

As soon as we had enough money saved we went into Leicester and bought her a lovely new child's accordion. Jan was overjoyed. The fact that she now had many interests and was also able to find pleasure in most things brought healing to our hearts. It was a joy to watch her progress, and also to see how close she had grown to her little brother. She became very fluent in playing the accordion, and played it in church and at a school for educationally subnormal children where I now worked as a speech therapist. She was allowed to go into a room where the most disturbed children were. As soon as Jan began playing her accordion they were peaceful. It was amazing to see these agitated children sitting calmly.

It was very difficult to keep a balance between our attention for Jan and equally for Andy. He was such a placid child who was happy with the simplest of things. In hindsight, I now realise that he was too good a child. Children quickly pick up on all manner of things going on in the home without us having to spell it out, and Andy had taken it upon himself, from a very early age, not to demand too much from us in any way. I discovered, as time passed, that this is quite normal in homes where there is a disabled child. I learnt that a sibling of a disabled child sees the problems that their brother or sister has to endure and the demands made on their parents, and either takes a back seat or alternatively becomes very disturbed. I wish I had known this at the time, but none of us are experts in child rearing and even less so when the child has such difficulties.

Andy never asked for anything at all, and if he ever had a problem he would keep repeating 'Don't worry mummy, please don't worry.' Even when, on a bitterly icy winter's day, he went out to play and slipped on the ice breaking his arm, he did not make a sound as he came in from the cold holding his arm behind his back. It was only when John asked to see what he had done that we realised he had broken his wrist and John rushed him to hospital. Andy's parting words to me were 'Don't worry mummy, please don't worry!'

Life settled down once again. Jan now came home from Lickey by minibus. We had moved house again into a different county, and they arranged transport for children.

I would wait with Andy at the window of our home, and as soon as we spotted the minibus coming down the road we would be out of the door and ready to help Jan climb down. She would clasp my neck and after kisses all round she would immediately make for her room and go round touching all her belongings to make sure that nothing had changed. Then she would get her records out and play music for a while, and next to the piano, or get the accordion out and play that. Noise abounded for the short time she was home.

The weekends were a hectic time with so much to cram into two short days. As Sunday teatime came around, the house would take on a sombre atmosphere. Jan would become very quiet and want lots of cuddles. We would watch her favourite programme on TV before the minibus came to pick her up. The show was called "Skippy the Bush Kangaroo", and Jan just loved the story. But, as time passed she would just say that she had tummy ache and that she wished she could stay at home. We had no choice. It hurt us terribly to put her onto the bus and wave her off. As soon as the bus had driven off I would go into the house and move furniture around and clean for hours. It was my way of dealing with my pain.

One Friday, I went to get Jan down as usual from the bus. I was aware that something was wrong. Her face was so ashen with red rims under her eyes. She did not seem to have any joy in her at all. I watched her edge her way along the bus and thought that maybe she was sickening for something. I lifted her down and she burst into floods of tears. The bus drove off as I took Jan into the house. She sobbed and sobbed before I eventually dragged from her the source of her tears. Very gradually she began to unfurl the story of what had caused her to be so upset.

Between sobs, she told me that she wanted to learn the game of chess. Her teacher knew of her desire to learn the game, and so on this Friday afternoon the teacher asked a young man, who she knew played the game, whether he would take Jan into a classroom and show her what chess involved. The classroom was empty. They had not been playing very long when the young man persuaded Jan to sit on his lap. She was a very friendly child and, of course, very tactile as blind people need to be. He then proceeded to bend her backwards and tried to kiss her. She screamed but it made no difference as he continued to do whatever was his intention.

Fortunately, a male teacher happened to be passing the room and heard Janis scream. He barged in and apparently pulled Jan off and then set about dealing with the lad. Jan told me that the teacher told her that he was tempted to hit him with a stick he was carrying. Unbelievably, Jan was put onto the bus home without an attendant and we were not contacted about the incident. She travelled the whole 45-mile journey in terrible distress.

It was soon time for John to come home from work. As soon as he heard what had happened he rang the police, who immediately came to our home. It was a terrible event. They questioned Jan over and over, and then asked whether we would object to undressing her as the woman police officer wanted to take photographs of her body if there were any bruises. The thing seemed to take hours. Then they left us and said that they would return in the morning after making inquiries.

I did not sleep. I kept going in to see Jan. Fortunately she slept through the night.

Around ten in the morning, a police officer arrived. He sat down and began to tell us about his enquiries. He said that the young lad in question was just eighteen years of age and was doing voluntary work at the school before going off to university. After the incident, the lad had caught a train to London and gone to the headquarters of the Mormons, of which he was a member, and confessed everything to the elders. The officer said that in his opinion it would be better to drop the matter, and explained that the case could go on for many months and then Jan would have to testify all over again in every little detail. He thought that, although the offence was serious enough, no actual bodily harm was caused and in his experience it would be wisest to let the matter go. Although we wanted the young man brought to task, we had Jan's welfare at heart and decided to go along with what had been suggested.

The time was fast approaching for Jan to sit the entrance exam for Chorleywood Grammar School. It was an eleven plus exam, but Janis was considered capable enough at the age of ten to take it. It had been explained to us that she would stay from Friday to Sunday, and during that time not only would she take the academic exams but she would be assessed as far as her personal care was concerned and whether she was able to look after herself.

Little did I know that Jan was petrified. If she passed this exam it meant that she would live away from home for a month at a time. It was also over a hundred miles away. John had taken time off work to drive us down to Rickmansworth. We were on tenterhooks all of the time and I guess Jan picked up on this. She had her fingers in her Braille book all the way, only speaking a couple of times to ask whether we had arrived yet.

The school was a huge mansion of a place set in the most superb gardens. We entered through the huge oak doors, and I stood in the massive marbled hallway in awe of this grand building. To the right of us was a very wide, sweeping wooden staircase. The excitement of the new girls mingled with the sound of echoing footsteps. I was surprised to see how easily some of the girls were navigating this on their first day as without hesitation they dashed up and down.

Jan clung tightly to my hand. She looked so very pale and lacking in her usual confidence. I was unaware at the time that the noise was horrendous for her. All she was aware of, because of her hearing problem which had still not been diagnosed, was the tremendous hubbub and clatter. It was many more years before we learnt that Jan had not been hearing very well from an early age.

Someone came to us and introduced herself as Jan's future house matron. I tried to explain that Jan was very nervous. I was too. I did not want to leave Jan and neither did I want her to be so far away from home. I have never felt so awful. It felt as though I was abandoning her into other people's care, to something which was beyond my control, and in which Jan had no choice. Suppose some of the people that I was to entrust her to were not trustworthy? But I had to remind myself that this was the best chance she would have as it was deemed to be the finest school of its type in the country and I knew that they only took the very highest achievers from the many schools for the visually impaired.

We were shown around the house – a huge sprawling building. On the way round I mentioned Jan's love of music and the house matron suggested I spoke with the music teacher, Miss Elgar, a relative of the great composer himself. Jan perked up at this. We were shown into the main hall where other parents and their children were having tea and biscuits. We joined them but Jan was very clingy, disturbingly so. The other girls seemed more confident.

Miss Elgar had been told about Jan's musical talent and the teacher wanted to hear her for herself. She took us into a magnificent music room and led Jan to the grand piano. She asked her to play whatever she wanted. Jan was now full of confidence and at home before the splendid piano. After she had finished Miss Elgar asked her to pitch certain notes. Then she turned to us and said that Jan was, indeed, gifted and had perfect pitch and she would do all that she could to further her musical talent. My pride swelled and new confidence emerged at the attitude of this teacher.

After this we were ushered into the house matron's room where form filling was taking place. After filling in the normal paperwork we came to some documents which we were told were for us to sign giving permission for Janis to be adopted. I was taken by surprise but the house-matron went on to explain that owing to the fact that the girls were away from home for very long periods they liked to place them with local families for weekend stays. She said that the people were well vetted and were upstanding professional people. It was considered to be good for the girl's experience and development. Reluctantly, and with the fear of abandonment returning, I signed the form feeling that I was signing my child over to another family. '*I* should be looking after her,' was a scream trapped within me.

It was suggested that we take Jan for a stroll around the grounds before leaving her for the weekend. It was an uncomfortable time. We walked on the manicured lawns. I tried to jerk Jan out of her serious mood, but she was not having it and remained in silence until it was time for us to go. She did not cry or attempt to hold onto us, which seemed all the more painful. She just stood with her arms hanging limply by her sides, not attempting to wave or make any movement. It was worse than if she had screamed at us for leaving her there. We drove off as the house matron took Jan indoors.

The weekend passed quite quickly and it was soon time to go and fetch Jan home. She was so pleased to see us, and was full of all that had gone on over the weekend. There was a change in her, she seemed more relaxed and confident and her usual buoyant comical mood had returned. She chatted for quite a good part of the journey. I chastised myself for fretting so much about leaving her there.

Janis passed the entrance exam and she was to start at Chorley (as it became known) after the end-of-term holidays. She received the news in a very quiet manner. I began to get all of her clothes ready and newly labelled, and tried to create some measure of interest for her, but this time I was having a great deal of difficulty.

The days flew past until the time came for us to take Jan down to Chorleywood. There were many cars parked in the car park and driveway. Janis seemed quietly apprehensive, but the positive manner of the staff and the house-matron. as we entered the building, calmed our anxiety. Jan was ushered up to her room to meet her dormitory mates and to choose her bed. She did not turn to wave us off.

CHAPTER 16

Andrew had now started at school and so the house was very quiet and empty for most of the weekdays.

I waited anxiously for the time of week when Jan was allowed to phone home. At first, the calls came regularly but then she began to miss calling me. I was concerned and rang the school. I was told that this was a good sign as it showed that Jan was settling down and was not worried about home. It brought some relief.

On one of our visits to pick up Jan for her monthly exeat we were ushered into a room by a member of staff. Her tone implied that there might be more bad news on the way.

'Have you ever noticed that Janis walks very badly?' she blurted out. I was shocked at her question.

She continued, 'We've been watching her for some time now and she has a most peculiar walking gait. We wondered whether you would agree for her to see a doctor at the school. We will then have a better idea as to the problem.'

I butted in with, 'Do you think it's serious?'

'We have no idea, but we are aware that Janis has mobility problems.'

My mind flashed to seeing Janis descend the large staircase, and I always wondered how it was possible for the other girls to dash down and back up the stairs with little difficulty and yet Jan was always very slow and precise in her movements. Then it struck me that there was a definite change in her mobility. She had always been so energetic and independent, but of late she had been less confident.

'Of course, yes, please arrange for whoever you think is the best person to assess the problem.'

She assured me that measures would be put into place and quite soon we had an appointment with the doctor. I knew that it was not good news as he asked, 'Would you be prepared for Janis to come into The Hospital for Nervous Diseases in London?' He must have recognised my reaction as he quickly added, 'It's not what you might feel. The nervous disease part I mean. It's a hospital that specialises in the nervous system. You can come in and stay with her as well.' He tried to put me at ease. 'It's purely to carry out some tests to try and find out what the problem is.' I agreed.

Arrangements were made with a friend that she would take Andy for a short time. I told her it would only be for a few days. She was to have Andy during the day and John would pick him up at night after he had finished work.

John drove us to The Maida Vale Hospital. A very old and rather dark place, it did nothing to quench the fluttering in my stomach. I was given a put-you-up bed in a spare space upstairs – not a bedroom. The tests were commenced almost immediately and went on and on. Repeatedly I was asked the same questions about every detail of Jan's birth and problems since, my family history and all manner of things. Day after day the same questions and further tests. Nothing was seen to be found, or if there was anything they didn't tell me. The days dragged into more than three weeks.

One day, the house doctor who had been carrying out the tests asked whether I would allow Janis to be presented in the lecture theatre at Queen's Square. This is one of the world's leading hospitals for neurological disorders. I discussed this with Jan, who was quite happy to go along with whatever. She was always reading or playing games and seemed to take everything in her stride. Arrangements were made. I had no idea what lay ahead. A nurse was to travel with us in the taxi across London to this huge antiquated hospital. It was an awesome building, and the sight of doctors and nurses going about their work in a very proficient manner, plus the magnificent marble wall-plaques engraved with the names of great physicians who had worked there over many years, filled me with a renewed confidence. Surely they could discover what problems Jan had. Maybe have a cure?

We were taken to the floor where the lecture theatre was situated and asked to sit and wait outside the room. The young house doctor appeared and asked Jan to get undressed and put on a theatre gown. He also, without explanation, put some drops into her eyes to enlarge the pupils. I was bemused by all that was going on. He said for us to be patient, and that when he was ready he would come and take us into the theatre.

Jan was busy reading another beloved Braille book when the doctor reappeared and said 'We're ready for you now,' turned, and led us into the room.

I was amazed by what was before us. There was a raised platform rather like a stage, with a tier of seats rising up in front of us. Seated in these were many doctors, some in suits and others in white coats. A spotlight shone onto the stage. Janis and I were introduced and the young doctor continued to address the audience with a monologue of medical jargon that I could not comprehend except when he told them about Jan as a small child and of my observations. He then asked me whether I would take Janis and walk her backwards and forwards along the stage. Next, he asked whether I could lead her by just holding her finger tips so that the doctors could see just how much she was capable of managing. Her balance was quite poor and I had to reach to hold her from time to time.

He requested that Jan climb up onto the bed on the stage. When I had removed her shoes and she was comfortable, he turned to the audience again and invited them to come down to examine the patient. I was still stunned by what I was experiencing. I had never known anything like this and had no idea that this sort of thing happened. They all came down from the gallery and took it in turns to look into Jan's eyes with their ophthalmoscopes, and did various tests on her legs and arms. One doctor and then another would conduct a test and speak to the crowd, and there was a lot of muttering and note taking. The young doctor thanked Jan and me, and we returned to the anteroom for her to get dressed and to get the taxi back to Maida Vale Hospital.

On another occasion, Janis was to see a psychologist at Queen's Square to assess her IQ. This time no one else came with us, and I was given Jan's case notes to hand in at the other hospital. This was the first chance I had had to read her notes, an ideal opportunity to take the thirty minutes or so to glance over what had evolved from all of the tests. Jan was engrossed in yet another book. I did not enjoy the results of my reading; in fact it caused me to have a very heavy heart. It had been discovered that Jan had a very rare syndrome. So rare was it that they could not trace another person with exactly the same condition. Notes had been sent around the world.

On the return journey I read what the psychologist had written. She had assessed Jan as having a very high IQ, although she had commented that she tended to be a rather 'cheeky child'. I was not shocked by this, as I knew it was a defence mechanism for Jan. If she felt threatened or scared she would revert to a rather impudent sense of humour and would often have people in fits of laughter, even though some of her comments were indeed a little cheeky. I gathered that Jan was erring on the gifted side, but this was nothing new as we had been told over and over that she was a very bright child. But it did nothing to console my troubled heart. I just knew that whatever was found to be wrong with Jan it was going to be bad news.

Eventually all of the tests were completed. We were sent home with only the diagnosis of 'peripheral neuritis' and nothing more. I had no idea what this meant, but I was told that she had no sensation in her lower legs up to knee level. This was so vitally important for a blind person, as their lower limbs were used as tactilely as were other parts of the body. Also they could sense vibration and use there feet and lower legs to help their mobility. John came to take us home engrossed in our own thoughts and feelings.

Jan was now feeling better about the fact that the school knew that she had mobility problems, and the chastising by her mobility teacher when on 'White Cane Lessons' ceased from then on. But another problem had arisen. Janis was now saying that she could not hear in class and in the dining room. One night during her weekly telephone call she told me that she was hungry. I asked her what she had for her meals that day and she said she had not had anything for lunch or supper. When I asked her why, she said that she did not know that the meal had been placed in front of her. Apparently the girls had been instructed that they must sit at their place with their hands at their sides and wait for their meal to be placed in front of them. She could not hear what was going on around her, and then she had been told off for not eating her meals. When she tried to explain she had apparently been laughed at.

Janis became quite low in mood and it was arranged, without our knowledge, for her to see a psychiatrist. She tried to explain that she could not hear in noisy environments. His response was to say, 'But you can hear me perfectly now, can't you?'

That night she rang to tell me she had been to see this man. I was appalled that we had not been informed or asked for our permission. But now Jan's tone gave cause for serious concern. She said that she had had enough. That no-one believed her and she was so unhappy. If she had to stay at Chorleywood she would kill herself.

There were other phone calls in which she would break down and sob that she wanted to come home forever. I tried to explain to her that it was not possible, but my heart was breaking in two. I ached to have my child back and to love and care for her, just as much as she wanted to be at home with us. It was too much to bear and I made up my mind to speak with the house matron when I next visited the school.

Jan was to be in the school Christmas concert as Joseph, and we had been invited to see the play. We did not see Jan before we went into the hall but as the play began I was shocked by her appearance. Jan's shoulders were right down, the corners of her mouth drooped. She looked so forlorn and it was obvious she was having great difficulty in hearing what was going on. She looked so sad and ill I could not wait to get to her.

After the play and tea was over, John was busy putting Jan's trunk into the boot of the car. I was just about to see to Jan and get her into her seat when a man came to us and introduced himself. We shook hands, but I noticed that Jan was looking very tense and moved away slightly. She had a cardigan in her hand and she offered it to the man saying, 'This belongs to your wife,' but he refused to take it, suggesting that Jan keep the cardigan and bring it with her to his house after Christmas. She did not answer, which I thought was rather rude. When I asked about this as we drove off she just shrugged her shoulders and continued to look very unhappy. Maybe when we got home she would tell us what was worrying her so much.

The Christmas tree was ready to be decorated and as always we waited until Jan came home so that she and Andy could put the decorations on together. But this year it did not give Jan the usual buzz. I kept asking her if she was OK, and she said that she was. When she went up to bed she asked me to sit with her. I was always pleased to sit on her bed and talk, but this time I felt that something was terribly wrong. I noticed a tear trickle down her cheek and as it dripped off her chin I wiped her face and said gently, 'Come on darling, you know that you can tell Mum anything at all. Has something gone terribly wrong at school?'

'No, not at school.' Her voice was quiet. 'It was at my weekend family's home!'

'Whatever has happened?'

She was now sobbing as she poured out the terrible story.

The man of the family was a teacher at a boys' school. On one of Jan's visits he had asked her whether she would like to go with him to see some of the instruments in the music room. She was so excited as they set off. When eventually she arrived at the school and was moving around the music room exploring the various instruments he came up to her and wrapped his arms tightly round her and tried to kiss her. Jan said that she screamed and told him to get off. But the school was empty, closed for the weekend. I hugged her as she tried to tell me through her sobs what else had happened. She begged of me not to say anything.

'Not say anything? Not anything? But why?' I demanded. I tried to control the anger rising up into my throat.

'Please don't send me back Mummy, please don't send me back.' Her sobs were breaking her voice. 'He gets into bed with me!'

She was now uncontrollable the sobs racking her body. I held her again, my heart pounding.

'When? When does he get into bed with you?'

'When his wife goes out to baby sit he makes me go and get ready for bed, and then he comes into my bed and touches me.'

I could not gather my thoughts. My mind was racing and I wanted to go to the phone. Instead I took some control and attempted to calm her down.

'Are you sure that it was not an accident?'

She almost shouted, 'No! No! He tells me he is tired and is going to get into his pyjamas and then he comes into my bed. One night he was doing it and his wife came back early and he jumped out and made me promise that I would never tell anyone. He said that if I did his wife would leave him and the children and they would go into a home!' she exclaimed.

Tears were flowing down my face as I looked at Jan's red and swollen eyes.

I hugged her to me saying 'There, there, sweetheart. I'll make sure that nothing happens to you. Dad and I will stop this and I promise that you have nothing at all to worry about. For now I'll go and make you a nice milky drink and bring you your favourite biscuits. Try and rest or read one of your books.'

Jan's body was still shaking with sobs as she felt across her bed for a Braille book to read.

I went downstairs and hesitated briefly before I went into the lounge to tell John what I had just heard. He reacted as though he was a madman, saying he was going to go down and kill the man. We did not even know his address so we could not find him anyway, and the school had closed for the Christmas break. I tried to calm John down and begged of him not to go up to see Jan in such an irate state. I made the drinks. John was pacing the floor.

How we managed to keep a happy mood in the house for Christmas I do not know. Looking back I cannot even remember why we didn't call the police. I guess that we needed to confront the man or speak with the school, or maybe it was to save Jan from any further distress. Hadn't she been through too much in her young life? I remember that as soon as I was able I made contact with the school to say that Janis would not be going back for a little time and explained why.

The next day we had a phone call from the house matron to say that incidentally she would be passing through Hinckley and wondered whether she might call in and say hello to Janis on the way. Of course I said that she could, but my suspicions were immediately aroused. House matrons did not do this sort of thing out of the blue like that. What about other girls that lived in her journey's path?

When she arrived she was very brusque and her official manner was much in evidence. She sat sipping her tea and immediately referred to the incident that Janis had spoken about.

'I really do think that Janis has let her imagination run away with her. She's such an affectionate child and I think maybe she has misunderstood the situation. Maybe when she was sitting with the man she may have brushed his penis accidentally as she reached out to him, and aroused him slightly.'

To say I was gobsmacked is an understatement. Not only was she talking through her hat and obviously, a middle-aged spinster who had no idea whatsoever about men. I lost my cool.

'That is a stupid thing to say. But even if that was the case would it entitle him to get into Jan's bed and touch her body?'

She moved uncomfortably in her seat and said that we should do nothing about it until we had spoken with the head of the school. She did not even talk with Jan. It was blatantly obvious why she had come. It was our opinion that she was not on her way anywhere, but had been sent by the head of the school to try to placate us. After a little more polite, stilted conversation, she bade us goodbye and was on her way.

When we arrived at the school we were shown into the head's room.

She was a round, fresh-faced, old-fashioned spinster type woman in her late fifties I would think. Immediately she went into a defence of the school and it's very good name, and said that a charge of this sort would bring discredit upon it. John was quick to say that he wasn't bloody concerned about the school but he was very concerned about his daughter.

The head continued: 'Well it's hard to believe what Janis is saying, You see this man is not only a senior teacher at a boys' private school but he is an upstanding member of the local community and a fervent church-going man, as are his family. I must remind you that there was a similar incident at her previous school.'

It was beyond belief that this woman was putting the name of her school before our daughter's interests and making subtle accusations at the same time. I sat staring at this so-called principled woman.

'I think you should call the police,' I said.

'No, no,' she responded briskly. 'Let me write to the man and his wife first. If I write to them both and say that a complaint has been made against him and that you are no longer prepared to allow Janis to visit them ever again, then if he does not reply we shall know that it is true and you must do what you think is best.'

'Are you doubting my daughter's word'? I quickly demanded.

'Well, no but I have to be absolutely sure,' she said as she wriggled uncomfortably in her seat.

Very reluctantly we agreed to this, I guess the main reason being that we wanted to resolve matters without bringing more distress for Jan and disrupting her attempt to get on with her schooling.

A letter was sent addressed to Mr. & Mrs.......... There was never a reply. We had to make a decision as to what we should do and asked Jan what she would like to do. She did not want us to tell the police. I do believe that she was very scared and wanted to try to put the whole matter behind her.

We had not realised the extent of Jan's unhappiness. She returned to Chorleywood, but when it was time for us to drive away she threw herself at the car as it moved off. I could not bear to see her in such a state, but had to grit my teeth as I watched a member of staff take her indoors. Was there no one anywhere that would listen? No one seemed to care that establishments of this type were not suitable for every child. We had no choice, it would seem.

The next telephone call from Jan was one appealing to me to get her away from Chorleywood. 'Please, please Mummy, I miss you all so much and I am so unhappy here.'

My voice choked in my throat as I promised her that I would. John and I would do whatever it took to get her away. I promised her that she would be home quite soon and to do her best to settle down for the interim period. But how was I to fulfil this promise? I had asked the social worker whether he could help and he had said the same as everyone else – that Janis was in the best school for her.

Through a local Retinitis Pigmentosa support group I heard about a family, in Nottingham, who had a blind daughter who went to a mainstream secondary school. Immediately I wanted to know more. I quickly found out as much as I could about them and contacted them by phone. Arrangements were made for us to go and see them at Jan's next visit home, and we duly set off to meet them.

It was a lovely busy home. The parents of the blind girl were both teachers. As we sat talking and drinking tea their twelve-year-old daughter was in the kitchen baking cakes. I was amazed at just how confident she was. I learnt that she caught three buses to get to school across Nottingham and I was most impressed, although I realised that Jan's mobility difficulties would never permit her to do a journey like that on her own, or so I thought.

They listened to Jan and us tell our sorry story and were amazed that we had been so long-suffering. 'The problem with both of you,' they said, 'is that you are too nice. You need to begin kicking up a fuss and demanding things for Janis.'

We explained that it had been drummed into us again and again that we had no choice and that if we did not send Jan to the school provided we could go to jail. This was in 1976, and Lady Warnock had only just looked into the integration of disabled children into mainstream schools. The couple told us that we were to use the Warnock Report as ammunition in our fight to get Jan into a school that she could attend from home on a daily basis. They were obviously much more clued up on the education system than we were.

Fired with a new determination, I started ringing people the very next day. First of all I contacted our social worker again. I might just as well have saved my breath. The same words again, that Janis was very privileged to be going to the best school etc., etc. Did we not want for her to achieve good exam results so that she would have some future? This was emotional blackmail as far as I was concerned. Of course we wanted the best for her, but the best in what? She was certainly not benefiting from being away from home. At what price was academia to be achieved?

I approached the education authorities, on the phone, and was passed from one department to another, from this extension to another. John had to get on with his job of bringing in the money for the home and so all of this was left to me. I persevered for days. Eventually I made contact with the person I saw as being the most likely to help us. I was asked to write a letter explaining all that had gone before, and the reason for wanting Jan back home. I was forearmed for this by the Nottingham family, who had given us lots of information and cited various statutes and the Warnock Report for us to quote in the hope that we might sound as though we knew what we were doing. I was very surprised when a letter arrived from the education authority by return, asking for us to attend a meeting with the educational chiefs.

Our new friends had told us what to do, even to the point of taking notes as to how the chairs were placed in the interview room. We were told that there would be a long desk with several people seated behind it. Our chairs would be on the opposite side and situated together.

'Take them and place them away from one another, so that when you are both making your points they will have to turn to look at first one and then the other of you. You will be in control.'

I doubted the suggestion but they went on, 'Whatever you do, keep control and do not lose your temper or cry. Show them that you mean business.'

It seemed a rather silly idea to be moving chairs, but at the very least it would show that we had some control over our situation. Nevertheless, when we left the meeting we felt as though we had failed. The meeting had culminated in John and me being told that if we removed Jan from Chorleywood it would be a very serious matter. They had no other option for her education, stressing that Chorleywood was an excellent school with high academic success rates. Surely, they too asked, we wanted the best for Janis? It never ever occurred to any of these people to consider whether the child was suited to the school or happy in the environment, or even whether her health was being affected by removing her from her family. Furthermore, we were told that if we were to persist and take her away, then we would have to face serious consequences.

We rose from our chairs and John assured them that we would be removing Janis from Chorleywood as soon as we possibly could.

As soon as we arrived home, John was on the phone to the head of Chorley informing her that we would be taking Janis away. All necessary arrangements were to be made for her to return to her home. She replied that we could not do this and were we aware of the consequences of our actions?

The education authorities rang several times to try to instil in us that we must not take Janis away from Chorleywood as there was no other place for her, but we were determined to bring her home no matter what the outcome for us. She was very unhappy, and no child should ever have to endure such torment. Her health was being affected now. I rang Nottingham, and our friends told us not to worry and that the authorities were calling our bluff.

On the day that John drove down to Chorleywood to bring Jan home there was a terrific thunderstorm. He was travelling along the M1 when a lady in a car went speeding past him in the outside lane. It was not fit weather for speed of that kind, and as John motored on and rounded a bend, there was the same car straddling the motorway with its bonnet into the central barrier. John tried to swerve but there was a car on the inside of him, the road was very wet, and as he applied the brakes the car just slid into the crashed vehicle. The first I knew of this was a phone call from John. He explained everything that had happened and said that our car was a complete write-off. I panicked. I asked him whether he was OK.

'I'm just fine love, honest I'm OK,' he reassured me, and then went on to ask me to ring a friend to meet him at a service station. John had already made arrangements to hire a car to continue down to collect Jan and her belongings, and he would then motor back and leave the car at the service station on his return. Hopefully, Eric would be there to pick them both up and bring them all safely back home.

I rang Eric as soon as John had said goodbye. He said he would set off immediately. All went relatively smoothly. John arrived at Chorleywood. The head was waiting with all of Jan's things and her trunk packed. Jan was by her side.

The head said to John, 'Well, she'll never make much of herself, you know.'

John ignored the remark and led Jan to the car and packed her trunk and all belongings in the boot. In spite of the head's remark, a happier child there never was!

While all of this was happening, I received a phone call late in the afternoon. It was from the education authority to say that they had secured a place for Janis at Exhall Grange – the school in Coventry that had sent her away when she lost her sight. The man went on to say that a new head had taken over, and he was partially sighted. It was his philosophy that no child should leave the school when their eyesight failed and he was to employ a teacher of Braille for Jan. I believe, with hindsight, that the EA had tested us to the limit to see whether we would carry out our threat of removing Jan from Chorleywood, and when they had the call from the head to say that Janis had left they then rang me. Why could they not have told us of this before and released us from so much anxiety? Why did it take them so long?

John and Jan were thrilled at the news I was able to give them when they got home. But our priority was to let Jan have a few days rest to recover herself, ready for her return to Exhall.

CHAPTER 16

We quickly made contact with Mr. Bignell, the new head of Exhall, who agreed that Jan should take a few days off to recover from the trauma. The other good news was that he had decided that children living in the vicinity of the school could attend as day pupils. How much better could it get? The E.A. also agreed to arrange transport to and from the school and this time a car and driver was laid on.

Jan was around thirteen when she started back at Exhall. Once again we were receiving good reports from her teacher. She was flying along with her lessons.

Life was hectic at times. Jan was now interested in the flute and again, the music teacher at Exhall advised us where to go to buy her one of her own. We had recently bought her a lovely new piano, which had cost us all of our savings. Now we were to have to stretch the budget somehow.

We went into Leicester, and it was a lot of money to pay out but we felt we had to encourage Jan as much as possible. She passed a couple of exams on the flute. Her love of the accordion was ongoing, as were those lessons and her piano lessons. Her main love was piano. She really seemed to excel in this and passed her exams quickly and with distinction.

Around this time, John had been made redundant from his job and we were struggling to manage. Some friends asked us whether they could help in any way. During this conversation I happened to mention that Janis missed being able to ride a bike. They set about raising funds with charity football matches and the like, and quite soon Jan had a tandem.

I had not been on a bike for years, but one Saturday John had taken Andy out to the park and Jan wanted to ride her bike. So without hesitation I obliged. We were doing very well. It was a beautiful sunny day and I was enjoying this new adventure as much as she was. Until, that was, we came to a downward slope and two very sharp bends in the road. As the tandem leaned to the left Jan, not being able to see what the cause was, leaned to the right thinking she might fall off. The bike became uncontrollable and eventually wobbled and crashed to the ground. My head hit the tarmac with a huge thump. My glasses were knocked off and I couldn't see, but was aware that the tandem was on top of me and Janis was shouting, 'Mum, Mum are you OK? Please Mum, speak to me!'

I tried to reach her but could not get across the bike. I tried to tell her I was OK. I was as concerned about her as she was for me, but she had fallen without causing any damage to herself at all.

Quite quickly a crowd of people gathered around us, and as I looked up I saw a doctor leaning over me. He had apparently been visiting an expectant mum and came out to see what had happened. The bike was lifted from me. Janis stood up and I managed to tell them she couldn't see. It must have been quite something to discover that the child on the ground was blind! We were taken into this stranger's house and examined and very kindly someone drove us home leaving the bike for John to pick up. It was rather battered but as soon as John restored it Jan was off on the back, though this time with her dad in front. I had learnt a lesson. I was black and blue for weeks afterwards.

Our involvement with the church had grown and John was asked whether he would like to be a Boy's Brigade officer. He felt privileged to be asked and was fitted out with his uniform. This, of course, involved yet another meeting to fit into our already busy schedule. We had also set up a Torch Fellowship Group for the Blind which we had been successfully running for over three years, and this took up a great deal of our time too. After seven years we left it to others to run, but it is still thriving to this day.

Then John's work began to involve many hours of overtime. It was not unusual for him to start work at 6 a.m. and work through until 9 p.m., and to work on Saturdays and Sundays. It was all beginning to take its toll on his health. I became very worried when he developed a very bad case of bronchitis and tonsillitis. He was very poorly, and off work for quite some time.

We were all getting quite used to what help Jan required, and she had reacted to everything as though it was second nature to her. That was until we attended Exhall for Jan's medical examination, which was an annual event there.

After the doctor had carried out his usual examination he called us into his office. Again I had a foreboding that all was not well. He wanted to know whether we had seen a specialist consultant about Jan's peripheral neuritis. I told him about the London hospital experiences.

'Did they offer you any cure?' was his reply.

'There is no cure and they don't know what has caused the problem.'

He went on, 'I believe Janis rides horses. Has she ever had a fall or damaged her spine at any time'?

My mind flew back to an event that had happened at Lickey. A boy had got hold of Jan by the arm and swung her against the coat pegs in the cloakroom. Janis was in agony and was eventually diagnosed as having a very badly bruised coccyx. I had put this out of my mind until now.

'This could be at the root of her problem,' was the doctor's opinion. 'I feel that there is something wrong with her spine and it is not her legs at all. Would you be prepared to take her to a consultant neurologist at Queens University Hospital in Nottingham?' he continued.

My hopes were raised and I reassured him that we would do whatever it took to get her well again. He persuaded us that it would be well worth seeing the consultant.

The appointment was made and it was to be on Jan's birthday. We were quite high-spirited in thinking that this man was going to put things right with her legs. Again Jan was into one of her books as we drove all the way to Nottingham. She did not seem the slightest bit interested in what was going on. Had she got so used to the routine and negative results? .

After a lengthy physical and neurological examination, the consultant asked the attending nurse whether she would help Janis to get dressed whilst he talked to John and me. His gentleness and sympathetic tone of voice shouted to me of the seriousness of the situation.

He asked us to take a seat in his office. My heart felt as though it would thump through my chest because I had been here so often. I knew that it was bad news. He began by asking us why we had brought Janis to see him. It was difficult to answer. I stammered out that the doctor at Exhall had suggested it, not daring to mention the word cure.

'When Janis was seen in London did they not tell you then what the problem was?' he asked, but did not stop for a reply. 'I'm sorry, but Janis has an extremely rare condition for which there is no cure. You would probably find maybe one other person in Nottingham with a similar syndrome, and even then it would only be similar, not the same. We do not have a name for whatever Jan's syndrome is. What we do know is that Janis will lose sensation, maybe up to her waist.' He held his head down as he spoke.

'What about her arms and hands?' I blurted out. 'She's a musician and also she needs her hands to read and for everything else.'

'Her upper limbs are fine. I don't think that there will be a problem there, but I would suggest that you prepare for the fact that Janis may, by the time she is twenty or so, be in a wheelchair. I suggest that you take her home and make her as happy as you can. You might also think about downstairs accommodation as it will be dangerous for her to climb stairs.'

I think I had taken in all that he said as he finished with: 'I would like to see her every six months, just so that I can keep an eye on things.'

John stretched out his hand and said, 'Thank you, and God bless you.'

I was physically shaken by John's comment but could not understand why his kind words bothered me to such an extent.

We left the hospital with Jan still in her happy, fun loving mood. It was her birthday and this news was a shocking present for her. She hadn't been told anything, and I knew that she would have to be told. But when? I also knew that she would want to know what the doctor had said.

As we got into the car I could contain the tears no longer. Jan was in the back of the car. Where was God in all of this? And then my mind wandered to John's parting remark. Why should God bless the doctor when he was allowing so much to happen to my child? How could John be so calm and benevolent in such a situation? God had brought John and me together, we had tried to follow his teaching but at every turn we got knocked down. The thoughts ravaged my mind and I could not control myself. For the first time my faith had been shaken to the core and doubts were gaining a foothold. Jan must have heard me crying and her hands, which were always so gentle, reached to touch my face. She caressed my cheeks and discovered the tears.

'What's the matter, Mum? What did the doctor say?'

How could I tell her? Could I lie? Never! I could not shatter her trust in me and so I told her as gently as I could what the doctor had told us. I explained that eventually she may need to use a wheelchair as to walk would be very tiring for her. I suggested that maybe she would like a bedroom downstairs with her own bathroom en-suite. In an attempt to lighten the blow, I suggested we buy a sign with her name on and the words 'Private Keep Out' and she would be in complete control. She could entertain her buddies whenever she liked.

I said that she could choose all of the furniture and the colour of her bathroom suite. Immediately she shot back, 'Please can I have a royal blue one?' I couldn't help but laugh. She was just so positive and never ever seemed to let any of this get on top of her. A royal blue bathroom suite I had never seen, but I knew that I could not compromise on this one.

'Don't cry, Mum. I'm no different today than I was yesterday!' Her comment and her ability to accept such bad news jolted me.

Janis returned to school and applied herself to her lessons, but the crack in my heart was now widening by the day as I watched for signs of this hideous syndrome taking its toll on her body.

Life seemed to settle down as Jan adjusted to life at Exhall. There were problems with her hearing but we had been assured that it was nothing to worry about.

We applied to the council for a grant for a large extension to the side of our detached home. It was accepted without question and within no time at all work was in progress. I was not prepared for the mess and horror of it all. It was an awful six weeks, but eventually the builders moved out and John and I began the interior work. It was a beautiful extension which increased our lounge to double the original size, and off that there was Jan's large double bedroom and en-suite royal blue bathroom. What a job that was, but I hunted until I found one. When we had finished and all the carpets were fitted it looked absolutely grand. Jan had her very own private door into the house where there was a ramp down into the garden. Her friends could now come and go as they pleased. It was a bonus for Jan.

She had been at Exhall for almost two years now and was doing very well and was very happy. But another problem was looming. Jan began asking us to repeat things, especially at the meal table. We learnt later that the noise of cutlery on plates was enough for her not to hear what was being said. I had also noticed that she seemed very vacant at church. This was because all she heard was a cacophony of noise. I was to learn later that she had almost always heard like this and to Jan it was no different. The only thing that had changed was that her detection of the spoken word was becoming less. The routine tests carried out at school and at hospital showed that there was little wrong. We tried to adapt to the problem and she just got on with things as best as she could.

Then Jan contracted chicken pox. I had heard that as you get older it can be more serious and Jan set out to prove the point. She was around fifteen at the time and was very ill. Her whole body was a mass of pox blisters and she was in such pain. Her temperature was worryingly high one day and so I asked for our GP to call in. He was shocked when he saw Jan but was honest enough to say that he felt useless as there was very little he could do to ease her pain except administer paracetamol. Slowly Jan recovered, but not to her old self. She became very depressed and could not walk very far. It was time to consider a wheelchair, and surprisingly Jan accepted this without question. She was obviously now struggling to walk.

One evening I had to take to my bed, as I was unwell. Jan came up to see me (she was still determined to climb stairs at times) and I explained that I felt really poorly.

'But I want you to come down Mum,' she said. I apologised profusely and turned to rest.

About an hour later, John came rushing into my room to say that Jan had taken an overdose of some tablets. I jumped out of bed as John made ready to rush her to hospital. He was out of the house like a shot saying for me to stay and take care of Andrew.

It seemed an eternity until he returned. 'They've pumped her stomach out but the doctor said not to worry, he felt it was just a cry for help. But they have to keep her in as paracetamol can cause liver damage and they need to be sure this is not the case.' He looked so tired as he related this to me. 'We can go and see her tomorrow.'

Why did she not say that she was so troubled? Had she kept so much bottled up inside? Our GP said that one of the side effects of chicken pox was quite serious depression. I can only assume that so much of the years of trauma and pain had spilled over and she had come to me for help, unable to express her innermost pain, and I had not recognised how troubled she was.

The next day John and I rushed to the hospital only to find that she was her usual happy self and was happily chatting to a boy of about her own age. Jan was discharged the next day.

We were advised not to talk about the matter unless Jan brought it up in conversation herself. It was never mentioned.

CHAPTER 17

Jan was now a very keen CB radio bod and would spend hours calling up folk around the area. Her name was Midnight Princess owing to her being awake until the early hours and chatting, Some of her buddies soon realised that she struggled to hear them and also had difficulty hearing the radio stations. They quickly raised money for her to have an adaptor fitted, which increased the volume of the receiver. She was thrilled. An offshoot from this was that the CB buddies would come and take her out occasionally.

Jan uses her new CB radio.

Jan was a typical teenager but I saw the pain she tried to hide when she wanted to go into town and do all the things that teenagers do. Sometimes the girls from church would pop round on Saturday mornings and then leave, saying that they were going into town to do some shopping. Jan never seemed to assert herself by asking whether she could go with them. I think that she thought that they did not want her because she would be too much trouble for them.

My heart ached so much as I watched Jan struggle with her limitations. She always tried to hide her pain and appeared so cheerful, but I was aware that she was doing a very good job of hiding her feelings.

There was an article in the local Evening News regarding the Hinckley carnival. They wanted applications for Carnival Queen. I asked Jan whether she would like to enter and she was excited about it. Of course she would love it. I had no hesitation in entering her. Firstly, I thought it would help her to overcome the depression that the chicken pox had left behind, and it would also enable her to meet more people.

The carnival was being planned and the applications for the Queen had piled in. On the night of the judging, Janis was placed second to the winner. The evening paper the next day was full of pictures. This was followed with letters from the public saying that Janis should have been the Queen. It was the year for disabled people and there were letters to this affect. We discovered that Janis had been denied the title of Carnival Queen because of her disability.

Quickly following on the tail of this was an appeal on a Blue Peter programme on TV. They were appealing for money to buy incubators for premature babies, as there was a shortage around the country. I had been narrating the programme to Jan and then asked her whether she would like to raise some money.

'But how can I Mum?' She was intent.

'I think that you might use your musical gift in some way.' I spoke before my brain had thought it through.

'Do you think I could? Really, Mum, do you think I might be able to do something?' She was beginning to get really excited.

When John came home and while we were eating our evening meal we all joined in a discussion of how we could raise some money. I suggested that maybe we could put on a concert. Janis had just composed another song called "I'm Glad To Be The Girl I Am", and the tune she played to it was lovely. I suggested we use that and other compositions of hers, and perhaps John could sing. He had a lovely tenor voice and had sung in the local amateur dramatic society. He agreed to this and Jan said she would play piano for him. But this was not enough to fill ninety minutes of time. We said we would all put our minds to it.

While the kids were at school and John at work my mind worked overtime on the concert. I thought we would have a gospel group, community hymn singing, a speaker, and John and Jan playing and singing. Next came the important task of getting the public in. Jan belonged to a church youth group and they soon rallied round and got their families to spread the word, and we got as many folk as we knew to do the same. It took up a great deal of my days in organising everything, but I managed to get together what I thought would be an excellent concert. We were amazed when we realised all of the tickets had gone. But would they all turn up on the night?

My doubts were squashed. On the night the people came in hoards, and the church was packed out. Now my heart was fit to burst as I watched Jan at the grand piano playing and singing her own compositions and then accompanying her dad as he sang "Morning Has Broken" and "Were You There".

The speaker told the audience how Jan had first of all lost her sight as a child and had now been told that she would lose the use of her legs. 'However,' he went on, 'she did not let this get the better of her. No, just the opposite. She composed this song "I'm Glad To Be The Girl I Am", and furthermore she wanted to help other people and this is why we are here tonight'

He did not finish before the audience burst forth with applause. How many tears does a mother carry in her heart?

The concert was a huge success and people gave to the tune of several hundreds of pounds. Janis took it all in her stride. When the letter arrived from Blue Peter to thank her for what she had done she was thrilled.

CHAPTER 18

LOURDES

Jan's friends took her along the canal for a walk and they got talking to someone who had a boat on there. Before long Jan was inside the boat asking lots of questions. Before she got off she had decided that she wanted to join the boating club.

She had also met a man called Fred who seemed very interested in Jan and asked what hobbies she had. Jan told me about him and that he was married with kids and such a lovely guy. I was a little disturbed but a few days later I had a phone call from Fred. He introduced himself and explained that he was married and had children but went on to explain the nature of his call. He belonged to the Catholic faith, and very tentatively he asked me whether I would have any objection to him asking Jan whether she would like to go to Lourdes. I told him that Jan was now of an age to make her own decisions. We made arrangements for him to come to see us at home and talk with Jan.

Jan was thrilled at the suggestion. Fred explained that she would be taken in the "Jumbulance" across to France. That it would be an overnight journey and that Jan and the other disabled young people would be put to bed and strapped in as they travelled.

When the time arrived for Jan to go we were asked to take her to the local Catholic church, and were invited to join in the Mass that would be taken before the journey. The only strange thing was that we were to meet in the early hours of the morning. However, it all added to the excitement.

We arrived at the church. There were many cars and the huge Jumbulance waiting. As we entered the foyer of the church the excitement was tangible. So many young people in wheelchairs eagerly wanting to venture off. After the moving church service we were ready for the young folk to be settled in their beds. It was a very emotional time as we watched the carers gently supporting their charges and making sure everything was just right, that they were comfortable and safe. It took an age as each person was very carefully and safely put to bed one at a time.

Fred was to be Jan's carer. These people gave up two weeks of their holidays to travel across to Lourdes to care for the sick and disabled. It challenged me deeply.

I think it was around three o'clock in the morning when we finally waved goodbye and the Jumbulance began to roll on its journey to France. John and I returned to our home to try to get some sleep, but sleep would not come. Such love and care so freely given had moved my emotions to the point where I could not switch them off.

When Jan came home we were there to meet her. She was so excited. Obviously I had prayed that God would perform a miracle whilst she was there. I prayed for them all.

We arrived back at our house and Jan began to tell us all about Lourdes. She said she had something very serious to talk about. She wanted to convert to Catholicism. We said that we did not see why she shouldn't, but suggested that she waited for a while before making up her mind. It seemed that she had had enough of the other churches and had decided she wanted to go to a different church to us. There had been many promises to call and collect her to take her, but time and time again she had been let down. I could see how she thought that this time she could depend on people's promises.

The next evening Fred rang to see how Jan was. I assured him that she was just fine. He asked whether he could come and see John and me. 'Of course,' I assured him. 'Anytime you want to.'

Fred arrived and began to tell us of various things that had happened. But he really wanted to tell of something quite special. In the chalet where they stayed they slept in large rooms with partitions between the beds. The sick or disabled person would sleep next to their carer. Any little thing that Jan wanted, Fred was there to get it for her. They had all gone to bed after visiting the grotto one afternoon, the grotto where 'Our Lady' had appeared years ago and which was where miracles had, apparently, been performed. Jan had been to 'the waters' and had been totally submerged. She had remained intensely quiet for the rest of the day. But at one o'clock in the morning she whispered, 'Fred. Fred are you awake?'

'Yes Jan, what is it?' he answered.

'Would it be possible for me to go to the grotto again?'

'Of course. When did you want to go?'

'Now please!'

'Now Jan? But it's one o'clock in the morning.'

'Can't we go now then?'

'I guess there's no reason why we shouldn't.' And Fred told her he would get dressed and be round to help her into her wheelchair.

Jan never spoke a word as Fred pushed her up a long hill. It was quite a long way away. When they got to the grotto Fred leaned over and asked her what she wanted to do.

'Please Fred, I hope you won't mind but could you just push me right up close to the statue of Mary and leave me there? I'll call you when I'm ready.'

'Of course.' Fred pushed her as close as he could, applied the brakes to the wheelchair and went a little way away to sit and wait.

Fred went on, 'It was a lovely night. So very quiet and all that could be heard was the spluttering of the hundreds of lighted candles that created a soft light against the dark sky. They lit up Our Lady. I was so pleased that she'd asked me to take her because it was so beautiful. I waited for over an hour or so. She never moved or uttered a word until I eventually heard her softly call me to say she was ready to go to bed. I didn't ask any questions and neither did she volunteer any information. I pushed her all the way back down the hill. She never spoke, not even when we went indoors. I helped her to her bed and she got herself undressed then whispered "'Night Fred". I never heard her mention it ever again.'

To this day Jan has never told me and I have never mentioned it. I will never know what happened at the Grotto.

A few weeks later we were invited to the Catholic church hall for a supper and film show of the whole event. It was a very moving experience.

CHAPTER 19

FURTHER EDUCATION?

Another problem had appeared on the horizon. At the age of sixteen Janis would have to leave Exhall. But where was she to go? She was now quite disabled and found walking very tiresome. She also experienced a lot of pain in her legs. I asked her social worker about a placement in a College of Further Education and he said that the normal succession to Exhall would be a college of FE for the blind in Hereford. I tried not to worry too much, but I had discovered that it was a rather rambling sprawling complex of buildings, and some of the classrooms were on the second floor and there were no lifts. There seemed to be no alternative. I shelved the worrying thoughts as best I could.

Janis was ready to take her 'O' level exams. She did not swat, although I kept saying that she should, but she felt certain that she had enough knowledge to be able to pass. She managed to pass three and was deeply disappointed. The educational system had failed her inasmuch as there was only one teacher of Braille at Exhall and she obviously had her limitations. Jan's biggest disappointment was that she was refused human biology. She was angry about the fact that the biology teacher had said that it would be impossible for a blind person to carry out the necessary scientific tests, and had asked Jan to sit at the back of the classroom and occupy herself whilst the class was taking lessons. This was another stumbling block that she was to overcome later.

Jan was capable of doing much better and wanted to learn everything about everything, but she had so many set-backs, the main ones being that there is no establishment in this country that is geared for the academic deafblind person. It was a matter of struggling through and grasping what any tutor was able or prepared to teach her.

The other major problem was that the peripheral neuritis was now causing a lot of pain.

The time arrived for Jan to leave Exhall. It was a huge wrench for all of us. She had been very happy there and had made many friends and had a few boyfriends. However, there was no option but for her to leave and apply to go to the college in Hereford.

I was watching a programme on TV about hearing problems. There was a unique device being demonstrated, which enabled people with an unusual hearing problem to cope better in the classroom or social situations. I immediately contacted the firm and we were invited to take Jan down to London to try the device. It consisted of hearing aids attached to a receiver. The other part of the equipment was a microphone type of gadget that the speaker wore around the neck. It was quite amazing to watch Jan's face light up as she tried the equipment. The demonstrator walked away down the passageway and talked to her and Jan heard clearly what he was saying. Of course Jan wanted one but the downside, once again, was the cost. The demonstrator explained the different ways in which we could raise the money. By the time Jan was ready to go to college she had the device.

Jan was sixteen when she began at Hereford. She was still anxious to learn as much as possible. She settled in quite well and her phone calls indicated that she was very happy there. I recall one adventure that she told us about, in which she had decided that she would find her way to the local chip shop and said she would take some other students with her. It was quite a way from the college, and unfortunately they became lost. Never daunted, she found the whole thing quite amusing. She roared with laughter as she related to me how she managed to get back.

She quickly made many friends. However, she struggled with the mammoth task of climbing the stairs and walking around the campus. She would have to go from one classroom to another up stairs and down again and back up again. By the next end of term she was having terrible pain in her legs. It was all too much for Jan to cope with. With great sadness for Jan, John, me and the head of the college, who had been impressed by Jan's academic achievement, it was agreed that she could not cope any longer and Jan had no alternative but to leave. The head suggested that we try a college for disabled people in Coventry.

Jan still had the burning desire to learn as much as possible. All of the time, she was reading and studying. She actually acquired a book on how to speak German and taught herself. She also had a poetry book in German and she would recite some of this to us, and would shriek with laughter and so would we at her pronunciation. It was so sad to see her wanting to be studying but having nowhere to go to be taught.

Jan asked whether I would contact the college in Coventry. I made all the arrangements for her to go for an interview.

This was very different. It was a very modern building and there was a lift and easy access to every room. The living quarters were self-contained flats, and there was a communal area for the students to relax, drink and enjoy music. Jan was quite impressed. The only problem was that they had not had a blind student before, but Jan was prepared to give it a go. It was a very short-lived experiment.

John, Andrew and I had gone on a week's holiday in our touring caravan. We thought it would be an ideal opportunity for us to spend some quality time with Andy. He so often took a back seat in so many things without intention. Now he was able to rock climb and do whatever he chose to do without many restrictions. It was a good holiday for each of us.

We had arranged that on our return we would go to Coventry and pick up Jan for her weekend at home, but when we arrived we were told she had left.

'Left? Whatever do you mean by left?' I shrieked.

We were told that Janis had packed up all of her things and hailed a taxi home. She had not told anyone of her decision. To say we were shocked is an understatement.

When I went into our home I immediately noticed, through the patio window, a line of Jan's washing hanging on the line. I was even more perplexed. What was going on?

I went into Jan's room and she was lying on her bed reading. She knew that we would be upset, as she was immediately on the defensive. I was very angry with her. The struggles and frustrations of the years of trying to get the right education for her surfaced. I just let rip. Fortunately, Jan did not hear all that I said. She did, however, detect that I was very angry and upset. When I calmed down she explained that she was not going to be patronised and treated in the manner that she had been at the college.

I cooled down and asked her to explain to us why she had walked out. She had not been there for very long and had tolerated a lot of things that she was not prepared for. She had been given homework to listen to on a tape recorder. She was given printed instructions to listen to such and such a chapter and give her comments on it. How was she to read this herself? She had beckoned a friend to help her with the reading part, but how could she find a chapter in a whole tape of the book? It was an impossible task, and when she returned to college she seemed to be in trouble for not doing her homework. The last straw was when she asked a member of staff to get her some painkillers for her neuritis and had the reply, 'I will put your wheelchair on charge for tomorrow.' And no tablets. She had been home for some days when we arrived.

I have to admit that it was another eye opener for me. I had always worried about leaving Jan on her own for too long. She had resented this and I knew that part of all of what had happened was to also make me take note that she was a young adult who was quite capable and wanted to be as independent as anyone else.

During this period of time it was obvious that John was having problems too. He became quite depressed. The pressure of his job and the emotional strains at home were once again beginning to take their toll. The strain of the years of problem after problem, as well as the anxiety over Jan's future, caused us to rethink our whole situation. John told me that he would give anything to give up his job, but at fifty-five years of age it was not possible. We discussed all sorts of things that we might do. We travelled around the country looking at various options. Eventually it was decided we would sell up and move to the coast and set up a guest-house.

We had seen an Edwardian terraced house quite near to the sea in Exmouth, Devon. It needed a great deal of work doing to it, but this seemed an ideal opportunity for the whole family. There was John's exhaustion, Jan now being at home all the while and Andy ready to move up into secondary school. We thought it would be an ideal new start for all of us. With hindsight, I know that we had really had enough of trying to cope and needed some respite.

While we were waiting for the sale of the house and the legal requirements to be finalised we had an appointment to visit the Nottingham hospital. Jan told the young house doctor about the terrible pain that she was in. He prescribed the drug Tegretol. It was an anti-epileptic drug but it had been discovered that it gave pain relief in certain other conditions and he suggested that Jan try it and if it suited fine, but if not then to throw it away. We did not have any paperwork as to any side effects and trusted the doctor. The tablets certainly cured the pain and Jan was able to walk much better.

A week or so later she developed a rash. Her face and neck were bright pink as though she had been in the sun too long. I took her to our GP who thought she had a viral infection. We waited a few days but Jan then developed a sore throat and felt sick. We returned to the GP who said he thought it would pass, as there were all sorts of things going round. I asked him whether it could be the tablets she was taking but he said he thought not.

The time had come for us to move to Devon. It was such an emotional wrench as we left the home we had loved for ten years, but the thought of the sea and a new school for Andrew, more time for John, Janis and me, drove us forward.

As we drove through Hinckley, Jan was calling up her CB buddies on her radio to say goodbye. It was a heart wrenching time. We passed the local college and there was Jan's ex boyfriend with another girl. I told Jan that I had seen Tim and she asked me to stop so that she could speak with him. I had to tell her he was with another girl and I watched her sink into her seat saying not to bother. It had been a lovely friendship and they were quite smitten with each other. Tim's parents were not at all happy with their son going out with a blind disabled girl and caused a lot of commotion in an attempt to stop the friendship. His father even came to our home to try and settle the matter.

Our arrival in Devon went without too many problems and we were soon in our new home, but most of the furniture was stacked in one of the large downstairs rooms. There was a great deal of work to do before we could open for business.

A few days after our arrival a friend arrived to bring us a welcome card and some flowers. As soon as she saw Jan she asked whatever was the problem. Anne was a nurse and immediately said that the rash Jan still had needed to be looked at by the local doctor. I guess we had got used to her red face and the rash had not unduly worried our GP. However, I decided to make an appointment. After examining Jan, she thought she might have glandular fever as some of her glands were swollen. I had also told her that Jan said it hurt her to swallow. The GP decided to run some blood tests, which came back negative.

Within a matter of days Jan was complaining of her stomach going into spasm and the rash was becoming worse. She was also looking very puffed in the face. Also she had missed a period, which was most unusual. I took her back to the GP, who asked me whether there was a chance that Jan could be pregnant. It was with great difficulty that I put the question to Jan. She seemed shocked, but by now she was feeling really ill and was not up to arguing with anyone. The GP said she thought it wise to do a pregnancy test, which proved negative. Jan was in no fit state to argue over anything.

Within the next few days she could not get out of bed and was swelling up. She was also now very deaf and said that her ears felt huge and her face was numb. She could not eat and drank little. We called the surgery and a male doctor came out. He decided to have another blood test done as he said that sometimes they showed negative when there was a possibility that she could have glandular fever. This test also came back negative.

Jan was now bedridden and had a commode by her bed. I had to lift her and help her with all of her personal needs. I was desperate as I watched her deteriorate from day to day. It was a Sunday when I rang for a doctor to come to our home. A locum doctor on emergency cover arrived. As soon as she saw Jan she asked how long she had been like this and I filled in the details. She immediately called a neurologist to our home and he subsequently admitted her to hospital.

All sorts of tests were carried out. The end result was that it was put down to her rare syndrome. Janis had swelled so much that she looked two stone heavier. The worst part was that she had become profoundly deaf.

Ann had been chatting to the social worker for the blind who was to be Jan's social worker. She had told her about Jan and her musical talents and other stuff, and Pam, the SW, wanted to meet her as soon as possible. It was arranged for her to come with us to the hospital. When we arrived at the ward we were told that Jan had gone to occupational therapy. My heart leapt. Perhaps she was getting better? We headed off to the OT department and there she was, on her knees making her way from one side of the pottery room to the other to collect things that she needed. She could not walk, but still she was determined to be as independent as possible. Pam was very impressed and introduced herself.

It had been suggested by our new GP that John and I needed a break. Janis had been transferred to the local cottage hospital and our friend Ann promised to look in twice a day while we were away. It was important that Andrew had a break away too. We arranged for him to go with an activity group on the Holiday Park where we were staying. He went canoeing, abseiling, rock climbing and lots of other sporting activities. It was lovely to see his rosy-cheeked face, and to smell the dirt and fresh air which boys accumulate from playing outdoors, when he arrived home at the end of the day. It was so good to see him enjoying himself.

I could not rest. I rang every day at least twice to find out whether there was any improvement in Jan. She was still the same. Anne told me that she was still deaf. I cried to John that her lovely musical ambitions would now have to go. How could she play and compose? I could not get back home quickly enough.

Janis came home from the hospital and our GP came in to see how things were. She could see that I was feeling the strain of it all and she knew that we had a business to get up and running. It was to be our livelihood. She called in the neurologist. He went into Jan's room and then returned to talk with John and me. He suggested that Jan went into a Leonard Cheshire Home. I was very shocked at his idea. He went on to say that Janis desperately wanted to live on her own. I knew that she had been talking about this for some time but now it was surely impossible? The consultant said that it was only fair for the whole family if Jan went for a short respite period. It was arranged that we visit the place to see what we thought about it.

My heart was so heavy and was almost at breaking point. I felt so impotent. I loved her more than life and could not stand to see her suffer so much, and there was nothing more I could do.

The Leonard Cheshire Home was truly lovely. It overlooked the sea, and the general atmosphere appealed to me and alleviated my anxieties a little, but the thought of Jan having to go into a home still appalled me. A few days later we took Jan to her new home. She was completely incapable of doing anything for herself and it was difficult for her to hear. As we approached the home Jan did not utter a word. Her silence was so painful to me. We went through the official procedure. Jan was made very welcome. I struggled to say goodbye as I kissed her on her cheek.

The next day I told John I wanted to go for a long walk on my own. I walked down onto the beach. Fortunately it was deserted. I walked in the sand along the edge of the lapping tide and began talking to God. My voice became louder and louder until I was shouting at him at the top of my voice. I lifted my fists and asked him what sort of a loving father was he to allow such suffering. I screamed at him, and on and on I ranted and flailed my fists at Him. I was gasping for breath. I must have walked about two miles before I finally collapsed onto the sand burying my face in my hands, and I sobbed and sobbed until I could cry no more. Slowly I made my way back home.

CHAPTER 20

At least this break from caring for Jan would allow John and me to get cracking on the house. There was so much to do. Walls had been pulled down, central heating put in, every room needed decorating, and the huge kitchen was yet to be fitted out to the standards laid down by the health and safety people before we could open for business.

In between all of this we visited Jan at the home. She had settled in quite well but it was soon evident that she wanted to come home. She stayed for four weeks. When she came home she was still in a very bad way and needed help to do everything, down to very personal matters. I could not sleep for worry. Then one night I lay thinking about all that had happened and how it had all begun.

Why did this decline in her health suddenly occur? My mind went back to the Tegretol. I strained my already exhausted brain to try and analyse just how Jan was before she had taken the drug. After her discharge from hospital she was still taking this, along with about five other medications, some of which were to combat the side effects of the Tegretol. I sat bolt upright and said in a very loud voice, 'That's it, that is what has caused all of this.'

John woke and I told him. I blurted out what I thought was causing Jan's problem. He listened and then told me to get some sleep and we would sort it out tomorrow. I fell into the deepest sleep I had had for ages. The next day I explained my thoughts to Jan and told her my reasoning and that I thought she should no longer have any medication. But we would have to wait and see what the results from this were. She was excited at my thoughts that the drug could have caused all of the problems and went along with my suggestion.

Amazingly, within two weeks the swelling had gone and sensation was returning to her hands, arms and face. I watched as Jan crawled to her beloved piano and struggled to find the keys to play. Play she did, but it was as though she to had to learn all over again. Her hands had a slight tremor but gradually, as the sensation returned, she was able to play as before albeit that the slight tremor remained in her little finger. My heart was swelling with hope and confidence that she would get well again. Sadly her hearing did not improve.

I told our new GP about my actions and that Jan was improving all the time. She did not say much, but said we just had to wait and see.

Janis had been going back and forth to hospital three days a week for regular physiotherapy. One morning she had said that the terrible pains had returned and she begged of me to get some Tegretol again. I had thrown all the medication away, so rang the surgery to ask what I should do. I was not entirely convinced that it was the drug that had caused her problems but I was soon to be. A prescription was given for the Tegretol without question. John fetched it and had it dispensed.

Ann had called in and I asked her to join us for lunch. Reluctantly I gave Jan a tablet just before she sat at the table, and we had all begun eating our meal when suddenly she said that she felt strange. We all looked at her. Her face had turned crimson. Now she was clawing at her face and throat. She was going mad with intense itching. She also felt sick. Immediately I knew that it was a reaction to the tablet and rang the surgery. I spoke to the GP who confirmed that it most likely was.

The doctor went on to explain that when someone has had a reaction to something of this kind and it is withdrawn and then later given again, the body recognises this immediately and screams out that it does not want it. I asked what I should do as Jan had an appointment at the hospital. She said to go with her and ask them to look at her there. When we arrived I was shocked to learn that there was nothing that could be done at the hospital as she was there for physiotherapy and not for any other treatment. For her to see someone for her rash she needed a referral from her GP. Jan was tearing at her face and throat and one of the nurses kindly went and fetched an ice pack and applied this to Jan's skin, suggesting that I rang our GP.

I rang as soon as we got back and it was arranged for Jan to have some Piriton. I gave these to her and in no time at all the itching eased off and Jan went into a deep sleep as a result of the antihistamine affect.

She woke up some hours later and said that she was in terrible pain in her legs. Was there no end to her suffering? I gave her some more Piriton in the hope that a good night's sleep would help her as the surgery was now closed and I had to wait until morning. The following morning Jan was in terrible pain even though the Piriton was causing her to be very drowsy. I rang the surgery and spoke with our GP. She said she would leave a script out for me to collect for some very strong painkillers. If these did not do the trick then she would need a morphine type drug.

I had tried to sleep in a chair next to Jan's bed. Her room was downstairs and I needed to be near her. Her distress became so bad that John decided we should bring a mattress down and put it on the floor by her bed. We slept like this for several nights holding her and reassuring her as best we could, until the pain eased a little. Eventually we moved back to our room and things seemed to be improving.

I was flicking through a newspaper or magazine when my eyes fell on an article by a woman whose daughter had a rare condition. She had managed to bring a lot of benefit to her daughter by testing and treating her for allergies. I knew that Jan was very sensitive to a lot of things, as she had had eczema since she was a baby and I had to look for colouring in drinks and food. The reaction to Tegretol was a further example of her sensitive system. I was quickly on the phone to the woman in the article. She was extremely nice and suggested I sent a piece of Jan's hair off to an address she gave me to find out whether she had other allergies. She also told me of a clinic in Southampton where the doctors treated patients with alternative medicines. Furthermore, she said that she would put some wheat-free recipes in the post for me to try out on Jan. I thanked her and then set about gathering a strand of hair and I also phoned the clinic in Southampton.

The hair analysis showed that Jan was not tolerating wheat and dairy products, and so the diet was set in motion. We took her to Southampton. The system that was used was most unusual. The doctor applied small glass vials to Jan's toes and the reaction to whatever was inside was registered on a machine. When I asked how it worked the doctor was honest enough to say that they had no idea. It was a German invention and all they knew was that it worked and they were having a lot of success in detecting problems in patients. However, he said that he did not want to build our hopes up as Jan's central nervous system was very damaged and although they saw patients with rare conditions he had never had anyone with so many problems.

My hopes were raised and dashed at the same time. He must have sensed this and said, 'I can definitely help her a little, maybe more than a little, but we will have to look at her over several months.' He continued to explain that the tests had shown that she was hypersensitive to many things and any medication she was given needed to be monitored very carefully.

We left the surgery with several homeopathic medicines, and stretching before me was the arduous job of nursing Jan back to health and trying to get the guesthouse up and running for the fast approaching season.

It was with great relief that I saw an improvement in Jan every day. She was beginning to be able to read her Braille books again. She struggled, at first, to play the piano, but quite soon she was back to enjoying her music again too. Sadly her hearing had now deteriorated to such a state that I discussed with Jan the idea of using the deafblind manual alphabet. We both knew a little about it. We also knew how to administer this, but for Jan to receive it on her hand was a different proposition altogether. Jan saw it as another thing to accomplish. Never once did she complain about all that had happened. In fact her sense of humour was as sharp as ever and she often had the family and visitors in stitches at some thing or other.

Sadly, one of the things she had to give up was her CB radio. She had tried to make contact but could no longer understand anything that people were saying. I did see her looking quite sad as she struggled to understand what was going on, but then one day she just said that she was going to sell her CB radio outfit as she had got bored with it, putting on a very brave face as she said it.

Jan was more proficient at the manual alphabet than I was. It is harder to receive on the hands than it is to give. Every word has to be spelt out letter for letter, and the process is very laborious and tiring. But Jan soon picked it up and I became quicker and quite soon we were able to converse fluently. I found this easier than trying to get Jan to understand conversation in the normal way. The down side of the manual language is that there is no intonation and neither did she see our body language. At times she took things the wrong way. We decided between us that if I was telling her something amusing or pulling her leg then I would tickle the centre of her hand and this did help.

I too had to learn new ways of expressing myself. For instance, one day we were chatting and I quite simply asked the question, why? How many ways can we say this word? Jan took it as me criticising her, when all I wanted to know was why she wanted to do a certain thing. I quickly realised that Jan often misinterpreted what I was trying to put across. But my tiredness and the fact that I had to get on with our business often meant that I just put information onto her hand and I did not have time to spare to re-interpret on occasions. Often this led to hard feelings between us with me not always understanding why, when I had placed a message on her hand, she had gone into a mood. We had a lot to learn.

We also had a visit from a social worker for the deaf. He, too, used the manual language, but fluently. He was to become very much a part of Jan's life.

We were able to take Jan out in her wheelchair now, and she was able to move around the home better. I continued with the diet and the medicines and we went to Southampton another couple of times. Then one day Jan said she would like to walk into town. We were quite surprised, but slowly, with dad on one side and me on the other to hold onto, she managed to do the fifteen-minute walk into town, shop and walk back. She was triumphant. If only her hearing would improve! It was wishful thinking. It never ever came back.

A social worker suggested that she attend a day centre for the disabled. It would give her something to occupy her mind and a change of environment, she said. Jan always had things to occupy her mind, as she was now able to read her many library books again. Very reluctantly she went along. She attended a few times but one morning she begged of me not to send her. I asked her what the problem was. She said she felt patronised and bored. I asked her why and she explained that she was made to pack plastic cutlery into bags. These were for use on airlines. Jan sat for hours doing this menial work and at the end of the week received 75p after her lunch money had been deducted.

I was shocked and felt that I had subjected Jan to a humiliating situation. How could anyone expect a young woman with a fine intellect and high IQ to do such menial work and expect her to be satisfied? Added to this was the fact that the pay was a pittance. This was work so that airline passengers could enjoy their meals on board a plane? The whole thing appalled me. She did not go again.

Now Jan spent a lot of her time on the piano. She would go over and over tunes, and really I guess we got used to what we thought was her messing about on the keyboard.

CHAPTER 21

When we lived in Hinckley, I saw on the BBC programme Tomorrow's World, that a machine had been invented called a Versa-Brailler. It was a sort of computerised brailling machine, but it stored Braille onto tapes and was capable of a great deal more that would enhance Jan's quality of life. It could also be connected to the phone, enabling the blind person to send Braille messages down the line which would be received in Braille if the user had a Versa-Brailler too, or as a printout on a screen for sighted users. The replies were received in Braille by Jan, enabling her much more independent contact. Of course it was only compatible if the person at the other end had the right modem.

It was a wonderful machine and the beginning of a new era of technology for the blind and deafblind. Later we took Jan to an exhibition where all sorts of equipment was on show. Among them was the Versa-Brailler. Jan was very keen to try it out and was over the moon. However the price was several thousands of pounds. It was a great deal of money and well beyond our reach. We explained to Jan that if we could raise the money somehow she would have one.

Another incredible piece of equipment called an Optacon, allowed blind people to read the printed word. This device involved placing printed matter under a sort of flat-bed scanner type machine with the result that the printed word was converted into pinhead type features. Jan had a try at this too, and because she knew what the written word looked like she was able to grasp this technique immediately. Again this cost several hundreds of pounds.

I am not sure how Pam got to hear about Jan's dream to own a Versa-Braille machine, but one day she came to see John and me. She asked whether we would mind if she attempted to raise the money to get Jan one. She said she was asking because in a small town like Exmouth, and because there would be press coverage, would we mind people wanting to know about some personal details? She went on to say that we would also need to become very involved, and she knew how busy we were at the time. We were not at all bothered about any of that, and in fact told her that we would do whatever we could to help raise money,

Quite quickly the article appeared in the Exmouth News. It seemed as though everyone had caught the vision and empathised with Jan and wanted to get her this marvellous machine. People just took money into the newspaper's office, schools held various functions, groups of children did whatever they could, we held a car boot sale, there were concerts held and all manner of things. It just snowballed, and Jan was so excited that her machine would soon be on its way. Even the editor of the local paper was astonished at what was happening and asked whether it would be possible for Jan to write a piece for the paper to explain exactly what the Versa-Brailler would enable her to do. There was a forty-eight-hour deadline.

They had no idea just how important that request was to her. She had never been asked to do something like this for anyone. She had always said that she would gladly give all her benefit money back if only someone would give her a job to earn her own money. Of course there was no fee involved, but as soon as she heard of the request she got out her typewriter – just an ordinary portable typewriter we had bought her for the previous Christmas present. It was no different in any way to the ones used up and down the country, and she began to type as though her very life depended on it. The words just tumbled onto the paper. She did not stop for a minute. Within a matter of a few hours the pieces of A4 paper were in my hands ready to go to the editor.

The next day, I took the story along and left it at the reception desk. Not long afterwards I had a call from the editor to say what an incredible article she had written and he was going to print it exactly as it was written and that he would give it the double centre page spread. Wow! Was Jan pleased! She could hardly wait for the edition to come into the shops.

We very soon had several phone calls about the article. One was from a freelance writer who wanted to know whether Janis would allow her to be her ghost-writer for a book. I told Jan and she pondered on this. Then I had a word with the editor of the paper and his reply was to tell the freelancer to go and jump, as Janis was more than capable of writing her own story.

The money came from all over. Sometimes hundreds of pounds and sometimes an old person dropped off part of her pension at the newspaper office or a note was sent to us with a pound inside. Children sold toys on a table outside their home. It was not long before the Versa-Brailler was on order.

But we had our business to run. We had had an excellent season and the house was often fully booked. A neighbour offered us three of her bedrooms for over-spill. It was a very busy time. Jan would amuse herself by reading, studying or playing her piano. Andy had joined sea scouts and had taken up sea fishing.

Although Jan could not hear conversation she still had some residual hearing and could hear certain sounds on piano or her electronic keyboards. One particular piece of music we heard over and over again as she played it on her electronic keyboard. She had used many (synthetic) instruments to bring about a lovely tune. One evening, John and I were very busy serving the evening meal as Jan played in her room just off the kitchen. John was clearing the tables in the dining room when one of the guests stopped to ask him what the piece of music was. John just casually told him that it was his daughter messing about on keyboards (she had two that she used at the same time). The male guest remarked that it was a lovely tune and worthy of recording, and he felt it would sell.

We were very busy but, in afterthought, John said that he would send the tape to Television SouthWest. The tune, called "Salute to The Royal Children", composed just after Prince Harry was born, was sent on tape and reached the hands of the head of music there, a Mr. Ed Walsh. He liked the tune very much and he sent the tape on to H.M. Royal Marine College at Dartmouth. He told them about Jan but asked for no favours saying, 'If you think it is worthy of your time then use it; if not just send it back.' Lo and behold, they thought the tune was excellent! Furthermore they were going to adapt it for a thirty-two piece band to play. Jan took this in her stride as though it was a daily occurrence and continued to compose more tunes.

Jan had been intent on the birth of the new prince and had decided to knit the baby a matinee jacket. She sent off for a Braille pattern and I took her to buy the wool, a lovely pale lemon. I am not a knitter so I was amazed to see, as the piece of knitting began to grow, that it was no easy pattern. It was an intricate shell pattern and on the odd occasion when she dropped a stitch she would call 'Mum, can you come and find a stitch for me please?' What a palaver that was. But she plodded on, deeply engrossed in her work.

Eventually it was finished and she asked me to sew it together for her, and wash and press it. When this was done she folded it and placed it in delicate tissue paper. Then together we wrapped it ready to go to Princess Diana.

The press was doing a great deal for the Versa-Braille fund, and now Jan had got other irons in the fire. We had a call from TSW to ask whether Jan could go to their studios where the band would play her music and she would be interviewed. Jan was thrilled, more by the chance to go somewhere different and meet new people, I think. But what was she to wear, she asked. I dashed out to get her a new dress. It was a lovely Laura Ashley corduroy type material in deep burgundy with a tiny turquoise rosebud pattern all over. It had leg of mutton shaped sleeves and a rose at the throat. As soon as I got home and Jan tried it on it brought a huge lump to my throat. She looked absolutely lovely, her waist-length auburn hair draped around her shoulders. I was so proud of her and I loved her so much it hurt.

The big day came and we all went to the Royal Marine College. First of all the interview between Jan, the musical director and me took place. Then we were seated in front of the stage and the band arrived. I tried to relay, for Jan, all that I could about the building, the stage, and how the band looked. When the trumpet players stood and started to play the fanfare at the beginning of Jan's tune her face lit up. As the rest of the band joined in she giggled. My heart was singing.

Afterwards, the interviewer asked what she thought of it and she replied that, 'It sounded quite thin on my keyboards, but now it is just great and I can't wait for all of my friends to hear it.'

We were told that it would go out on TV the following night. All of us sat close to the screen anticipating that Jan's slot would be a few seconds only. Were we surprised when the local news programme began with Jan's tune and pictures of Princess Di holding her baby and the presenter talking about the remarkable Janis Revell from Exmouth. She went on to tell what had provoked Jan into composing the tune. Then the interview at the College was shown, followed by the band. More pictures were flashed across the screen of Princess Di with the new baby, then of Charles and Di and the baby, and one of the whole family together. Fresh tears now dripped down my face but these were tears of happiness and joy.

The next day we were very surprised to receive an invitation to a concert at the Royal Marine College at Dartmouth. We were told they were going to include Jan's tune in their programme. We could hardly wait, and when the time came it was such a unique and wonderful night. A great deal of attention was given to Jan. As we entered the foyer people recognised us from the TV programme and smiled. We made our way to our seats and I immediately picked up the programme and quickly glanced through. Boldly printed a little way down was "'Salute to the Royal Children' by Janis Revell". My heart swelled with joy and pride.

Before the concert began, the conductor said that he would just take a few minutes to introduce a special piece of music to be played that night, and went on to explain a little about Jan's tune. He did not mention her deafblindness but said that a very special young lady had composed it.

The band played their set pieces and then came the time for Jan's piece. When the tune had been played the conductor once again addressed the audience. He then explained that Janis was in need of a special piece of machinery to enable her to study for a degree at college. He explained that she had first of all lost her sight and now she recently had become profoundly deaf. He turned to the band and asked a very handsome Marine to present Jan with a cheque for £200. The band was in full dress uniform and looked very smart. The young soldier walked down from the stage, along the gangway and up the steps to where we were sitting. It was a breathtaking time and you could have heard a pin drop. He was carrying the biggest bouquet of flowers. As he stood in front of Jan he placed the flowers in her lap and then bent and kissed her gently on her cheek. Finally he handed her the cheque.

I had been relaying all that was happening to Jan and I had said what a dishy bloke the soldier was. She blushed and held the flowers up to her face. The bandmaster finally said that they were going to keep her piece of music in their repertoire forever. The audience applause was so loud, and went on for quite a while. What a marvellous night it was.

A short time after this we had a call from TSW again. This time it was to ask whether Janis would appear on the Highway programme with Sir Harry Secombe. They said that they would give her a contract for £80. This may not seem much now but in 1983 it was considered to be quite a nice sum.

When I told Jan her mouth fell open. 'I'm going to get paid?' she gasped as she clapped her hands in front of her face and screeched with delight. She was very thrilled that she was required to sign a contract. And so we had another big event to look forward to. Things were certainly looking much better. If only her hearing would return, was my constant thought.

The fundraising was still ongoing and there really was not a dull moment. It was all happening at such an alarming rate, and on reflection I realise that little Andrew was very quiet and unintentionally in the background. He did not make any demands and seemed quite happy to go along with whatever was happening. Also we were very busy with the business and we had no idea just how badly he was feeling left out.

The great day of the Highway programme arrived, and the filming was to take place in Plymouth. It was a bitterly cold day and snow lay on the ground, but our hearts were warmed by the excitement of all that was happening.

On the first day we were taken to a beautiful little theatre called The Globe. It is based inside the Stonehouse Barracks of The Royal Marines at Plymouth. Inside, it was all red plush and elegant gold, and it held a beautiful atmosphere. There was the well-known composer Peter Knight, playing the piano. He was to be interviewed before Jan. When Sir Harry had finished he turned to the camera and said, 'And now from one composer to another.' My heart swelled with pride!

Janis was taken to have some makeup applied, and then she was seated at a grand piano. While she sat chatting I brushed and arranged her hair which I had curled the night before. Now it hung in curls around her shoulders over the white and gold suit she had bought especially for the show. Peter, Jan's social worker for the deaf, had rehearsed with Jan some of the things that Harry might ask her and they worked out how they could cut down on the manual alphabet so that there were not too many long silences while he translated. Peter had reassured Jan that all would be well, but she was very nervous.

Now Harry came and joined them and began to ask Jan about her hobbies, how her blindness affected her and also her deafness and whether she would like to see again. She answered with humour and had Harry in stitches. His shoulders shook with laughter. She told him that she enjoyed bowls, archery, swimming, horse-riding, gliding, reading, music, poetry and composing music and that she would love to be a poet and a musician and nothing else. 'Oh yes,' she added, 'I'm hoping to get a degree in English.'

Then she talked about her eyes and said that she would not want her eyes operated on even if they could, but she would love to have her hearing back, Then she added that she didn't think she would let anyone mess with her hearing, either. This was typical of Jan. Nothing was ever straightforward. She was laughing as she said this and so was Harry.

Then Harry asked her whether she would play something for him.

Jan answered, 'I'll play the 1st movement of Beethoven's Moonlight Sonata, that is when I've found my place.' She giggled as did Harry, and tapping the high notes of the piano to find her place she began to play and then the cameras faded.

The rest of the programme was to be filmed the next day on the Ho at Plymouth. It was a cold but bright sunny day. Harry was waiting to sing and the Royal Marine Band was in full dress uniform. How spectacular they looked. Harry had introduced Jan's tune and now it was time for them to play it again. It all went so well, and was beyond our wildest dreams. Jan sat in the sidelines in her wheelchair. Harry had detected that poor Andy was lost as he stood watching all of the attention bestowed on Jan. He took off his hat and placed it on Andy's head chuckling in his unique way as he did so, saying, 'Try that for size lad.'

I often wonder whether he caught the nits that, a couple of days later, I discovered Andy had.

Following this, Jan was asked whether she would appear on a programme called "See Hear" for the deaf and blind. It was a small magazine programme and during this they asked Jan about her ambitions and her appearance on the Highway programme. She was asked to play some music. The interviewer asked her however she managed to play the piano and she replied, 'With both hands of course.'

It was all good fun and the whole family was treated very well. A few months later she was asked to appear on this programme again, but this time she was to appear with the well known Evelyn Glennie. Evelyn was just starting out on her professional career but nonetheless at the end of the programme, in which they both played their own instruments, they were asked whether they would play together at the piano. Of course we had no idea at that time that Evelyn would become so internationally famous.

Jan meets the HM Royal Marine officer during the filming on The Ho.

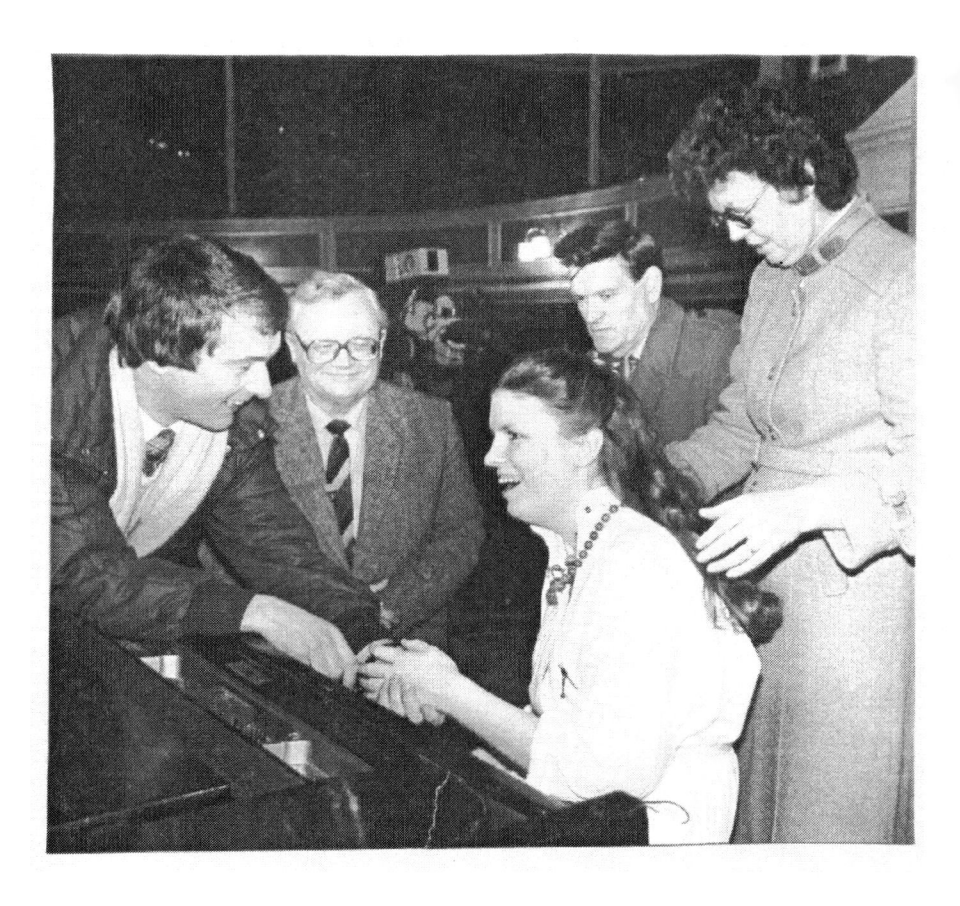

Preparing for filming. Jan's social worker, Peter, talking on her hands. Sir Harry, John and me.

CHAPTER 22

Jan was not content. Her active mind and her hunger for knowledge meant that she kept on about learning and getting her degree. English Literature was her great love and she swallowed books for breakfast. I promised her I would do what I could to find somewhere for her. I had always stressed to Jan that no matter how people treated her she was to always remember that she was a person who had rights just as anyone else – a person with all the same desires and ambitions as any other person, but who happened not to be able to see or hear.

When Pam came round I mentioned to her that when Jan was in London being fitted for the hearing system (which later proved to be of no use to her) the gentleman there had mentioned The Star centre in Cheltenham. He told us it was a fine college for the disabled and they had some hearing impaired students too. We had not paid too much attention because Jan had been quite upset at the other college experiences and then all sorts of other things had gone on so we hadn't given it much thought. But now it was worth looking into. Pam agreed and said she would enquire.

The Braille machine was due at our home and Pam had asked us not to open it or to tell Jan when it arrived, but to ring her. She wanted to be there when she received it, and of course, the press wanted to take pictures too. Jan was late getting up that day and had no idea what was in store. Pam arrived and made out that it was a normal routine visit, as did the photographer who had become a friend. We sat round chatting, and then John brought out the huge box. Jan looked very puzzled as John took her hands and laid them on the top. I think she knew what was in the box but could not allow her feelings to be raised too much. After peeling off the layers of packaging with the help of her dad, she reached the machine. As soon as she got her hands on it there were whoops of laughter, her hands high in the air clapping and shouting, 'It's here.'

The Versa-Brailler she had waited years for had arrived.

We all wanted to see just how this machine worked, but as soon as Jan plugged it in she was away typing her Braille into it and fingering its response. Her fingers were flying across the Braille dots as they appeared.

'Now I can take it with me to college,' she excitedly pronounced.

I glanced at Pam and the glint in her eye told me that she had fixed it for

Jan to go for the interview.

Jan's love of books such as Anne Frank's Diary, Grimm's Fairy Tales, The Iliad of Homer, Living French, Voices part one and two, could now be indulged. An anthology of French verse and more were now within her reach as the Versa-Brailler could store 400 Braille pages on one C60 cassette tape. However, it should be explained that for her to have a Thesaurus it would consist of 47 volumes in Braille, and when I say volumes they each measured about 12"x 10". Her Bible consisted of about 26 of these and her hymn book of about 12 volumes. We had quite literally run out of shelf space, each shelf holding maybe half a dozen of her books. She took her hymn book to church in a suitcase.

But much more than this, the Versa-Brailler was to change Jan's quality of life in a huge way. Her love of literature caused her to eventually purchase over 300 specialist print books. Of course she would never be able to read these, but for her to just have them in her home was heaven to her. She would label each book on the spine with the title and author's name, and every time she discovered a book of further interest, onto the shelf it would go. Of course, for her to be able to read books fluently she borrowed Braille books from the RNIB, and these would arrive in large sacks at our door. She also had newspapers and magazines in Braille, so not much information passed her by.

Pam had made the appointment for the college interview. She told us that she would drive both Jan and me to Cheltenham and asked me whether I would contact someone we knew who was into technical equipment for the blind and deafblind – it was his job. Pam wanted support for Jan's application, and he would be able to explain fully how this equipment would help not only Jan but the staff as well. He was to sit in on the interview if necessary. He was himself blind.

The interview at the college went very well. It took all day and we joined the staff for a lovely lunch. Jan was full of questions and the head of the college was extremely impressed. After meeting various members of staff and having everything explained and shown to us, the head of the college said that it would be unkind not to let Jan go there. He felt that she had been cast away on a scrap heap and it was a terrible thing that someone with such a fine mind and desire to learn had been treated this way. We all agreed.

On the way home I recalled all that had happened to us in the short time since we had arrived in Devon. I felt as though my chest would burst with thanksgiving. There was to be more. Following on from the TV appearances, we had many phone calls asking whether Jan would take part in various events or concerts around the county. Her diary was filling up fast.

Then TSW rang to say that they had had what they thought might be a very important phone call. They gave us a number to ring. John rang it and it was a music foundation in Jersey. Someone with connections there had seen the programme and had discussed Janis with the funding board. Jan's main interest of wanting to become a professional composer was discussed. The outcome was that the sum of £750 had been allocated for Jan to find a teacher so that she could fulfil her ambition. Just to remind you, we were still in the year of 1984/5 – this was a relatively large amount of money.

Jan was absolutely thrilled. At last she was being taken seriously and given credit for her abilities. Sadly she never did draw the money because she could not find a teacher who could comprehend how someone who is both deaf and blind could compose music. Janis never gave up though, and was always composing something or other by herself.

Jan started at Cheltenham and was soon doing some really serious work. There was a tutor there by the name of Dr. Gilbert Childs. He was the author of several books and an advocate of the Steiner method of education. We met him on our first trip to fetch Jan home at the end of term, and he told us that he was in awe of Janis's ability to absorb so much information. He said that he normally had to plead with other students for their homework with little result, but not so with Jan. He said that she was a joy to teach and gave so much back. When he asked us whether we realised that she could obtain a doctorate quite easily I was taken aback. Yes, I knew that she was bright but I had no idea just how bright. Once again Jan took this in her stride and as we journeyed home she had her fingers in yet another book.

There were many venues that Jan would be invited to play, and often John would sing while Jan accompanied him on piano. During the Exmouth Carnival, the Royal Marine Band led the parade and amongst the tunes played was "Salute to the Royal Children". Leading the procession was the musical director whom we had met at their college.

There were many phone calls from other organisations such as retirement homes and care homes asking whether Jan would be prepared to play for their residents. Jan was only too happy to oblige. She was also asked whether she would play in the concert room at Bicton Gardens – a local place of beauty and a big tourist attraction. It was a lovely event. As people were leaving they played Jan's tune "Salute to the Royal Children". They also presented her with a cheque towards the equipment she needed to further her education.

The big one for Jan was to play at The Theatre Royal in Plymouth. She had a wonderful reception there too. After she had finished playing various pieces of music on her two keyboards she was presented with a bust of Bach. Her fingers traced the features, as she stood on stage as the audience applauded. oblivious to what else was happening.

One day we had a phone call from the manager of The Deaf-blind League (later to be renamed Deafblind UK) based in Peterborough. She wanted to know whether Janis would like her to come down to see her and discuss the Versa-Brailler and the Optican (the print reader) in more detail and maybe give her any help that they could. She said that she would like to bring the director, who is also deafblind, with her. Janis was never one to turn down any new adventure and so they were invited to come down and stay from the Friday until the Sunday.

It was a general getting to know one another and enjoying the fellowship, but over the weekend I was aware that something was going on in Jan's mind. The woman had mentioned that the League was situated in Peterborough and that there was a complex of self-contained flats in the grounds. They were for the more able deafblind person who was capable of looking after him or herself. Jan had said over and over that she wanted a flat of her own, but social workers had instilled in me that it was not feasible owing to her limited walking, etc.

CHAPTER 23

Jan was back at college. She rang and sounded very excited as she told me that she had met a very nice boy. He had visited the college to do some voluntary work. He was a Leo, a younger member of the Lions Club. He fell for Jan immediately and asked whether she would go out with him. One of his hobbies was gliding and, of course, Jan was keen to know whether he would take her too. It was not long before she was up in the glider with him. She wanted to know whether she could bring him home to meet us. It all sounded very serious.

We were pleased when we met the young man. We all got on very well. After just a few weeks Jan said that they wanted to get engaged. We were invited to meet his family, and again we all got on tremendously well.

It was coming up to Jan's twenty-first birthday and I asked whether she would like an engagement and birthday celebration together. She thought this to be a splendid idea and quickly set about asking all of her friends from around the country that she had made either during her early schooldays or through the "blind world". She got to work on typing out the invitations. The numbers rose daily, but we said that we would have all the family and all of her friends and that we would sleep as many as possible of those that were coming a long distance.

The guest-house was packed. Presents lay on every available surface. Every room downstairs was heaving with people and the music was belting out. The atmosphere was electric. John had to dash out for more bottles of wine as our stock had been swallowed up within a couple of hours. Jan looked radiant. My family was thrilled for her and us. The whole weekend was a huge success.

It was a very exciting time. John and I were thrilled. We had dreamed that Jan would one day get married. Russell and Jan were now talking about where they would live and what sort of house they would have. Russell returned to his home in Cheltenham and Jan stayed with us for the rest of the end of Christmas break. Russell came back to join us at Christmas and we all had a really lovely time. Andy was in his element because he had many more presents than usual. He now had an extended family.

Jan returned to College for the New Year term. We were happy that she was getting on so well. She rang quite frequently and seemed to be very cheerful, but I became a little concerned. She had been to see the flats at the Deaf-blind League and was full of talk about them. When she came home at half term she broke the news to us. She and Russell had decided that she should move to Peterborough and live independently. Why he was so keen was beyond me because he was still living at home. I guess it helped for Jan to include him when trying to tell me as she knew that I would be very worried about her. John and I sat and talked things through but there was no doubt in our minds that whatever we said it would not make any difference as she had made up her mind.

Once the news had been broken to us it seemed that plans were quickly in motion for the move. Russell arranged for the van to come and collect all of Jan's belongings. I was very apprehensive, but when I saw the piano, the last thing to leave, being lifted onto the back of the van I could not hold back the tears. Not only would we miss her so very much but also there would be no more music around the place. We waved them off and returned to a very quiet and what seemed like a half empty house.

It was not long before Jan was on the phone telling me all about her new home. She was so excited, and I couldn't quite believe that it had happened. She told me about the size of the rooms, and what she was putting where, and what she intended buying. I caught her excitement and quite soon my apprehension or anxiety – I was not sure what my feelings really were – were replaced with happiness for her.

At last my heart was beginning to heal. We now had more time for Andy and to really get down to building on the business. The new season was closing in on us. But then we had a phone call from Andrew's school. We were asked to go in to see his teacher. Yet another shock was in store for us.

Andy had been getting into all sorts of petty trouble. His teacher informed us that his lessons were suffering because of his unhappiness. I became very concerned. Unhappiness? I did not think Andy was unhappy. But the teacher went on. It had been discussed among the staff and it was thought that with all that had been going on around him and the attention that had been focused on our daughter, Andy was rebelling and trying to make a statement that he was not able to put into words.

I was shocked and felt very guilty. Andy had always been such an easy child and never demanded much at all. Because of his easy ways it had enabled us to get on with so much. I was to discover that this behaviour was often the case when a child had a sibling who was disabled. The child assumed that he had no rights because the disabled sibling needed so much more and was not able to enjoy things the way he was etc., etc.

When we got home, John and I decided that we would take a holiday and try to make it up to Andy. We booked a flat in Dartmouth. Then, after a week, we went back to Hinckley to visit friends so that Andy could see his old pals back there. The fact that we could focus entirely on Andy meant that we became aware of just how far we had let matters go. Andy was very unhappy. We managed to get him to tell us a little of what he was feeling.

It was not just about Jan, in fact he never mentioned Jan, but he did say that he felt as though he had lost his mom and dad.

'We don't go on picnics or away in the caravan now. We never go anywhere. You're always so busy.' His face was flushed and nervous.

I realised for the first time that we were never available for him. When he went off to school we were getting the guest's breakfasts, and when he came home we were busy getting the evening meal and after that was the clearing away and setting up for the next day's breakfast. There was always so much to do. It was a 24/7 job with no time off at all during the lengthy season. What time had we given him in over two years? He was now coming up to the difficult teenage years.

What were we to do? It was obvious that we could not allow things to go on as they were. Even though things were quieter without Jan we still would not have much time to do things with Andy. We would sell up. There was no question about it. The guesthouse was lovely; all freshly decorated, the rooms all colour matched with beautiful bed linen. New Axminster carpets were fitted throughout. Everyone who entered said how lovely it was, and tourists from as far as Australia, Canada and America came and complimented us on the quality of everything. Now, after just two years, we were to sell it all, but what would we do?

John picked up the local free paper and was glancing through when he called me to come and see something. He showed me an advert. It was a café that was for sale in the town of Sidmouth, a short drive away. It was a leasehold lock-up property and quite reasonable. We both thought that this could prove to be the answer. It would be more normal opening times and we could arrange to close after Saturday lunch and have Sundays off, thereby returning to some normality of family life. We would buy a house and endeavour to rekindle the lifestyle we once had. John rang the estate agents to make an appointment to view.

It was called The Copper Kettle, but much to our disappointment it was rather a greasy spoon sort of place with the strong smell of grease to prove it. We learnt later that the neighbours had often complained of the smell of stale oil. Undaunted, we saw through all of this with a vision to change yet another building into something really lovely. We offered our price and this was accepted by the vendors. We then placed the guesthouse on the market and the very first people to walk through the door to view bought it at the full asking price.

At The Copper Kettle, it did not take long for the local people to come in to look over the premises and savour our wares. I was really enjoying this new venture when I went down with a very bad dose of flu. It was enough to put me to bed for days. When I did not pick up after three weeks I went to see my new GP. He began by asking me what I had been doing. I tried to explain all that had happened. I was crying and apologising for making a fool of myself. He said to cry as much as I wanted and handed me a tissue. He went on to explain that my body was letting me know that it had been through too much. He said it was about time I started looking after me for a change. He said that I must take several weeks to recover. I missed Jan so much that it hurt.

The café had taken off and we were beginning to derive the benefit of a better income. Andy was getting on well at his new school and also enjoyed helping in the shop after school for some extra pocket money. He got on very well with the customers. He also took up golf and quoits. Sidmouth was a lovely place to live. The golf links overlooked the sea and the quoits were near to the seafront.

Then one day Andy came in and said he had been watching the lawn bowls just at the rear of our café. He asked if he could play. It was a strange thing for a young boy to want. John contacted the sports pavilion and it was agreed that Andy be given a try to see whether he would enjoy it and whether he was any good. When Andy came back from his trial period an elderly gentleman followed him into the café. The man said that the bowling club was very impressed with Andy and that he had a very good eye for the sport. But, he went on to say that there was some concern as they had never ever had a youngster join them before and that they were going to call an extraordinary meeting to discuss whether they should form a junior club. This was duly agreed.

There were offers of equipment made to Andy. We soon had him kitted out, and very smart he looked too. We went to watch him play. He was obviously very good at the game. He had a very unique way of holding the ball up to eye level before bowling. Of course there were always crowds of holidaymakers as well as local folk watching, and Andy would get loud bursts of applause. He looked so very special – this small ruddy-faced lad amongst a group of elderly men. He, of course, enjoyed all of the attention and we went along with it. He was now enjoying being in the spotlight.

The café was a lovely business to run and the town was picturesque. Everything seemed to be going well until we received a call from The League in Peterborough to say that Jan had given up college. I was very annoyed, as such lengths had been taken to get her into education again and we thought that everything was going well. But apparently she was unwell and could not cope with the institutional life. We sped up to the college and spoke with Dr. Childs. He explained to us that Janis was rather like a wild bird, that she would never do well in such an institutional type place and needed to be set free. Her health was suffering as a result. We had a great deal of respect for Gil and he had many years of experience. When we saw Jan we were convinced that she was right to leave.

Also, it seemed that things were not going well between Jan and Russell. I didn't know what the problem was, but Andy had gone up to stay with Jan and when he came home he said that Russell had been there and there had been several rows. He said that he did not think Jan was very happy. My stomach lurched at the news but I tried not to worry.

CHAPTER 24

Janis went to Switzerland with the organisation SENSE and had a wonderful time. She was asked whether she would write a description of her holiday for their newsletter. This is what she wrote.

Adelboden 1985

Foreword: Janis Revell, who is totally blind and profoundly deaf and has difficulty walking, recently went on the Mobility International holiday to Adelboden in Switzerland. Janis was a member of the British party organised by SENSE. Here she writes vividly of her experience:

Adelboden is a mountain valley village surrounded by snow capped peaks and avalanche fences. When the clouds are low you are completely closed in, and when they are high above there is a marvellous view of the blue sky and snowy mountain-heads.

There are beautiful birds singing outside the hotel windows and there are the sounds of cowbells and bleating sheep to lull one into peacefulness. Not that we lazed around and soaked up the atmosphere without plenty of entertainment. There were trips out every day and we got to know people from other countries.

But the beginning of all the new experiences for me was the flight over to Switzerland. I'd never flown before, save on a holiday trip of twenty minutes. It was exhilarating and a great beginning to a superb holiday. We didn't reach Adelboden until late, so we had a meal and settled down.

On Sunday there was a meeting to get us to meet each other. I was introduced to Jan, a Dutchman, and his mother Bess, who spoke English and quickly learnt the English manual alphabet so that he could communicate with me. The Dutch manual is too complicated for me to learn.

I am not sure of the order the events happened in because it was such a full week, and there was something exciting happening every day. However, I think it was Sunday afternoon that we went up the mountains for a cable car ride. There was a splendid view of mountains and waterfalls and we stopped at a pub for a drink at the other end and where there was also a miniature village.

On Monday some of us went to a folk museum and some to the wood carver's shop. There were many fascinating things to be seen at the wood carver's. Bears, cows, rabbits, and pigs, puzzle boxes with hidden key rings and many other things.

There were many shopping trips too, and we bought many unusual items between us. Beautiful music boxes in the shape of a Swiss house for example.

One night some Swiss ladies in costume came and showed us folk dancing and there was a huge horn that wound around the room like a giant serpent which many of us had a go at blowing – not with particularly musical results!

One day some of us went for a trip in a horse-drawn carriage but the horses were not too friendly, as I discovered with the result of a swollen finger for a few days afterwards. But the ride was good and we met more cows and soaked up more of the local atmosphere.

To me one of the best experiences of all was the day we went for a chair lift, and as we were riding along, hearing all the cow bells and sheep, sometimes an occasional bird and the rumble as we passed over the pylon. That was bliss, so still and full of local sounds. That was also the day we went rowing, many of us taking turns at the oars.

On Thursday we went to a place where there were Swiss houses from different periods of time. Some of us went into town in the afternoon. One thing I enjoyed that day was the peaceful rest by a lake where we fed the ducks and swans. The whole group met up again for a motorboat trip. There were many waterfalls to be seen from the boat and it was a marvellous trip.

There was dancing and drinking quite regularly – almost every evening – and by the end of the week we'd all had such a marvellous time that some of us (including me) were quite exhausted.

There were snowball fights too, of course, the day we went on the cable cars. And many new friends and overseas pen pals made. All in all it was absolutely marvellous – I've never enjoyed a holiday so much before.

Though I couldn't see it, one thing I shall always hold dear in memory is the picture painted by two friends in Adelboden. The mountain peaks with the snow-line not too far above the village; the waterfalls; the fast flowing stream, the strength of which I was able to feel; the low lying clouds that hemmed us into the world entirely contained in the valley between the peaks. I know I certainly won't forget those cowbells.

A BABE OF MOUNTAINS
By Janis Revell

A babe of mountains I lie alone
Singing through my loud speakers, the birds,
My head is lulled upon the fields, which like silken rags
Cushion me gently on their greenest threads.

And God lay by me a riverlet of looping lace,
Which shines, reflecting the lamp-light of the skies,
Which chatters to my outstretched arm as it lies
Its head upon my shoulder, and chuckles and churtles
As it calls to its little ones to follow along their own courses.

And in my collar of soft white linen,
That makes me hold my breath for fear of its melting,
Upon this cotton neck-band God has pinned
A brooch of crystal, cold and smooth against my chin.

Upon the brim of my clear iced hat, God has placed feathers
Which wave their heads in solemn worship and prayer
Of hissing a messenger that moves among them.

And where is my lover in all this?
Alas! He stands helplessly at my feet like an ant beside a pencil.
He can no longer kiss
My forehead gently, for he is
A man, and I, a mountain.

My thoughts are no longer full of his love for me,
They are full of fear as I watch the conquered lie down to die,
And know that one day I
Will be conquered by man too.

Later followed another remarkable holiday with SENSE in Scotland. Part of this was filmed by the BBC2 'See Hear' programme.

A WILD RETREAT
By Janis Revell

Many of us spent hours on planes, trains, buses and boats. Yet it was worth it all, all the falling up steps and being jarred in not-too-cosy minibuses. Our goal was St Nithians in Crieff, which is near to Methven.

Methven is situated halfway up a hill, which has two groves of trees encircling its summit, visible from the road, which winds in and out of the forestry and field. Crieff is surrounded, just as the hill on which Methven stands, by varied farmlands, hills and woods.

Saturday was travel and settle in day, and most of us were glad to retire to our rooms pretty early.

Sunday was a day of recovery. We could walk, go hill-climbing, swimming or just dally around soaking up the atmosphere. For me, however, Scotland held some memories – memories of challenges; I was there not to surrender to a day of luxuriating in fresh air and fair sun. I was there to capture again a typical Scotland, a country I had dreamed up as a rough hardy romantic but fierce land. The least I could do was climb a hill....

I don't normally leave my wheelchair out-of-doors. Knock Hill was a fair-sized one. There were two gates – narrow difficult things for someone with a wheelchair, so I abandoned it at the very foot of the hill – the other side of the donkey field. The donkey seemed quite contented to let us pass unaccosted, but the track, Knock woods and clumps of country scented mud had other ideas for me at least. The track was steep, especially where the trees were, and clinging to an old oak tree did not stop me slipping backwards. Reaching the top of that hill, with the kind, tender cheering of my companions, was a thing of great joy to me. The wind was brisk and cool, the view stunning, and although it was 'out of sight' for two of us, I could feel Scotland stretched, austerely beautiful, around me, beckoning...Scotland gave me a reward for my fierce obsession with it and its inhabitants.

Hitherto I looked upon most museums and castles as lumps filled with lumps, in other words, just things that bored people looked at for relief of boredom. I was to leave Scotland not only with the prize of great friendships made, but also with a burning lust of castle-history. I can't stop reading Scottish history, and whenever a castle comes up in it I am all ears!

Monday was the day that created the foundation of that love for me. Glamis Castle, home of a very gracious, kind, hospitable lady – Lady Strathmore – was our first outing. The previous evening while sampling my first wee dram of whisky in a local pub, the tour organiser, Gill Morebey, had dropped the clanger that Macbeth had been murdered in this castle. Now I had studied Macbeth at school, and again at college, and yet still forgotten the name of his castle. So in a way it is thanks to Gill that I now have this passion for castle-history. I went in search of ghosts and possible bloodstains, just for proof. I was told there were many ghosts – some of which I'd read of in a biography of the Queen Mum (whose bedroom we were allowed to peer into) and of course I met Macbeth's present guardian – a huge real, stuffed bear.

I wouldn't say it was 'strawberries and cream' weather, but some of the group certainly tucked into all sorts of delicacies outside the castle. Before we left there was a visit to the gift shop. I bought two key rings of the castle – my love was beginning to kindle…Lady Strathmore had a photo taken with us, and kept chatting with individuals. She seemed as happy to meet us as we were pleased to meet her, and there was much complimentary talk in the bus on the way home on our hostess of the day.

Tuesday we went to glass blowing and pottery, a whisky distillery, trouting and on this occasion, Russell, my fiancée, and I saw how moulds were made with plaster of Paris for various vases, models of whisky bottles, and other things. We saw how the transfers were placed on vases before firing, how they came out smooth and glossy. We met a worker who attached handles to jugs, and a huge, wet, revolving cushion on which work was wiped to remove blemishes.

I think that it was probably this evening that the disco was arranged. For me it was to be an experience never to be forgotten. I had, for five years or more years, despised myself for being too wobbly to dance. I'd been fiercely jealous as Russell, many times, got up to dance. This time proved too much – my sorrow was conspicuous – and rewarding. A friend danced with me, and I discovered that by placing a hand on one shoulder I could balance! Russ soon came back – maybe drawn by the sight of me having a dance with a dishy guy from London? It was thrilling. I never quite got over the fact that I had not only just danced, but had attempted (though rather unsuccessfully) to keep up in the Conga. Aaaaaah well!

Wednesday was the day the BBC joined us on a motorboat trip across

Loch Lomond. It was a lazy day, a day more of relaxation – a break in the whirlwind of other days. But there were picturesque houses by the loch side to photograph; a caravan site with many boats moored along the shore, a few little shops selling fudge, key rings and toys.

There was a concert that night. Most of us did something or other. Some Irish boys played tin whistles (Incidentally I am now the possessor of two so they didn't go unnoticed). Julia, a friend who lives just across the street from me, played her electric guitar and sang. And several of us played the piano; all of us sang and clapped. It was a merry get-together.

Thursday was again a choice of whisky tasting (I'd had my taste buds amply satisfied, but had discovered greater pleasure in Bacardi and Cokes, hitherto unknown to me), pottery and glass blowing, trouting or horse-riding.

We chose trouting. It was laborious at first, sitting on a rustic bench with little back support and waiting for the fish to sniff us out. But soon I was reeling in a wriggling specimen which I had not the guts either to unhook or stone the head off. That was man's work.

It was amusing to Russ, though, to have me recorded on TV screaming as a wriggling, still alive trout was placed in my hand and I was advised to 'grip it then'.

That evening there was bagpiping and accordion playing and a singer, Jim Emery, at the hotel where we ate the trout we had caught in the morning, and as well as knocking a tune out of the accordion, dancing with some friends, I won a kiss from the singer himself – for making a din on the accordion, I suppose? I left clutching my best memento of Scotland – a Scottish sound…Jim Emery plus accordion whirring along a tape which has since been played many times. I am glad to have enough hearing to hear that, with a personal stereo and good-quality headphones.

I wasn't quite so joyful over Stirling Castle. We stood at the castle wall, surveying the peaks, including Ben Lomond, hiding the lake from us, and the River Forth. Below the wall the sheer cliff of a hundred and fifty feet and more fell to the valley bed.

That night we had our own, belated Burns night. He was the son of a poor peasant farmer, and haggis, turnip and potatoes were a luxury enjoyed only on special occasions. Now every year, Burns' birthday is celebrated with a haggis, turnips and potato supper. The haggis is lamb's liver and heart mixed with toasted oatmeal and suet, stuffed into a lamb's stomach. When glimpsing the recipe at home I'd felt rather nauseous, but whether it was the spirit of the evening or the fact that I was leaving the next day, I had to have some.

A piper traditionally pipes the haggis in, the stomach is slit, and the haggis dished out onto piles of stewed, mashed turnips and boiled potato. I loved it and had two platefuls. 'Like it?' I asked Russ. 'It's gorgeous!' he enthused. 'Well I'm glad to tell you I've several recipes for it at home. 'No thanks,' he said emphatically. 'You've got to get it into a lamb's stomach first!'

A piper showed me how to play the chanter I'd purchased in Stirling. Also from Stirling I'd received a present from a shopkeeper – a leather purse. As we caught the train from Stirling station the following day, I felt the sickness inside of someone leaving the home they truly loved inside me. And in my ears rang the words 'Don't forget Scotland.' We won't.

LAUGHTER
By Janis Revell

Laughter, she echoes down the valley;
Laughter she dances on the stair;
Laughter, she rings through the hills and the dales;
Laughter, she's everywhere.

Laughter she sits in the tree-tops,
Weaving her spell of pure joy;
Filling kind hearts with enchantment
That nothing can destroy.

Laughter, clothed in long, soft dress
Of white with sweet flowers of pale blue;
Her eyes are twinkling emeralds;
Her tears are clear, fresh dew.

Laughter, her hair soft, warm and fair,
As laughing she glides through the skies,
Floating, light hearted, on the cloudless air,
Or laughing through people's eyes.

Laughter, she chuckles in the sunshine;
Laughter she dances on the moon;
Laughter, she's merry from day-break
Through morning and way after noon.

Laughter she echoes down the valley,
To ring in your ears all day through;
Laughter, she's never found sleeping.....
She's laughing all night long too.

I had been on The Weekends Away with SENSE and was Jan's escort interpreter. These were wonderful breaks when parents and their children would gather. Various workshops were arranged if one wanted to attend any of them. Some were informative, others relaxing, such as aromatherapy sessions. At night there was entertainment, mainly by the deafblind youngsters and it was truly amazing to see.

On one of the mornings we attended the plenary session which started the day. Janis was really intent. I was laying down as much information, on her hand, as fast as I could. The deafblind manual alphabet is mostly laying one letter at a time on the hand, so you will imagine the amount of information one has to condense and remember as the speaker talks at the normal rate of speech. However, I must have done a good enough job because at the end of the opening there was question time and as Rodney Clarke opened this up to the audience Janis shot her hand into the air. I was quite surprised. Rodney pointed to us, at the back of the large hall, and asked Jan if she would like to come to the platform. I had no idea what she wanted to say but she wanted to respond to a speaker – a mother – who had been told that she would have been better off to have her child aborted. She chose not to and the child had been born deafblind, brain damaged and other major problems. The poor woman was in tears as she told of her now having doubts at keeping her baby.

Janis spoke of her life, of her capabilities her disabilities, and she went on about the joy her life gave her. Then she touched on the matter of abortion. More or less, she said that she was against this. She went on to say that research was on the brink of detecting the gene responsible for her problems and that one day they will probably be able to detect this in the unborn child. 'Supposing my mother had had the choice of aborting me?' This was her theme and when she had finished there was thunderous applause.

After the meeting had closed several people came to gather round us and fired questions at Jan. There were several social workers among them. Jan answered as best she could. I interrupted to tell her a special friend had arrived whom she had been wanting to meet up with. She excused herself and asked me to take her to him.

To say I was stunned is an understatement. When transcribing I was never exactly sure whether Jan was grasping everything. Words tumble onto the hand one after the other and the deafblind person has to make sense as the fingers are tapped in whatever order, letter after letter, word after word, often without breaks. It takes a great deal of intelligence, and I must add hard work, for the translator too.

* * * * *

Another call came to say that Jan was not well again. She had requested that she go into Maida Vale hospital and this was quickly arranged. She was most upset. I asked whether she wanted me to go with her into hospital and she said she would like that. It meant that once again I had to leave John and Andy to cope with the business.

When I arrived at Jan's flat I was so shocked. She had lost a lot of weight and looked terribly ill. I stayed at the flat before going down to London with her. She told me how unhappy she was about her relationship with Russell and said that she had tried to break it off with him but he would not listen and kept coming to the flat. For the first time I saw her cry tears of unhappiness.

We were admitted to the hospital and I was to sleep on a put-you-up in the staff room. We were in hospital for about three weeks. There were several phone calls from Russell. He wanted to come down to see her and I could see that Jan was really worried. She begged of me to stop him but it was not for me to do. Eventually he got the message and left her well alone, but it took some time for this to happen.

Meanwhile Jan was undergoing more tests. We had been to the hospital for a flying visit after her Tegretol illness and had been seen by the professor who had researched into her illness. He confirmed that Jan had had a typical reaction to the drug but in a very severe form. He also said that her hearing would always remain as it was now. On this visit she was to have a muscle biopsy, lumbar puncture and all manner of tests. I was still amazed at her resilience and cheerfulness throughout.

On this visit to Maida Vale there was a big treat in store for Jan. She absolutely adored Princess Diana She was due to visit the hospital while we were there. Jan was to be presented to her. When Princess Diana came to the ward Janis was wheeled to the front of the group of patients gathered to see her. A tall man stepped forward saying to the princess that Janis had composed a piece of music called "Salute to the Royal Children". Diana seemed a little uncomfortable, but then said, 'It was very nice and when will you compose another one?'

Janis replied, 'When you have your next baby.'

Diana blushed, bowed her head and looked sideways at Jan over the top of her eyelashes and answered 'You will have to wait a very long while.' (This was when rumours abounded about her marriage difficulties). She chatted with the other patients and then made her way downstairs. It was all over in a very short while.

All of the many tests, some of them involving Jan going into theatre, still revealed nothing that would throw any light on her problems.

Some months later she was to learn that she had been awarded a grant by The Lord Snowdon Fund, for her achievements and her ability to overcome her disability and progress with her studies. She was to receive her award at a special luncheon in London and Lord Snowdon was to give it to her personally. I think it was for one thousand pounds.

It was a grand occasion. As we entered the building we were searched. It was at the beginning of bomb blasts around London. Janis was rather reticent to give her bag to be searched and nudged me saying that there were some personal things in it. However she had no choice. The search was very brief anyway.

There were many speeches and people with disabilities of all kinds. Lord Snowdon came down from the stage to present the cheques to each individual, and it therefore took about two hours to get through all of the presentations. Then we were all invited into the dining room. How splendid everything looked. There were several very large round tables covered with white damask tablecloths and all laid out beautifully. The food was scrumptious. Lord Snowdon came to our table to talk with us and asked John to bring him another glass of wine! He was extremely friendly.

Next to Janis sat a young woman who had no arms or legs. She told me that she was doing a university course and had her own home. I could not begin to know how she coped. She asked me to apologise to Jan for not being able to take her hand and talk with her. I offered the apology to Jan but undaunted she said that she would like to talk to her and would I interpret for the girl. They chatted like old friends.

When we had finished our main course we were invited to collect our pudding from a large table that had been set out in the corner of the room. As I rose to my feet the young woman asked whether I would bring her the profiteroles. Placing them on the table in front of her I hesitated, unsure as to how she would eat them. I plucked up courage and asked her whether she needed any help. She assured me that she was OK and quite naturally for her, bent forward and lapped the food up.

Chapter 25

I don't know what caused me to be so disturbed, but Jan's guide-help had been talking with Jan about her lack of friends and social life. They decided between them to place an advert in the paper with a picture of Jan asking if there was anyone who would like to make contact. I thought it very dangerous but the guide-help seemed to be a sensible woman. She assured me she would vet anyone that replied. I tried to quiet my uneasy mind whilst at the same time recognising that Jan would see it as interfering if I said anything.

I didn't hear anything for a couple of weeks. I was pleased because it was a sign, usually, that all was well. The next I heard was that Jan had a boyfriend. He had answered the article in the paper. I was unsettled, to say the least of it. She was very keen and laid my mind at rest by saying that she was going to church with him. He was much older than she was, but from what she told me all seemed OK. He played in the band at church and was very involved in church life.

The phone calls were now very infrequent. I put this down to the fact that she was getting on with her new life. Then she asked whether she could bring her new man to see us. Of course we wanted to see him.

As soon as I set eyes on him I took a dislike. He had very shifty eyes and some of the comments he came out with seemed very far-fetched. He was also in the habit of boasting about the good deeds that he did. I noticed that he seemed to keep his distance from Jan and was looking around him all of the time. The only time there was any contact between them was when he offered her his arm to guide her, and even then he looked most uncomfortable.

We arranged to go to church on the Sunday of his stay. As we were all busy getting ready he sat in the armchair with his head down. I asked him about getting ready and he became very fidgety and looked embarrassed, saying that he had not brought Sunday clothes so couldn't go. We persuaded him that he looked decent enough. He was very reluctant and acted very strangely. Very reluctantly he said that he would come.

What stood out for me was the fact that for someone who attended church regularly he seemed to be very out of place. His reluctance to join in with singing and other things was tangible, but I gave him the benefit of the doubt by thinking that maybe he needed more time to get to know us. Of course Jan could not judge any of this. She was at a loss because she could not see his body language or hear his comments.

It was soon time for them to return to Peterborough, but the man's car would not start. It turned out it had a major fault. The man uttered something about not having brought any money and that he had left his cheque book and cards back home. John lent him the money to get the car fixed, thinking he needed to get back to his job. I asked him whether he wanted to ring his firm or his mother and he made the excuse that it was no problem at all. He said he was in a position where he could go into work at any time and his mum would not worry.

In conversation he had mentioned his mum. He said that if his mum had any more worry it would kill her. This had come up a couple of times. I did not question him on this as he explained that she had had much worry over the years. He talked about his sister and his dad but I always felt he was fibbing. He was also very keen to read the Bible and pray and kept repeating how busy he was in church. Jan had mentioned that he had stopped taking her with him. Immediately I asked him why this was. His excuse was that he had to get there very early to set up the musical instruments as he was in charge and had the keys. The fact that Jan needed help would delay him from his duties. Jan accepted all of this but I bit my tongue.

We waved them off. I was most unhappy about the relationship. I knew that this man was up to no good.

The next time Jan rang, she began by asking me to try and understand.

'Understand what?' I almost yelled down the phone.

She said they had been to a solicitor and officially changed her name. She had been christened Janis Lorraine but she said she had always hated the "is" on the end of her name as it always sounded to her as though people were hissing. She had changed it to Lauren Jan. It was a pretty name and it suited her, but it was difficult to come to terms with. In fact John never ever called her by her new name.

Jan said that everything was OK. But she would often say that her man had not turned up or that he was always late, and at times she said she had no food in the flat. When I asked why, she would say that she was waiting for her benefit money to come through. She had always had money and I was worried. It was a very fraught time, to say the least.

Time passed and it was nearing Christmas. Jan had never been away from home for Christmas. She wanted to come home and said that her boyfriend would bring her and drop her off. I asked whether he would like to stay and she said that he couldn't as he always stayed home for Christmas. I said I understood but perhaps he could stay overnight and then drive back. She said he needed to get back quickly.

They arrived and Jan looked OK. Again I was unsure about this man. He was quick to say that he could not stay too long but gave no reason. We made him a cup of tea and offered him a sandwich but before he ate it he suddenly dropped down on one knee in front of Jan and asked her to marry him and produced a ring. As he pushed it onto her finger her face shone. He obviously meant a lot to her. He turned to us and said that she must get the ring insured because it was very expensive. It was all very showy and unreal. It was as though he had rehearsed it down to the last letter. I cannot explain how uncomfortable it made me feel and I was very embarrassed.

He finished his lunch and then kissed Jan on the cheek saying he had to dash, and without hesitation he left.

After seeing him off we returned to the house where Jan sat in a daze placing her fingers over the ring he had given her.

We had a quiet Christmas and Jan did not mention her man too much. I did not want to appear too inquisitive, but I tried to find out a little more about him. I was more concerned when Jan said that she knew that he had had a very hard time and had some problems and had to be very careful. She quickly added that she believed everything he had told her. I knew that if I attempted to ask too many questions she would clam up completely.

Jan had asked me to ring the man at his home on Christmas day. His father answered and said that his son had gone to Jan's flat to repair a piece of furniture. I rang the flat and the phone-line was engaged. I rang throughout the day and it was always engaged. I later rang his home again and was told that he had not returned. I was becoming very concerned. Jan dissolved into quietness and had her hands inside another book.

It was soon time for Jan to go back. Her man came and said he couldn't stop and they were off. There was no mention of the money John had lent him.

The next call from Jan was to say that they could not visit again because he had to get rid of his car. Apparently it had a lot of problems and would cost too much to repair. I just knew deep down inside that this man was telling a lot of lies and was deceiving my daughter.

A friend who belonged to our church had overheard John talk about another member's car saying that he had always liked them and would love to own one. Within days of hearing this she also heard that the man was selling it. She came in to tell John. John told her that no way could he afford it. The next thing we knew was that she had bought it for him. She would not take no for an answer. John was over the moon. He had never been able to afford a very expensive car, in fact most of our cars were quite old and John would do them up. Our old car was still very smart and in good condition.

It was not a difficult decision to make. Andy was too young to drive and so John and I decided it would help Jan and her boyfriend. I rang Jan to ask whether she would like the car.

'A car. Do you mean I am to have a car of my very own? Oh Mum. I never ever thought that would happen. Tell Dad thanks everso, and I love you both very much.'

She was thrilled and within no time at all she and her man were down on the train to collect it. It was lovely to see her being driven off in her own car. Her face shone with pride and happiness. But it was not long before we had a call to say that the car had been sold. He had told Jan it was too dangerous to drive and had put it in the auctions.

John was very angry about the situation and could not understand how this man could convince Jan so easily. Would a father let his daughter have a car knowing that it was unsafe? He spoke to Jan about it. She said that all kinds of things had been found wrong with it. She said that they would buy another with the money they got for it and John accepted her explanation but was very suspicious.

It was a heart-wrenching call that came soon afterwards. Jan said that she had something very serious to tell me. It was to say that her man friend had asked her to choose between him or us and she had chosen him. I was shocked at this news. I felt ill at her words. Why did this man make her choose? Furthermore, why had Jan gone along with him? Something was very wrong. I managed to say that if that was what she wanted then there was nothing I could do about it. It was so difficult to talk over a telephone line and via a machine.

Some weeks passed. Then Jan rang as though nothing had happened, to tell me she was going into hospital for an eye operation. She had congenital cataracts on her eyes, which had got slowly worse. The doctors at Moorfield had refused her the operation several times. Now she had persuaded them, as she was becoming more and more in the dark. They reluctantly agreed. She wanted me to go down to London with her. I admit to a feeling as though I was being used.

She said that her man friend would take her and drop her off, and would I meet her in the lobby of the hospital. I agreed and began to make provision for someone to fill in for me at the café.

I waited in the lobby of the hospital and eventually Jan was brought in by this man. He could not look at me. He quickly kissed Jan on the cheek and was gone. I just knew that he was a bad lot; I felt it in my bones! He could not get away quickly enough.

Jan was excited about the operation. She had it in her mind that her sight would be improved but the doctors tried to explain that it would make little difference and although it was quite a common operation it still had its risks. They even went so far as to say that she could get an infection and then the eye may have to be removed. But she had made up her mind.

It was time for Jan to go to theatre. I asked whether I could go with her, as I was able to interpret with the manual language. We reached the ante-theatre where I was asked to put on cap, gown and overshoes before entering. I talked to Jan as she waited for the injection to put her to sleep.

Gradually her eyes began to close and she had a smile on her face. I was full of anxiety and as she became unconscious a nurse put her arms around me and the tears coursed down my face. She walked back to the anteroom with me and advised me to go and get a coffee.

'She'll be just fine. We'll look after her, don't worry.' Her care and sympathy caused more hot tears to course down my face and sobs caught in my throat.

I went into the foyer of the hospital looking for the hospital shop. I wanted to get something for Jan for when she regained consciousness. There was a stall selling toys. I wandered over and bought a tiny teddy bear to give to her when she woke. As the woman gave me the change she said what a lovely teddy it was and she hoped that the recipient would think so too. My thoughts were that it would be a miracle if, when Jan came back to the ward, she could see it. I almost choked on the lump stuck in my throat as I tried to thank the woman.

I went to the machine and pushed in the coins to extract a hot coffee. Quickly I sipped the drink and went back to the waiting area. I had been told that it was a very short operation and Jan would be back out within the hour. They had decided to do both eyes at the same time. I did not want not to be there when she arrived back. I waited and I waited. It was over two hours before a nurse came to me to say that they had had problems bringing Jan round from the anaesthetic. She tried to reassure me that she was now doing well in recovery and asked me whether I would like to go to her. Of course, I was up and on my feet. I desperately wanted to be with her, my mind going back to another time in the Birmingham hospital when we had had difficulties bringing her round.

Her eyes were bandaged but apart from that she was just fine. She had been talking and had lapsed back into a deep sleep. I sat at her side holding her hand and praying with every breath I had that she might recover some sight at least.

I later learnt from Jan that she had heard them trying to tell her something and had thought they were trying to tell her to go to sleep; in fact they had been trying to wake her up.

We went back to her private room. I had a put-you-up bed by the side of Jan's. Within no time at all she was asking for a Braille magazine to read. She had been told that she had to rest for a couple of days until they took the bandages off, but Jan did lift the bottom of the bandage and was excited because she could see light. I tried to persuade her not to build her hopes up, but really needed to persuade myself.

It was the day the doctors had arrived to take the bandages off. We were taken into a small examination room. Jan was sat at a table with an examination machine. The doctor sat opposite her. The bandages were gradually removed. She was asked to place her chin onto the machine and look straight ahead. Jan did not say a word. The atmosphere was electric and my heart was pounding. I silently begged for her to be able to see. It was apparent that, although the doctor had said there would not be much to gain from having the operation, he was anticipating some good result. Jan blinked as she said how bright everything was. The doctor glanced at the junior doctor. He then asked her whether she could see anything as he held up his hand.

'Just a lot of bright light,' was her answer. The doctor said that the operation had gone very well and that she needed to take care that she didn't bend too much or knock her head for the next couple of weeks.

I was so disappointed. Perhaps I expected too much. Jan had not said anything much. On the way back she wanted to go to the toilet. I pushed her wheelchair into the bathroom and immediately she asked, 'What's that, Mum?'

She pointed to a large mirror on the wall. I was surprised.

'Can you actually see it, Jan?'

'Well I can see something shining and it is very bright.' Her eyes were dashing all over the room.

When we got back to our room and we were lying on our beds she said that she could see fingers if she held her hand to her face. I could not believe that this operation would be so important. Even a tiny bit of improvement was worth having it done. Then, the next day when Jan was in the bath, she said that she could see her hand beneath the water. As the days went by she commented that she could see the shadows of people as they came into her room. This was a big improvement and Jan was absolutely thrilled.

I happened to mention to a nurse that Jan played piano. She told me that at the end of the hall was a conference room and there was a grand piano in there and Jan could use that if she was inclined to. Jan was thrilled when I told her, and we were quickly on our way. We met the surgeon who had operated on Jan as we walked along. We asked him if it was OK for us to go into the room and he was overjoyed for Jan to be able to occupy her time happily.

She was in her element playing so many tunes from her vast repertoire. I was sitting at the side of the room lost in my thoughts when the large door opened and in came a young woman carrying a small child of about two years of age. He had headphones and he was obviously quite disabled, as one of his eyes was quite low down on his cheek. It was another rare genetic syndrome and his mother tried to explain. He had very limited sight and hearing and also had learning difficulties. I persuaded her to sit the little boy on the piano as Jan played. I interrupted Jan to let her know that the little child was sitting there and gave her a brief description of his problems. A smile crossed her face as she started to play "Nellie the Elephant". It was such a joy to watch as the little boy bent and placed his hand on top of the piano, his face lit up by a huge smile. Janis continued with little children's tunes and he obviously knew some of them. It was a really precious moment and a fellowship of suffering, as my eyes met the young woman's and tears melted down our cheeks.

We had many visitors during our visits to hospitals in London. Most of these were from the organisation SENSE. On one such occasion, Mary, a campaigner for people with Usher Syndrome, invited me out for a meal while Jan went off with a young man called Graham Hicks, who was also deafblind. Later Mary and I returned to collect Jan to return to the hospital. She had had quite a lot to drink.

It was about 10.30 p.m. as we entered the dimly-lit ward. The patients had all been pleased that she had been able to go out and some of them were still awake as we tiptoed into the ward. I kept pressing my fingers against Jan's lips and saying shhhh. She thought this extremely funny and was in fits of giggles. As I went to lift my arm up again to say shhhhhh she would beat me to it and say shhhh! Followed by loud laughter. My attempts at silencing her were futile. Now most of the ward was awake. It was a very good night out.

Eventually we returned to Peterborough. We had to arrange for a car to come and pick us up as Jan's man friend said that he could not collect her. He dropped in to see Jan after work but didn't stay long; he had an excuse to leave and promised to call another day and to take us both out for a ride. They had another car so that had calmed our suspicions a little.

The days passed and he didn't come. The weekend came and it was obvious that Jan was getting more and more depressed.

Jan's home help came once a week, but the boyfriend had said that nobody else was allowed to call. Not even her friends. He had attempted to alienate her from all contacts with family and friends in a clever psychological manipulatory way. His excuse was that he didn't want anyone taking advantage of her. My worries were now becoming quite serious, especially when Jan said that she had been obliged to pay for some goods he had had out of her catalogue, worth several hundred pounds.

The home help arrived and I was introduced to a very pleasant young woman. She began to get on with her work but when Jan disappeared into the bathroom she asked whether she could speak with me. She said she had some concerns and thought I ought to know what was happening, and then went on to tell me that Jan was signing open cheques every week for this man. She told me that Jan was always short of money and had been going without food on occasions. I recalled the phone calls I had received when she had said she had no food in the house. Had she been trying to tell me something then?

Two days later he showed up and asked if we would like to go for a ride. He was looking very agitated. Jan was relieved and pleased that he had arrived. We walked down the drive. He was guiding Jan and I walked behind them. We stopped at an old ramshackle rusty car. When he opened the door to let us in I was gobsmacked. He had sold our lovely car and bought this? I did not say a word but squeezed into the back seat. The drive was frightening. The car was such a wreck that it banged and bumped along. I was glad when we got back home. He did not come inside with us but stood by the car and pecked Jan on her cheek, and was off like a shot looking all around him as he went.

I could hold my tongue no more and decided that I had to have this out once and for all. It did not take much coaxing and what I heard took my breath away. He had been taking regular sums of money from her because he did not have a job. He told her that his benefit did not leave him with enough to pay his mum his full board money and that his mother was ill and he could not worry her. I asked about the car. He had bought this from a garage on hire purchase and he had got Jan to sign the agreement. But I really was not prepared for what Jan was about to tell me. He had just come out of prison after serving a sentence for sexually molesting his teenage daughter.

Jan was now sobbing and came to me for a cuddle. I wrapped my arms around her small frame and we cried together. It emerged that this man had convinced Jan that it was an accident that he had accidentally brushed his daughter's breast whilst squeezing past her in the kitchen and she had told her mum. He was arrested at school the next day. He was a lab technician or so he had said. Could we believe anything?

Then more awful stuff began to come out. Jan was sobbing as she told me that he had abused her in many ways. That he had been dressing up in her clothes. The fact that she could not see or hear what he was getting up to was even more abusive in my mind. I felt physically sick. He had said that she must keep everything secret otherwise it would kill his mother. I wanted to scream as loud as I possibly could. How I managed to contain the raging emotions inside I will never know. Janis was in a terrible state. At least it was now out in the open and we could begin to build up from all of this.

I rang John. I had to let him know, and discuss what we should do about the situation. How terrible was it for John to be stuck so far away. He screamed down the phone 'I'll kill the bastard......I will. Look love I can't do a thing until the weekend and then I'll come down and bring you both home.'

We had a few days before John came for us. Jan asked me to ring a married couple who were friends of hers. I had met them once before. They were a kind of surrogate family for Jan and had been raising money to buy her the Optican machine she so badly wanted. The husband had been sky diving among other things to raise money. They were a lovely couple.

I tried to explain a little of what had happened over the phone and was surprised that they knew Jan's man friend of old but had made allowances for him. They also knew about his prison sentence. It had been in the local paper. They suggested that we went to them for a meal and the husband would fetch us.

Over the meal, I was to learn more of this man and his lies. The wife began to tell me that a short while ago he had gone to them and said that he was desperate to get his car repaired so that he could bring Janis down to Devon to see us. When I told them they had not been to us, they flicked glances one to the other. I asked Jan about the car repairs. She knew nothing of it, nor that he had been to them to ask for money. They said he had seemed so genuine and they were concerned for Jan to come to see us. He had asked if he could borrow some money out of the fund money and he would pay it back within a week. They loaned him £350. I saw in their expressions that it was bad news. They were very shocked and felt betrayed by this man. It was very upsetting for all of us. We stayed with them for some tea and then the husband drove us back to Jan's flat.

Then I discovered that this man had been taking quite large amounts from Jan's bank account. I asked to see her cheque books and it amounted to about £2000. There was also the matter of the several hundreds he had got for our car, plus the debts he had incurred in Jan's name.

John rang a solicitor and made an appointment to see him for advice about getting the money back. The solicitor was shocked at what John had to tell him and suggested that John drew up a letter setting out the amount that he was to pay back to Jan. The solicitor then added to the sum quite a large amount of interest. He asked John whether the man was working. He was. He had applied for a job with a national charity and had used Jan on his CV as experience. He got the job and it was quite well paid.

The solicitor stated in the letter that he was to pay the money back at so much each month. There was the proviso that if he missed a payment court action would be taken. John was to get the man to sign the letter and bank mandate and John was to return it to the solicitor. John then rang to say that he was coming up to Peterborough and would I arrange for him to meet this guy in town. A letter was sent to him but we wondered whether he would turn up. John had asked that he meet him at a café in the Queensgate shopping centre.

The day was arranged. Jan, John and I went into town. Jan had asked for her engagement ring to be valued while we were there. We were early, so John went into a large jewellers shop. He had asked me to wait on a seat outside with Jan and he went in by himself. When he returned his face was tense. Very gently he told Jan the result. The ring that this guy had said was so expensive and had to be insured was worth no more than a few pounds. Jan put her hands to her face. 'Oh no, Mum!'

John continued on his way to meet with the man. Jan and I waited. I gave her a hug and she held my hand. John was not gone for long. When he returned he looked furious. I thought the guy had not turned up.

'He turned up OK. He even greeted me with his hand outstretched. As if I would shake hands with him? I showed him the letter and all he said was, 'That's fine.' He even had the nerve to ask for a paint roller and half pot of paint that he had left at Jan's. I told him he could collect it from the porch. It took all of my will power to stop myself from hitting the bloke.'

I had to relay to Jan what had happened. It was necessary for her to comprehend the horror of what the bloke had done. It was heartbreaking to see her face sadden, her shoulders slump right down, as she struggled to accept the truth. He was a rogue and he had conned and abused her in the most awful way. Later, he even had the bare face to collect the paint and roller.

Every penny of the money was paid back and the debts to the catalogue company were taken over by them.

A while after this I was driving through Peterborough in a district where I knew that this man lived. I was in a stream of traffic when I saw a car trying to exit a road on my left. I signalled for the driver to come out. Only then did I realise who the driver of the car was as he held up his hand to acknowledge me. When I saw that it was the man who had abused Jan, the anger I felt was so alien to me. It surged into every part of my body burning through me. I was blinded by rage and tears coursed my face. I drove some five miles home and to this day I cannot recall how I did it.

After John had sorted this awful guy out we decided no more time should be wasted. Jan was ill and needed to come home so that we could look after her. Very quickly we packed her things and piled into the car.

We were all completely shattered when we arrived in Devon after almost a seven-hour journey, and Jan did not hesitate when I suggested she have a warm bath and get into bed and that I would bring her something to eat and a nice warm drink. I seemed to have gone into automatic mode. It was maybe that I needed to shut out the raging anger that had been swirling round inside of me. When Jan was settled I came down and John and I sat having a drink. John kept saying, 'I'll kill him, I'm sure I will. How I kept my hands off him I shall never know. It's a good job we met in a public place otherwise who knows what I may have done.'

I was scared. I had never seen John like this, ever. Fortunately Andy was out with his mates. How we had managed to keep the business going during all that had happened is beyond me.

* * * * *

After six months, Jan had recovered her health and had lots of time to think through many issues. She wanted to go back to Peterborough. We were very worried for her and did our best to persuade her to stay in Sidmouth. We told her we would try and get her a flat, but she was most insistent that she wanted to return.

You can imagine the dread that was in our hearts as we drove up to Peterborough with Jan and all of her belongings. She seemed quite undaunted at the prospect of starting afresh there. But I had to admire her immense courage and determination to pick up her life again and go forward. What lay ahead was anybody's guess.

However, things began going quite badly for us in Sidmouth. We were struggling as far as the business went. The recession of the late 1980's was hitting us badly and customers were very thin on the ground. We were sliding more and more into the red. Any profit was little and went to pay off the overdraft. We decided that we would have to sell the business.

I do admit to being rather relieved. It had been such a struggle with me travelling up and down the country and being unable to just pop round to make sure that Jan was OK. Andrew now had a job at the Methodist Holiday Home and was living in, so he decided to stay in Sidmouth. John and I decided to move to Peterborough. My health was not at all good and while this was happening I was admitted to hospital for a hysterectomy. It confirmed that we could not keep the business up and running. I was so tired. John was now of retirement age and so we decided that we would have to try and live on our pensions.

Jan was still living at The League and I stayed with her whilst looking for a house for ourselves. I looked at a place to rent for the interim period. I viewed a lovely little house but it was too small, however when I told Jan about it she said that she would love to move out of The League and live completely independently. And so it was that before we had a place of our own we were helping Jan to set up in hers.

Quickly following on from that we were moving into our own new home. It felt very much as though we had gone full circle. Not long after this Andy rang to ask whether he could come back home to live. He quickly got a job and loved Peterborough.

John and I took up voluntary work. John was driving for the ambulance car service and I worked for the Social Services. It started out as a part time job but quickly turned into a full time one. We did about 1500 miles a week between us. However we loved the work and it gave us a great job satisfaction. I love children, and my work was mostly with very young children and it fulfilled me. We all seemed to have found our niche.

However, Jan was having great difficulty walking again. I had seen on TV a pioneering operation for youngsters with cerebral palsy, which enabled them to walk better. It showed a boy who had been in a wheelchair now walking. I wondered whether this doctor could do anything for Jan. I talked it over with her. We agreed that we had nothing to lose. I wrote to the surgeon. He asked for us to take Jan to see him. I was aware just how much hope Jan had pinned on seeing this doctor. I tried to calm her and said that she must not build up her hopes. She had joked that she might be able to be a ballet dancer.

We arrived at The Orthopaedic Hospital in Oswestry. There were quite a lot of babies and young children waiting to see the doctor. It was a long wait to see him, but when he came to us I immediately saw what a lovely man he was. He took us into his examination room and after interviewing Jan asked her to get up onto his examination couch. Jan was laughing and joking but soon her mood was to change dramatically. He helped Jan to sit up and he perched himself beside her. He asked me to explain to her, for him, that there was nothing he could do except offer her cosmetic supports for her lower limbs. Tears shot from Jan's eyes.

The doctor put his arm around her shoulder and sat waiting until she had quietened down a little. Then he asked her why she did not want the splints. She explained that her blindness and then her deafness had brought increasing social isolation, her wheelchair even more, and now he was suggesting that she wear cosmetic splints? He did not disagree; in fact he said he understood fully. But he continued to explain that because her balance was now so poor it was dangerous for her to walk unless she had these supports. He said that she should never entertain going up stairs or walking across a road on her own. He then said that he had to go and see another patient and asked her to sit quietly.

'If you want to talk with me again or ask me any questions I will be just a room away.' He patted her on the shoulder and she continued to cry.

I took over his seat and tried to comfort her. What could I do? Always it was the same result. After a little while she lifted her head and asked to see the doctor again. When he came back she said that she would give the splints a go. He was very pleased and gave her shoulders another hug and said goodbye.

As a result of wearing her splints Jan was able to walk much better. So much better she was later able to walk over twenty miles to raise money towards research into Retinitis Pigmentosa. I never ever thought that she would accomplish such a feat.

Jan came from the walk to our home. She was vibrant, in fact glowing from her efforts. Unfortunately she had had to concede defeat just two miles before the end of the sponsored walk. She fell into my arms and I took her to the settee. Taking off her shoes and leg supports I discovered that she had several blisters, although Jan could not feel these. I took her upstairs and she had a warm bath and then I persuaded her to lie in my bed. But it was very short lived. She wanted to come downstairs and tell us about the fun she had had on her walk. Apparently cars had hooted their horns; some stopped and threw money into buckets. The group called at a pub for lunch and again money poured in. She and the group of friends raised several hundreds of pounds.

Jan was still studying at home but badly wanted to gain her 'O' level human biology. So, undeterred as ever, she got her guide-help to ring the local CFE and ask whether she could see the head. Arrangements were made. Jan went into town to buy a new coat for the occasion. She had always wanted a leather jacket and this was the chance for her to show off! She wanted to impress the head of the college in every way, she told me.

The day of the interview was a hot summer's day. Jan had on her new leather coat. She said the smell and feel of it was lovely and she felt a million dollars, but as the interview was in progress she became hotter and hotter. She interrupted the head by asking whether he would mind if she removed her jacket. She told this story with great guffaws of laughter as she told of the confidence she tried to exude, but in fact she was trembling with nerves and at the same time sweating like a pig. Nonetheless, the head was very impressed by her enthusiasm as she told him how much she wanted to study human biology, which had proved futile at her previous schools.

The head said that he was very keen for her to join the college but as they had never had a deafblind student there he would have to ask whether there was a member of staff who would be prepared to teach her. Jan had explained about her Versa-Brailler and that it could be connected to an electric typewriter enabling anybody to type in information and she would be able to read it in Braille and vice versa.

The next day she received a call to say that her case had been put to the staff during the staff break. There was one teacher, called Beryl, who had volunteered to try and teach Jan. The woman had no experience of either deafness or blindness let alone the two together.

They worked well as a team. Brenda was another teacher inspired by the fact that Janis was so keen to learn, absorbed information in a flash, and produced excellent homework. Janis sat her 'O' level biology at her home. When it came to doing scientific tests she used the help of her teacher to place certain items in the vessels and pour on the necessary liquids and tell her what happened to them, or what colour they had become, and other visual tasks. Annoyingly, the exam people omitted to send out Braille diagrams and so Jan had to cope as best she could to answer questions about certain diagrams without the diagram. Her teacher was very annoyed. But they decided to do whatever they could. Jan did pass but I think it was at grade C and she was not a happy bunny.

Jan always came home for her Sunday lunch. She had also taken to coming home every Wednesday after college, when she would rest and then have a meal before going home. She was happy with this for a little while but as she got stronger in health she decided that she would go straight to her flat.

John and I were very tired and needed a holiday. We booked a caravan through a friend and asked whether Jan and Andy would like to come too. Andy had to work but said that he would like to come for a long weekend. Jan wanted to come for the week.

Just prior to going on holiday, Jan had persuaded her guide-help to take her along to a meeting of the IVC (Inter Varsity Club). She had discovered them on her computer and found out that there was a local group. Pam took her along to the meeting, which was held in an up-market hotel. Jan and Pam sat together all night within the group without anyone making direct contact. Pam told Jan that she did not think she would fit in with the crowd as they were, in Pam's opinion a lot of OK Yah folk. Jan was annoyed, and insisted that she would go again.

The next time, Jan was determined to get one or two people to speak with her. She introduced herself to whoever was sitting beside her and asked whether they would like to talk to her on her hands. She explained that a tap on the hand was yes and a hand across hers, as though wiping it clean, was a no, and she demonstrated. Before long she had made an impression. Not one person refused her. On one occasion a young man was sitting beside her. She asked him the same question. He took up the challenge and she taught him the manual alphabet. Then she asked him to tell her his name and after that they were chatting as if they were old friends.

It was the annual beer festival on the embankment in Peterborough. Jan had been invited to go along with the IVC and she was thrilled. She was introduced to real ales and loved them. Thereafter she would drink it by the pint.

Whilst sitting on the grass in the big marquee Nick, the man she had met before, came to sit by her and chatted. She had taken her Polaroid camera with her and asked him if she could take his picture. This was something else she refused to be denied – photography. She would ask the person to clap loudly and she would follow the direction of the sound and shoot for a picture hoping for a good result.

The following Sunday she showed me the picture she had taken of Nick and asked me to describe him. I said that he was bald, wore heavy glasses, was short, fat and quite ugly really.

She looked so shocked as she gasped 'Oh no, Mum. Really?'

She felt my body shaking with laughter and she joined in. She then asked me to tell her what he was really like. When I told her that he had a very handsome open face and nice smile she snuggled down contentedly. I added, 'But he is grey haired.' She was not a bit bothered about anything now. I glimpsed the first sign of romance.

It was time for our caravan break. As soon as we arrived Jan asked whether there was a telephone kiosk on the site. (This was before we had mobile phones). I said that there was and she asked whether I would mind taking her to ring Nick. Of course I didn't. But if we went once we went about twenty times and every time the phone was engaged with a corresponding look of dejection from Jan. My heart ached so much for her and I hoped with all of it that this was to be a true romance.

The night before Andy was to go back home, Jan very tentatively asked, 'Mum, I've got something to ask you. Would you mind if I went back with Andy?' I had a good idea why.

When John and I arrived back home and met up with Jan again she was full of excitement. As soon as she got home she had tried to ring Nick but his phone was still engaged. Not one to be deterred she persuaded her guide-help to take her to his house and push a note through his door. It transpired that Nick's phone was off the hook without him realising. He rang Jan as soon as he got her note and she invited him to go to her flat to listen to her play her piano. The date was fixed.

The next time I met Jan she was vibrantly beautiful. I had not seen her look so happy for many years. She had fallen in love and Nick had fallen in love with her.

Jan was quick to bring Nick to our home for Sunday lunch and in front of him enquired as to our opinion. I responded by saying how nice he was, very nice. He seemed so caring and wanting to do whatever he could for her. She laughed, saying, 'Hands off he's mine.'

It was not too long before she moved in with Nick. His house was quite small but in no time at all they were looking for something much bigger. Jan had said that she would like to help to pay the mortgage. Again she was wanting to be able to do what most of us take for granted.

They moved to a bigger, four-bedroomed detached house with en suite bathroom, in a very nice district near to Nick's place of work. It was lovely. Jan loved the fact that it had a walled garden. Another attractive feature for her was that there were no downstairs doors on any room, but only archways. Doors are a hazard to a blind person, especially when left ajar, as the person often puts their hands out in front to feel whether the door is open. If it is halfway open, then a hand could go either side and to walk ahead would cause a nasty bump.

All seemed to be going well. Jan had continued at college and had taken 'A' level Governments & Politics. Whilst on this course she was taken to the Houses of Parliament and shown round by the MP David Blunkett. He was very taken with her attitude. Before she left he gave her some headed paper and envelopes. How Jan enjoyed writing to all her friends and family on this parliamentary notepaper. She rolled with laughter when one, then another, said they were surprised when they received a letter with the parliamentary symbol stamped on the back of the envelope. The letters were all hand written in the type of writing a child of six would use. This was the age at which Jan had stopped seeing, and so her handwriting remained that of a child.

Jan completed the course in just twelve months and passed at grade 'A'.

CHAPTER 26

My life was now completely changed. Jan did not ring so often and her demands on me were becoming less and less. I was thrilled because it was obvious that she had met a good man and that they thought the world of one another. It was good to be in their presence, as their love was tangible.

The very first thing that Nick bought Jan was a pair of shoes. This might seem quite an unromantic thing to most people but Jan had for some time had to wear shoes two sizes bigger and often in a man's fashion because of the bulky splints that she wore under her socks. She must have confided in Nick that it bothered her. He booked an appointment with a specialist shoemaker in Cambridge and took Jan to have shoes made to her choice. She was thrilled.

Their outings were many and often, and so were their holidays. She would often ring to say that they would like to take us out for a meal. Jan would put on dinner parties, preparing the food during the day while Nick was at the office, and he would attend to the finishing touches when he came home. She was a very good cook and made all sorts of cakes and lovely scones.

Life took on a new meaning for me. At last I could lay down the heavy load of years and take up a life of my own. I was coming up to sixty and the new freedom was quite alien to me.

I decided to look into counselling. First of all I did a six-week course and then after enjoying it very much went onto a 12 month experiential one. This was tough. I learnt such a lot but I also had a great deal to give. I would have loved to continue but the cost of several years of training to become a professional counsellor was steep. Not only the cost, but also I would be getting towards seventy by the time I was fully qualified. I felt that by the time I had passed all my exams I would be too old.

However, something else came along. 3D Decoupage was becoming all the rage. I went up to Sheffield to learn the craft. It stole a part of my heart. I began doing many pictures and then had an exhibition in the public library. It evoked a great deal of interest. I wanted to teach. I applied for a business grant. I had to go on a course and be assessed at the end of it. There were grants from a hundred or so pounds to a thousand, and I was granted the top amount. This, together with some money from an insurance policy, set me up in my own little business. I had a lock-up shop with a room at the rear in which to teach up to ten people at a time. It took off very well and I was in heaven. Then a lady called into the shop. She was the wife of the head of a college in town and wanted to know whether I would teach there. After taking that on, I was asked to teach at night school at another college. It was a hectic but wonderful time for me.

Things with Nick and Jan seemed to going along fine. We would see them most weeks. One Sunday they came unexpectedly in the late afternoon. Jan burst into the lounge, loudly saying, 'Meet your son-in-law!' She was shaking as she held out her hand. I thought it was for me to see a new ring.

'Mum, I'm married!' She was still shaking.

I think Nick recognized the look of shock and said that they had gone to the registry office on Friday and had two witnesses. Then they had gone to Sherringham for their honeymoon.

Now I was shaking. All manner of emotions were racing through me. John looked ashen. He could not speak. I remember trying to appear pleased for them and said to John, 'I think this calls for a toast.'

Still John said nothing as he brought out some wine.

I managed to ask why the rush, and Nick explained that they had recently given a dinner party and a solicitor friend had turned up and announced that she was married. She had just gone off and done it without a word to anyone, including her parents. Jan had already asked Nick to marry her, and on that night he said that if she was prepared to do it like that then he would marry her. We just had to come to terms with the marriage the way it was. But to deny us this after the years of trauma and pain was almost too much.

Nervously joking and for want of something to say I said that it did save a lot of money and Nick agreed.

Nick asked whether we would join his mum, dad and brother for a meal on the following Tuesday at his home. We accepted, but when they left John and I were in tears. John so badly wanted to walk his daughter down the aisle. It had been his dream from the moment she was born. I was worried because he looked so ill. He was on medication for his angina and tests had shown that he badly needed a heart by-pass operation.

A year or so later, on a Sunday lunchtime visit, Jan brought us the news that she was expecting a baby. We were overjoyed as well as being apprehensive. But they both assured us that they had thought it through and looked into everything and they were confident that they would cope. They were so happy.

It became increasingly obvious that Jan wanted a space between us. After twenty-eight years of needing my help she was now able to be more independent of me. Any offer of help or suggestion of things that we might buy for the baby was refused. I was hurt. To be disallowed another joyful occasion was almost too much to bear. I tried to get my head round things and realised that for the very first time Jan had entered into something that no one else could do for her and she was totally in control.

However, it was all very confusing and I have to say heart-wrenching at times. Her behaviour caused me to be very concerned about her. She became quite argumentative and mistrusting of me and others. Then strong arguments erupted between us. I well remember us all going to a friend's induction ceremony at a church in Hinckley where we once lived. Jan did not stay for the ceremony but walked out and went to a pub with Nick, returning for tea and even then became quite aggressive. On the journey home a huge row broke out and I was reduced to tears. I could not understand why Jan had changed so much in such a short time. Was this the beginning of worse things to come?

I was enjoying my business. It had really taken off. I enjoyed the decoupage so much that it did not seem like work but pleasure. We were very busy. John bought in framing equipment and the framing side was a great success, so much so that Andy was able to come into the business full time. Andy was an ace at the framing side and also helped me on the craft side too. He too, thoroughly enjoyed the work. Everything in the garden was lovely. Jan's pregnancy was going without any problems and the time was approaching for the birth.

The baby arrived on New Year's Eve, 1995. She weighed in at 8 lb 12 oz. Jan had wanted a natural birth and refused all painkillers until the very end. She did everything very well and needed no stitches at all. We could not wait to see our first grandchild.

Holly was lovely. I could not take it all in. Everything had happened so quickly and our dream of Jan marrying and having a child had been fulfilled. Jan and Nick were very proud. Jan was such a natural mother and Nick an excellent father. From the very beginning of the pregnancy I was aware that Jan wanted no help from me at all and no more than was absolutely essential from anyone else. She did not voice it, but I knew that this was one thing that she had to do herself and she wanted to be as independent as she possibly could for the first time ever. She rejected all the offers of help from social services.

I was becoming more and more concerned that Jan was cutting her family out of her life, or so it seemed. John was beside himself with worry over the situation, and I tried to help him to accept what was gong on. I loved her unconditionally.

* * * * *

'Love, I am in a lot of pain.' I clicked on the bedroom light and looked at John. He was propped up on his pillows and he was clutching at his chest. I did not hesitate but grabbed the phone and rang for the doctor. Then I jumped into the clothes I had laid at the side of the bed the night before. I panicked and rang my neighbour, David, who came straight round. Surprisingly, within ten minutes a doctor and an ambulance turned up. As John was taken away David followed behind with Andy and me in his car.

John was taken into the intensive care ward and immediately tests were started. The result was given to him the next day. He had had a near escape. His heart was still OK but he had had a very bad angina attack. The consulting doctor asked whether he had any stress. John told him that we had a business to run and the doctor immediately said that it had to stop. I did not even need telling twice, nor did I question how we could keep going. The next day the shop was closed with a notice that at the weekend there would be a closing down sale. Andy set about ringing all of my students. The shop was swarming with customers on the day of the sale. All of my lovely stock was going for a pittance, we sold all of the framing timbers and framing equipment for a fraction of the cost, the fixtures and fittings all went for a song. My ambition and attempts to do my own thing were short lived. I was pretty miserable about the whole affair.

John was not a man to rest or sit around doing nothing. He had always been so very active. So he pottered around the house until the angina attacks became too frequent and he was rushed into hospital twice more before his operation took place.

There still seemed to be a distance between Jan and us. But she regularly came to see us and brought Holly, the Sunday lunches with us were resumed and we all had some delightful times together.

When Jan rang me to ask whether I could take her out I was over the moon. She wanted to go to a garden centre to look at plants and trees. Andy had a day off from work and so Jan, John, Andy, Holly and I set off for the centre. It was lovely to sit alongside Holly in her high seat with Jan at her other side. She was around ten months at the time. We had a delightful morning, having lunch and then taking Holly to her nursery and Jan back home.

A couple of days later Jan came on the phone complaining that I had bought a tree that she did not ask for. I thought it was a case of crossed communication. She asked whether her dad could go over and put the tree in the garden. John was not able to, and so there was a rumpus yet again.

She was asserting herself in ways which were alien to all of us and which caused a lot of pain to her nearest and dearest. She had been a favourite of my sister Peg who was Jan's godmother. They corresponded regularly for years. But quite out of the blue Peg received a very abrupt letter saying all sorts of unkind things about her. She was distraught. I tried to comfort her by saying that Jan was trying to distance herself and become more independent. But I could not persuade her. Neither could I persuade myself. It was a very different Jan to the one we had known for over thirty years.

It was obvious that as Holly became a little more independent Jan wanted to be more involved in her studies again. But it was more than that which was causing me to be disturbed. She began having weekends away with friends, without Nick and Holly. She was heavily involved with the Socialist Workers Party and she seemed to have picked up a lot of information to do with her rights.

She had also taken to smoking cannabis for relief from the awful pain of her neuritis. She had mentioned her intentions to a GP and he had said it was a harmless substance and he had used it at university. It was harrowing to see the change in Jan. She seemed to be very gullible and was easily persuaded by this new crowd that she mixed with.

Then one day she rang to ask whether she could come on the following Sunday for lunch. Of course she could come. She said she would be coming on her own. I asked where Nick would be and she said he was going to his mother's for lunch. Something was very wrong.

She arrived by taxi. After we had finished lunch she said she had something to tell us. She blurted out that she had decided to leave Nick. We were absolutely flabbergasted and very angry as she did her best to discredit him. We would not hear a bad word about him. She said that we did not understand and that Nick had taken over where I had left off and tried to wrap her in cotton wool. She needed to do her own thing and was setting up on her own in a bungalow. This was the biggest blow ever. There was a terrible row and Jan became very abusive and called me some horrid names.

Andy drove her home. John and I just sat and tried to gather our thoughts. Was all of this the result of the stuff that she was smoking and her new friends' influences? What had got into her to change her from a fun-loving, caring girl, a girl who expressed her love for us in so many special ways, to become so estranged from us? Was it that the years of trauma and suffering she had been through and pushed down inside her had finally exploded? I did not know and nor could I talk to anyone, because it would have to be a mother of a child with all of Jan's many problems. Where or how could I find one? It was impossible.

Along the years, many people had said what an incredible girl Jan was but never did they know or acknowledge the amount of hard work and effort her parents had put in to bring out the best in her. If we chastised Jan in front of anyone it was always looked on as something we should not do because of her deafblindness. She could not have it both ways. She had always wanted to be treated as anyone else and she had to accept that some types of behaviour were not acceptable.

We did not hear anything from Jan for months. Nick brought Holly to see us after the separation and was able to tell us how Jan was getting on and what was happening. He said that she appeared depressed at times. Access for Holly and her mummy had been arranged. Holly remained with her daddy at night and at weekends. Jan made many friends in the SWP and often went away to stay with one or the other.

Nick looked quite ill and I was concerned that it was all going to be too much for him. He was continuing his work as a senior computer analyst with a large building society, looking after Holly, taking her to be with Jan for access during the week, which meant a long trek across town before he started work and then again at lunchtime. He would then take Holly to nursery and go back to work. He was looking after Holly at weekends, doing the weekly shopping, washing, ironing and all the household tasks, and he also made sure that Jan had all she needed. I thought that it was all too much for one person to carry on their shoulders.

During this period John was getting much worse and the effects of the upset with Jan was bearing down on both of us.

Christmas came around and it was agreed that Andy would try and build bridges and arrange a meal for all of the family. Janis, at first, refused but then decided she would come. Sadly John was too ill to join us as he had contracted bronchitis. The evening was rather strained but Jan gave us a Christmas present. She wanted me to open it there and then but I said I would wait until Christmas day and open it with her dad. It was a lovely gift. She had taken six of the best photographs of Holly, since her birth through the first twelve months, and had them blown up and put onto tablemats. We caught a glimpse of the caring thoughtful girl we had known. But it was only a glimpse.

After Christmas, John was very ill. We still heard nothing from Jan and could only assume that she was getting on well and did not wish to come to us. She was back at college doing a foundation course in the hope of going to university to read English Literature.

John went into Papworth for his by-pass operation. He was down for a triple by-pass but ended up having a quintuple. The surgeon told him he was very lucky to have survived as long as he had. He seemed to recover well and was out of hospital on the sixth day. Jan did not appear. Nick told us that she had asked him whether she should go to see her dad. He replied that she did not take his advice usually and he was not prepared to give it now, and that she had to make up her own mind. This was so unlike Jan. She loved her dad and was always considered to be a daddy's girl. What had caused her to become this type of person I had no idea. I had enough to cope with in nursing John and could not dwell too much on this.

Just after John came home from hospital I received a phone call from Nick asking me whether I could go to see Jan, as she was very depressed. I asked him whether she wanted me to go and he said that she did. It was Sunday so I said I would go after lunch. I cooked our meal and made sure that John was OK. I plated and covered a meal for Jan and headed for her place.

When I arrived I was shocked to the very core. I had never ever seen Jan in such a terrible condition. Her eyes were very red and sore from crying, and she was agitated. I put the plate of food on the table and rushed to hug her. She crumbled into my arms and sobbed. Never, but never, had Jan ever shed tears of this intensity. Suddenly she would stop crying and sit up and start to giggle, and following on from this she began shouting at someone as though another person was there.

'Stop it, stop it you are hurting me' she screamed. And then she began giggling again and then crying. I looked at the social helper who had been placed in the home for round the clock care by social services, and asked her how long this had been going on. She replied that she had been like it for about two weeks.

I took Jan into my arms again. She had not slept for nights, apparently. Then she started all over again the same thing over and over. I took her shoulders in mid sentence and shook her telling her to stop but she carried on. She then turned to the window saying, 'Who said that I was going blind? I can hear, you know!'

I was trembling. This was most out of character and worse than I ever imagined when Nick said she was unwell. She jumped up and said that she needed a fag. She stubbed it out halfway through and went to the bathroom. She came back to the settee and the ritual started all over again. I rang her GP who had already been out to see her several times. A duty doctor turned up and diagnosed depression and prescribed tablets. The helper told me that Jan had been taken to outpatients on three occasions and seen by a psychiatrist, who had found nothing wrong with her psychologically and sent her back home.

It took me twenty minutes to get the prescription filled. As soon as I got back to Jan's place she took a tablet. The crying, screaming at someone, then the giggling went on and on. Then she jumped up and said, 'I need food, that's what the problem is, I need food.'

The helper took my plate of food to the microwave, saying as she did so that Jan had already had a large meal just before I arrived. Jan began to tuck into the meal. She managed a couple of mouthfuls and pushed the plate away and returned to the settee. I guess I was there for about four hours and the ritual of giggling, crying and screaming at someone to stop hurting her continued. Suddenly Jan turned to me and said, 'If you don't come with us you will be left alone, so get out, just go, get out of my house now.' She was screaming into my face.

I had no control, I was so very tired and the tears cascaded down my cheeks. What was I to do? I picked up my bag and made for the door. The helper asked whether I was OK. I could not speak as sobs wracked my body.

I reversed the car into a brick wall and badly dented the bumper. I could not see nor concentrate. I managed to get away from the bungalow and park a little way down the road where I sat and cried and cried until my tears were spent. Then I tried to gather my thoughts. I must not let John see me like this, nor could I tell him what had happened. It would be too much for him and so I had to conceal it as best I could. We had never ever kept anything from one another and yet just when I needed my man the most I was unable to talk to him. I waited until my eyes had become less red. I knew that I could go straight into the bathroom and splash cold water on my face before going through to John.

Of course John wanted to know what was happening. I told him that Jan was very depressed and that I had called in the doctor and that she had some tablets to take. I rang Nick when John could not hear me and told him what had happened and that she had bawled me out. I told him that I must get on with looking after John and leave things in the hands of the social services. My heart was almost broken.

About a week later John said he did not feel well enough to get out of bed. I knew that I had to encourage him because for him to sit for too long was not good for him after his operation. He did manage to get from the bedroom to the chair in the lounge. As soon as I saw the result of this minor effort I summoned our GP, who came in immediately and said that John had to go back into hospital. It turned out that John was very anaemic and needed to have two pints of blood. It amazed me that as soon as a little of the blood went into his veins it was as though his lifeblood had returned; he improved minute by minute. He was back home in a few days and more able to begin getting around. He was not able to drive but had to go for little walks and gradually build up each day. I drove him to local beauty spots and we walked together hand in hand. He did not know just how heavy was my heart.

This went on for a couple of weeks and down he went again. Again he had to go back to hospital. This time they put him on some tablets to increase the quality of his blood and thereafter he made a rapid recovery.

Meanwhile Nick had rung to say that Jan was in hospital. She had been found wandering the streets at night only partially clothed, and someone had called the police. When Nick phoned me I was almost out of my mind with worry. I told him that John was not to be told too much as he was still quite ill and that I would only go to the hospital when I was sure that it was what she wanted. Andrew went to see her and said that she was OK but very sleepy as the hospital had been sedating her because of her now violent outbursts.

Then I had a phone call from Jill, Jan's social worker, to say that the hospital could not cope and that she was taking her to a specialist clinic for the deaf. She asked whether I wanted to visit Jan before she went. I told her that I was nursing John, exhausted, and that I felt that it was best for Jan to be settled and for her to decide whether she wanted me to visit her. She said the clinic was over a hundred miles away. I said if she needed us we would be there as soon as John was well enough.

Later, Jill rang us to say that Jan had travelled quite happily without any trouble at all and that she was her usual chatty self. Thank goodness, I thought as Jill went on to assure me that she was in an excellent place. The next call from her was to ask whether we could go to visit. Jan had said that she would like to see us.

John had to go for his two-month check up at the hospital at the same time and was given the all clear and told that he could now drive. He was told to take things easy and avoid stress. My mind was quick to grasp the good news. I felt that once again we were on an almost even keel. The fact that Jan was in hospital seemed to cause me to worry less. That is until we went to see her.

Chapter 27

We arrived at the hospital a week or so after Jan had been admitted. She did not know that we were going because I wanted to make sure that she was pleased to see us and for it to be a surprise for her. We went into the patients' lounge and found Jan sitting in a wheelchair with her head slumped on her chest. I went and took her hand and spelled out the nickname she had given me – BAGS (after she bought me a shopping bag with BAG-IT written on the side). I had subsequently called her "Fags", after the cigarettes she insisted on smoking). Slowly she sort of rolled back her head. I was very shocked by her appearance. When she spoke I was alarmed. She slurred her words so much that I could not understand her and had to keep asking her to repeat. Her face was flushed and swollen. Her forehead seemed to bulge and her lips were puckered and very red.

She was obviously overjoyed that I had arrived and immediately asked whether Dad had come. Her face lit up when he took her hand and spoke on it.

Jan was waiting to be taken to the local pub for a meal. The staff nurse and an auxiliary nurse were going to take her. We asked whether we could join them and they said it would be good for Jan.

As we walked along, the staff nurse said she had forgotten to put sun cream on Jan. I asked what the problem was and she said that she was taking the drug chlorpromazine and Jan's skin could be photosensitive and needed protection, but added 'It should be OK.'

Immediately, I asked about the drug and said that I thought Jan was having a bad reaction to it. I told her how alarmed I was at the condition she was in, and how she had deteriorated. Nothing was said. When we were having our meal, Jan asked me to cut her food and she began feeling for her tools. I was beginning to notice that she was having more trouble than usual, and as she began eating she seemed to have difficulty finding her mouth. She had a pint of beer beside her and asked where it was. I placed the glass in her hand and she raised it as high as her forehead and gradually slid it down her nose until she found her mouth. What was going on? My stomach was in knots. Then she asked for her serviette. I handed it to her and she dropped it but continued to raise her hand and went through the motion of wiping her face and then handed the missing tissue back to me saying 'Thanks Mum.'

We continued our meal and I told her the latest joke that I had heard and she roared with laughter. We shared many funny moments and I noticed the staff nurse talking to the auxiliary about Jan behind her hand and staring across at us. I was perplexed.

Then Jan asked me to tell her the joke again as she had forgotten it. I was most surprised at this as she had always had such a fine memory. She explained that she could not concentrate now. What *was* going on?

Jan was far from the usual high-spirited girl she had always been, in fact she was like a zombie and I knew from past experience that she was probably having a serious reaction to the drugs she was being given. I asked the staff nurse whether the drugs had caused her symptoms and she said that they did sometimes have that affect but she did not comment further or seem concerned. I asked that Jan be taken off them. I was surprised when the nurse said it wasn't possible, but when I stated firmly that I wanted them stopped she said that she would have a word with the psychiatrist who ran the unit.

We returned to Jan's room and sat with her. When I asked her whether she liked the 3D-decoupage picture I had sent her she said that she could not feel it as her hands were damaged. I pressed her for more information and she said that her hands were numb but hurt her. I was still having great difficulty in understanding her speech, but with time I did get more used to it. She had always used speech very effectively and because she had heard it into her late teens she spoke very well.

The senior nurse asked whether we would attend a case meeting on the Monday. We were staying in a house that belonged to SENSE. It was to become a retreat for us on many occasions and we will always be extremely grateful to the many people who showed such love and concern to Janis and us.

We visited Jan again on Sunday and she seemed even worse and complained about her hands, which were paining her.

On the Monday we attended the team meeting. In the room was the consultant psychiatrist, a staff nurse and auxiliary nurse, occupational therapist and a counsellor, and I think one or two more. The meeting started by me being asked what sort of a child Janis was. I tried to explain a little. I was asked whether she was strong willed. I said that she was and that I thought it had held her in good stead owing to all of the disabilities that had come along one by one. I was questioned as to how I handled this when she was a child. But there was no discussion about side effects to the drugs she was being given.

So I asked about the medication. I explained about Jan's previous reaction to Tegretol. The consultant said that she knew and that Jan's records were marked to this effect. I asked again for the drug not to be given and I was told that the drug chlorpromazine would have to be withdrawn gradually.

We returned home but rang almost every day to see whether the drug had been stopped. It had not. Nick made his usual Saturday visit and said he was concerned that the speech and numbness was still the same. The doctor arranged for speech therapy and massage. Why was it never questioned why this was necessary? When Jan was admitted to the hospital she spoke perfectly and was able to use her hands without any problems and read her Braille books fluently. Things got worse, and special tools were brought in for her so that she could feed herself. These utensils had bulbous handles to enable her to grip them. Then a plastic guard was placed around her plates so that she didn't push the food off. She had always been meticulous in her eating and never ever made a mess, but now she was grovelling around the plate and spilling food down herself. Why did no one realise that this was probably a severe reaction to the drugs?

Initially I wrote a letter to thank the staff for the care that Janis was receiving, but as the deterioration went on my phone calls became more frequent and I made it quite clear that I was not happy about the amount of drugs they were giving Jan. Now my calls were taken with polite conversation, but I was aware that things were not going well. I became more and more concerned that Jan was not able to read her Braille books and would spend a lot of time on her bed. This was so out of character. The drugs were still being given to her.

We had the SENSE house for the August bank holiday weekend. This was only a few weeks after our first visit. When we saw Jan we became even more worried, because her speech was now dreadful. When we arrived we were shown into a room and asked to wait as the nurses were helping Jan to get dressed. I had never known Jan to need help when getting dressed and she would resent it if anyone ever suggested that she needed such assistance. Perhaps she might mislay an article of clothing and need help to find it, but always she attended to all of her personal needs. Every day she took a bath after breakfast and would then choose her clothes, which were all colour matched by having a different shaped button representing a colour inserted somewhere on the clothing. She was very independent and now she was being attended to like a child. I was very concerned.

Eventually they brought Jan to us. She was attempting to walk with a nurse either side, and as she came down the corridor she literally threw herself onto the floor and was screaming indecipherable stuff. The nurses waited until she had calmed down and then lifted her onto a wheelchair and brought her to us. I immediately asked whether she was still on the drug (I didn't know then that she had been given several) and I was told that she was. I asked to see the doctor and eventually she came to us. When I asked her about the drug and spoke of my concerns, her remark was, 'Well she's not the only patient, you know. I have 200 more besides and I had to give her something.' And with that she was gone.

It was from this moment that I was to become increasingly disturbed as to Jan's treatment.

We took Jan to a local park. It was a lovely day. We pushed her round and explained all that was happening. Then she smelt food. There was a barbecue area and John asked her what she wanted. She asked for a hot dog. John came back with a huge hot dog wrapped in tissue and oozing tomato sauce. He gave it to Jan and she began eating and it began to crumble; the sauce was all over the place. John went to help her, whereupon she suddenly threw the thing down and began rocking, and then she was jabbering and her jabbering got louder until she was shouting. Now she was shaking her head furiously from side to side, then her whole body. We could not understand a word of what she was saying but she was like a mad woman.

John grabbed hold of the wheelchair as other parents gathered their children to them, staring at us as they did so. We had to go over a humped bridge to get to the car park and John was pushing as fast as he could. Jan was still flailing around, her arms waving and her head swinging from side to side. We managed to get her into the car. I shouted in the hope that she would hear me. I held her as tightly as I possibly could but she fought me off, she was so strong. She was babbling as though in a foreign tongue.

John managed to put the wheelchair away and then fell into his driving seat. He was gasping for breath. He drove off and asked me to try to calm her down but she was not of this world, she was completely out of control. She was foaming at the mouth and from her nose. She picked up the bottom of her blouse and blew her nose into it. Then she wanted to get out and undid her seat belt. I tried to restrain her but she was too strong. I screamed for John to put the child safety locks on – we were in the thick of Saturday traffic on a main road of a busy city. How John managed to drive safely while all of this was going on is beyond thinking about. The only words I could decipher from Jan were, 'Handicapped, hate it hate it.'

As we reached the hospital she had quietened down but was gasping for breath and physically exhausted. John got out of the car telling me to sit tight and wait. He went into the ward to tell them what had happened. Two nurses came out and quite casually helped Jan out of the car and as they did so she slid to the floor. John got the wheelchair from the boot and Jan was eventually hauled into it and pushed into her bedroom. We were asked to go and sit in the waiting room. We were exhausted and I was very concerned for John. It was only a few weeks since his heart operation. About twenty minutes later we were ushered into Jan's room. She was lying on her side on the bed. She looked much calmer. As I took her hands and spelt BAGS on it she turned as though to look at me and said 'I'm sorry Mum, I can't help it.'

Where did all of my millions of tears come from? Was there no end? Someone said that God had a special place for a mother's tears! I asked why he needed to see so much distress in the first place. Was there no end to Jan's suffering?

It was Sunday. As we approached the mental health unit I felt sick in the pit of my stomach. How much more was Jan to have to take? We went in to see her and it was obvious that she had been sedated. We could not get any information from the staff except that it was becoming more evident that they thought Jan just had behavioural problems.

We did not stay long. We needed a break too, and assured Jan we would be in on the Monday. We were to attend a meeting anyway.

At the Monday meeting I told the psychiatrist and her team about what had happened in the park. It was as though I was talking to a stranger. There was not a flicker of surprise or comment. I told them I was very alarmed at her condition but the words behavioural problems were bandied around all of the time.

We went in to see Jan but she was very sleepy and so we didn't stay too long and made our way back home leaving Jan with a promise that we would soon be back. She muttered, 'Please Mum.'

Nick visited every Saturday without fail, and if he could he took her out for a snack which they ate in the car. The doctor eventually stopped the chlorpromazine drug and Janis began improving. Her speech was better and she was able, with a struggle, to read her Braille books although only a dot at a time. We had experienced all of this when she had the drug reaction in Devon.

She had even asked to be taken to have her hair done and to get some smelly goods as she called them. Then she wanted to go to the museum and other places of interest, and was out for pub grub. We thought that the worst was behind us and she would get well.

What was still puzzling me was that our alarm at her condition and the fact that she had deteriorated so quickly did not seem to concern any of the staff, nor the doctor herself. It was still considered, and the diagnosis given, that Jan was suffering an adjustment disorder following the birth of Holly and then the breakdown of the marriage. It seemed more than this to us.

Jan had her own personal counsellor and one day he called us to one side and asked whether we were aware that Jan had been smoking cannabis. I replied that she had told us and then he asked whether she may have taken anything else. I was shocked but I guess he was doing his job. I replied that I had no knowledge of this at all.

Just after this conversation there was a double page article about a young woman who had taken ecstasy and she had been rushed to hospital. Eventually she was placed on life support but only after her brain had swelled so much that severe brain damage had occurred. After her recovery, although she was quite severely disabled, she employed a

London barrister and sued the hospital for compensation on the grounds that they failed to recognise that she was suffering organic brain damage. There was a list of symptoms she had and was still experiencing. I was really scared – alerted to the fact that Jan was displaying most of the same symptoms.

The next time I spoke with the psychiatrist I mentioned the article to her, giving the date of the paper and hoping that she would, at the very least, read it. Her reply was that the drug mentioned was a highly dangerous one and dismissed my concerns yet again.

I was so sure that something of the same nature was happening to Jan. I managed to track down the barrister through various channels. However, once again I was told that evidence would be necessary. It seemed that every door I tried to open was slammed in my face.

I later discovered an entry in Jan's diary which she wrote a few months before being admitted to the mental health unit. It reads:

> When I was eighteen I was prescribed Tegretol. This was a drug for controlling epilepsy. I am not an epileptic, but the neurologist in Nottingham gave me the drug experimentally to see whether it would benefit my symptoms of acute neuritis and involuntary muscle spasm in my arms.
>
> The drug was, according to my mother, prescribed in June 1983. I can remember the tingling and numbness that I began to experience; the burning pains, and certainly my hearing deteriorated rapidly at this point.
>
> Three weeks into September I was admitted to The Exeter hospital suffering such acute pain that I could barely move; so hard-of-hearing I could barely communicate any longer, and suffering such a sever deterioration of the sense of touch that I could no longer read Braille.
>
> My memory of this period is hazy. I was so ill that clear recollection is impossible.
>
> But something I do remember clearly. When my mother decided to stop the drug Tegretol some months later I suffered so badly that I still have nightmares all these years later
>
> The withdrawal symptoms included shortness of breath, agonising pains that left me gasping and crying and would respond to no pain relief, and mood swings so violent that they were horrible to watch.
>
> I remember rolling about all over the floor; hurling myself at windows and doors; biting myself and other people; screaming, begging and pleading to be put back on the drug.

> *If this doesn't amount to a physically hard, addictive drug, then I am hard put to it to understand what amounts to addiction.*
>
> *The company (who manufactures Tegretol) has written a letter of apology to my mother saying that it tries to warn people of the possible side effects. (Nothing was given by the hospital at the time of prescribing this).*
>
> *I am aware that I leave myself wide open to attack by coming out so boldly about my experiences. But this itself raises the vital question...*
>
> *If so many toxic substances are available legally, some of them for recreation (alcohol), and we hear very little about many of the medicines with such horrific side-effects, then why are less-toxic substances with such medical and recreational benefits illegal?*
>
> *This is an interest I am determined to get to grips with. Could cannabis help my condition? It looks to me, from the evidence, that it could well do for me what the experts and their supply of dangerous toxins would not.*

Janis was still distressed at night time. Therefore the doctor was now administering other drugs and an antihistamine because Jan had developed a rash. A dermatologist was brought in from another hospital and he said the rash was a reaction to the drugs she was being given. The antihistamines made Jan feel ill and she asked for them to be stopped, but they continued to administer them. She was on them for a very long time until one Saturday Jan asked Nick to wheel her down to the staff room and they both demanded that she not be given the tablets anymore.

But now Jan was having more and more pain. She kept saying that she could not concentrate and that she felt sick. A cocktail of painkillers was given without relief. Jan was still having shouting bouts and I believe that more sedatives were administered.

Because we lived so far from the hospital I had asked the people at SENSE whether they might have someone working for them who would be willing to visit Jan. A young woman called Elaine and her friend Mary, who were both carers, jumped at the chance. They became very good friends to Jan and saw it as a joy to visit and take her out. Elaine would phone me and keep me informed of any changes. I repeatedly asked whether Jan was able to read and the answer was always no. Without the use of her hands her life's quality would now be very poor. My concerns grew by the minute.

Jan kept on repeating that she wanted to go to Sheffield University. She had talked about this with her tutors at college, and wanted to go to Sheffield to achieve an English Literature degree. The consultant wanted for Jan to be out of the hospital, so she had her staff look at places for her aftercare. One of these was at a place for disabled people in Sheffield. It was thought by the doctor that with it being near to the university it would give Jan reason for the fight to get better. She was still of the opinion that Janis was just strong willed and determined and her behavioural problems were because of that.

I think Jan saw going to Sheffield as a way of returning to the outside world and her chance to get the education she so badly wanted. But, following her assessment there it was decided by the manager of the place that they could not cope with someone needing so much care. If only they knew how capable Jan had been before her illness and admission to hospital.

It was coming up to Jan's birthday in December. She had been in the hospital for almost six months and she was so much worse. Elaine asked Jan whether she would like to go out for a birthday meal and Jan jumped at the chance. Elaine rang me to tell me about the evening. She said it had been lovely. However, whilst they were eating she realised that Jan had almost lost the use of one hand. She could only use one finger and her thumb. Also while she was eating tears started to trickle down her face and Elaine asked Jan what the matter was. Jan replied, 'Thank you for treating me as a human being.'

I began to shake uncontrollably. As I type this I am crying. The pain is just too much. A mother should be able to fix things, and here I was a hundred miles away and exhausted. I had collapsed and our GP had warned me that I must rest and leave others to look after Jan. How or what could I do?

I cannot say exactly when Jan was sectioned under the Mental Health Act. It was around Christmas time. She had begun self-harming. Then followed section II, as she had become aggressive.

On one occasion when Nick visited with Holly she gave her mummy a card she had made at nursery school. Jan took the card and, Nick said, tears rolled down her cheeks. She asked Nick not to bring Holly any more. Also she told Nick that she felt as though half of her brain had gone and cried, 'I've had enough, I really have had enough.'

He replied, 'I know, I know.'

The whole family had said that they would visit her on Boxing Day. I guess it was the exhaustion we were all suffering which caused Nick, John, and me to contract a nasty flu virus and we were all in bed over the Christmas holiday. During this time I had a phone call from Jan. She was still unable to speak except in the most dreadful drawl and I had difficulty in understanding her. But she had someone by her side to repeat to me what it was she wanted and then to give Jan my answers. It seemed she wanted to speak with the then director of SENSE, Rodney Clarke, to see whether he could get her out of the hospital. He was a lovely man and had been a friend for years. I said I would try to contact him. However SENSE was closed for the holiday. I rang back and left a message to tell Jan the position, gave Rodney's telephone number and to let her know when he would be back in the office. I assured her of our love and apologised for not being able to visit her. I learnt, weeks later, that she had rung Rodney but he could not understand what she was saying except that she wanted to go somewhere.

The drug amitriptyline was administered for pain relief after Christmas. This was arranged over the phone between a nurse and Jan's neurologist 150 miles away. She now became very aggressive. The drug was only given for about two weeks but it is my belief that it was the final nail in her coffin.

We were called to attend a team meeting at the beginning of February 1999. There was to be a discussion about Jan's discharge and aftercare. A more senior psychiatrist from her previous hospital was to attend, and Jan's social worker was also summoned. The consultant was still insisting that in her opinion Jan had behavioural problems and an adjustment disorder. She said that Jan was very unhappy in the unit and needed to be out in society.

We arrived early for the meeting and stayed at the SENSE house again. When we went in to see Jan she was in bed. She was now considered to be not attempting to do anything for herself. She lay on her side with her now paralysed hand poking out from under her. I spoke with her on her other hand but she did not turn; she just lay there. She told us that she was in a lot of pain. She said she needed help and that she was to have an operation on her hands that day. No one had mentioned anything about an operation. Her speech was a terrible drawl and she was drooling.

As we sat in the room the psychiatrist came in and said a cheery 'Hi' and went to leave. I quickly buttonholed her and said that Jan was in a lot of pain. She just tersely said that we should address it at the meeting and left.

There was a huge team in the room as we entered. The visiting doctor was to arrive later in the morning. As the meeting began I started by saying that Jan was in terrible pain and also paralysed in her right arm and hand. The meeting progressed and various members read their reports. I was very shocked by the report read out by the occupational therapist. She had conducted an assessment of Jan's ability to look after herself, and it seemed that she now had great difficulty in showering and dressing herself. But her determination to get well was evident, as she had taken to using her teeth to pull on her clothing. Jan had to rest after each item of clothing before continuing to dress, and was exhausted when she had finished. The therapist went on to say that the deterioration was continuing.

After the morning session, the therapist gave me a copy of her report. I showed my concern. She volunteered that they had had another young woman like Jan in the clinic, and she had died. I did not want to hear this. I was aware that Jan was seriously ill but the psychiatrist had always upheld that it was behavioural and that she was unhappy in the hospital and we would see a great improvement as soon as she was out of there. The problem for this doctor seemed to be where she was to send Jan for aftercare. No one ever seemed to question or discuss why there was such a deterioration in her health.

For the rest of the morning, both John and I hammered home the concern we had, and that something needed to be done quickly and to alleviate the pain. The doctor said they could not find that she was in any pain. I pressed on about the medication, but it seemed that it fell on deaf ears literally. The consultant is profoundly deaf and uses interpreters for some of her work. I wondered how a psychiatrist could make assessments of her patients when she could not hear the slurred speech or intonation, the level of screams or their nature, whether the patient sounded in a depressed mood or anything of that nature? In fact I was now more aware of the fact that she did not hear for herself that Jan had perfect speech and excellent grammar upon arrival at the clinic so how was she making any judgements? There were many profoundly deaf members of staff too.

We broke for lunch. The visiting psychiatrist had phoned in to say he had been delayed. It appeared that the staff were in awe of this man.

I went back in to see Jan and she said she was hungry and hadn't had her lunch. I went to the office and it was obvious they were not happy to hear this as I was told that lunch had been taken to her but she had refused. I took the packet of sandwiches, which they had put in the fridge, and went back to Jan. I handed her the sandwich and she took it with her good hand and began ramming the food into her mouth to such an extent that it was bulging. At this moment, one of the staff from SENSE who had come to the meeting to see about setting up a placement for Jan at the SENSE site, came in to see Jan because she had never met her before. As Jan tried to push more and more food into her mouth the woman turned to me and said, 'My goodness, she must be hungry!'

Jan began to choke. I was alarmed and asked for a sick bowl. I had never ever seen anything like this. Was I in hell or was I going mad? Just what was happening to my daughter?

Eventually I went for lunch with some of the others and asked Jan's social worker to go in and see her. Her reply was that she thought it best not to, as too many visitors would tire Jan. Even at this time no one seemed to be hearing our concerns. This was the social worker that had arranged for Jan to go into this hospital. It seemed that no one was listening to us that our daughter could possibly die. Was no one going to take our concerns seriously?

I pinned my hope on Rodney Clarke who had said that he would like to call in to see Jan on the morning of the meeting but could not stay as he had another one to go to. He sat by Jan's bedside for about two hours and I was, unexpectedly, to discover his opinion on Jan's condition later in the day.

The team meeting resumed. However, the minutes secretary was not there in the afternoon, which I found rather strange. We all sat around waiting. Jan's consultant had taken the visiting psychiatrist into her office and they were in there for a long time. Maybe, I thought, he would bring us some good news?

As he entered the room he came and sat directly opposite John and me and ignored the rest of the people by addressing us first. How he knew us from everyone else we do not understand. He began by saying that he had been told that we had stated that Jan had been damaged by the drugs that she had been given. I can only assume that there had been some discussion about this when they were in the office. Furthermore, he said that she had not been given any psychotropic drugs, but if she continued in her behaviour they would have to, otherwise she could become incontinent, paralysed, catheterised and dead! There was no explanation for this diagnosis; he just burst forth with it.

'Of course,' he went on, 'We could perform brain surgery if you would prefer that?'

He was looking straight at us and was so arrogant in his manner I was struck dumb.

John took over by asking him about the terrible pain that Jan was in.

He replied, 'There is no pain. I have held her hands and there is no problem. She talks about an operation but there ain't gonna be an operation.' These were his exact words.

John said that we would be happier for Jan to go to see her neurologist and the doctor replied that if that was what we wanted he would arrange it and meet us there. We never heard another word about this.

He turned to the rest of the people in the group and said that they were to treat Jan as they would when training a dog. When Jan started screaming they were to come out of her room and leave her until she quietened down, and only then were they to return and stroke her on the head and tell her that she was a good girl. I discovered later that this regime was used as therapy and one can only try to imagine the horror of Jan crying out in pain or for someone to help her and being shut up in a room alone not being able to see or hear and with no-one coming to her aid. She must have been absolutely terrified to say the very least.

I was completely lost for words and felt that I was on another planet. It was as though I was watching it all from a distance and had no control over anything anymore. Whenever we had anything to say, and whatever we said, it was never acknowledged in any satisfactory way at all.

Then the discussion immediately turned to Jan's future placement and aftercare. The woman from SENSE said that they could arrange to have Jan but the adaptions, accommodation and after-care would be very expensive.

The visiting psychiatrist blurted, 'Let's have it then. She has cost us thousands already.'

I thought his arrogance was dreadful and beyond belief. I was gobsmacked.

Everything was going at such a pace and I felt so completely impotent. This was my daughter that they were talking about as though she was some wild animal that needed to be tamed, controlled and shipped elsewhere.

The meeting eventually closed. I went in to see Jan. She asked what was going on and I assured her that we would do our best to get her out of the place. But I could not mention SENSE as she was against going into any institutional type building. It had been agreed at the meeting that plans and costs would be drawn up and Jan would only be told when it was all ready for her.

She was still lying on her side with her knees pulled up. I kissed her. My heart had never felt so close to breaking. I told her we were leaving and she drawled out that she would like to see a specific nurse. I said I would contact her on the way out.

I called at the office. The nurse was leaving her job that afternoon. She cried on my shoulder and said how fond she had grown of Jan. This was another nurse who told me that another young woman had died on the unit. Never once did anyone say that they were aware that Jan was dying. They refuted our claims again and again. But I have often wondered why two members of staff needed to volunteer this information.

We arrived back at the SENSE campus and as we got out of our car I saw Rodney. I ran to him. We hugged and I blurted out what the male doctor had said. Rodney's response was not what I wanted to hear. He told me that he had sat by Jan's bed for a long time, and throughout it Jan had been talking to herself as though she was enacting a play and enjoying it. He said he had serious concerns that she would die because she had 'gone in on herself'. I panicked.

John and I decided to return home the next day, but before we left I wanted to go in and see Jan again. I got to her bed and said, 'Hi Fags.'

She replied, 'Hi Mum. Can you fetch a nurse? I've started a period and need help but please ask for a female nurse.'

I went down to the office and saw the ward manager. He went down to Jan's room with two female auxiliary nurses. They helped Jan to get out of bed and into a wheelchair. I had never known Jan to struggle like this in her life. They wheeled her to the toilet and John and I waited in her room. There was a terrible howling noise. It was Jan making this terrible noise as though she was in a lot of pain. We went into the corridor and the manager was telling the two nurses that they were to come out of the bathroom and wait until she had calmed down. I asked to go to her and he said that I was not allowed, as this was part of the therapy. We were asked to go to the lounge.

The screams and shouting went on and on and after about twenty minutes I could stand no more and barged down the corridor and into the toilet. Jan was thrashing backwards and forwards and from side to side in her wheelchair her face contorted. She was wild; there is no other way to describe her. I held her and slowly the rocking stopped. I put my face to hers. She was silent but suddenly she took hold of my hand and bit it, screaming again. I was scared out of my wits. No one seemed to have a clue as to her true condition. I didn't know what was happening. I was told to come out. We seemed to have no alternative; my mind was groping around to find some comprehension about the whole situation. She was like a mad person. I had never been close to anyone in this state before.

We were absolutely out of our depth and could not influence the situation one way or the other. We returned to our home. I decided to keep a diary of all of the events and messages and diagnoses that I received from the hospital. I still have this.

Chapter 28

Our GP and other people, and a nurse at the hospital, had all suggested that John and I needed to take a holiday. We were both completely exhausted. John had been told to keep stress away and yet had been through all of this since his operation. I was worried about him too.

We booked a five-day coach holiday to Torquay. Nick said he would go to see Jan the next week. As we settled into our seats I heaved a sigh of relief. I guess it was relief from having to think about food, cooking and general matters. But it gave more room for thought about Jan.

When we arrived at the hotel the driver asked everyone to wait while he checked in. He came back and asked for Mr. & Mrs. Revell to please leave the coach as we were urgently wanted. My heart leapt into my throat. We were shown into an office. The member of staff said that the hospital wanted to speak with us urgently. It turned out that Janis was even more aggressive and they wanted to apply section three under The Mental Health Act. John asked what this meant and was told that it would mean that they could hold Jan against her will and that it would also enable them to administer whatever drugs they saw fit. They needed John's word for this to be done and John vehemently refused. The house doctor said that if he didn't agree then they would have to take the matter to court. John still refused to agree.

Why they had left this until we had gone away for a few days is still beyond our comprehension. John said for them to ring Nick, as he was her husband. The doctor explained that because Jan was separated from Nick, John was the next of kin under the rulings of the Mental Health Act.

We went out on the coach every day. I did not see the countryside. Tears streamed down my face causing everything to become a blur, and my mind was all over the place. I sat with my face to the window and let the tears fall and held John's hand. I knew that he was in a dreadful state too. All was beyond help, or so it seemed as gradually Jan's life ebbed away. What would it take to stop this downward spiral?

Every day when we returned to the hotel there was a message from the hospital. John would ring and the same words were exchanged. This went on for three days until we were told that a court order would be applied for. At six o'clock one morning I was writing out a fax message. In this I wrote that we would agree if they gave us a solemn promise that they would not administer any more drugs. The fax went to them before breakfast and later that day the house doctor gave his word. We arrived home on the Friday night feeling very much worse than before we had left. Nick was going to see Jan the next day and so we decided that we would rest. I couldn't, as my mind was turbulent. I decided to begin my search to do whatever it would take to get Jan into another hospital.

Our worries grew by the day. When we got a call from Elaine to say that she would advise us not to go and see Jan, I asked what she was talking about. She said that she had been in to visit Jan and that she was now on the floor in a padded room and could not do a thing for herself and was unresponsive.

I rang the hospital and was told that Jan was still behaving badly. I asked for an explanation and was told that she was abusive to the staff and very aggressive. They said that she was refusing food and not bothering about anything at all. They further inferred that it was Jan's fault that she was like she was.

We went immediately to the hospital. Jan was lying on her stomach with her knees drawn up. She had a peculiar rash high up on the cheekbones and her lips were pursed and looked swollen and purple. Her features had changed. I tried to rouse her but she did not move. I did all I could to get her to wake but I couldn't. I asked the auxiliary nurse, who had been sitting in the room to guard Jan so that she did not hurt herself, what had caused her to sleep so deeply, and was told that her sleep patterns were all over the place. I replied that this was no ordinary sleep, it was as if she was unconscious. The nurse said it was probably the injection.

Immediately I was on the alert, as we had been told that no more drugs apart from paracetamol would be administered. I asked what injection the nurse was referring to and she said she had no idea but it had upset her because she was one of the nurses who had to hold Jan down while it was done.

She then asked me what had happened. I was very surprised by her question but she went on to say that Jan was doing quite well up until just before Christmas and had showed signs of improving. I said, 'Linda, you know what has happened don't you? It is the drugs that have caused all of this, isn't it?'

She replied, 'I think so, but I have to do what the boss tells me to.' We fell into silence again.

John and I had been by Jan's side for some time. I was kneeling on the floor beside her when she stirred. I was able to speak on her hand. I asked her if she would like some food that we had brought for her. She asked what it was and I told her. She asked for a packet of cream cheese biscuits and I let her feel the packet. She took it from me and tore it open with her teeth and then gradually eased out one of the biscuits with just one finger and her thumb. She could not use her other hand at all. When she had finished just two biscuits she started to go to sleep again. I asked her whether she wanted us to go and she nodded her head. We kissed her goodbye and left. The doctor was not on duty and the staff all seemed to be unconcerned at her deterioration.

I began in earnest to try and get Jan into another hospital, but I met walls of bureaucracy. I rang a solicitor and poured out my story to him. He did no more but to send me forms for making a claim against the doctor. I rang the daily papers begging someone to take notice and to help me in my plight but it was to no avail. I rang the Health Council and the woman on the phone was all but useless. All she wanted to know was how long Jan had been blind and what had caused it and on and on. In the end I swore at her and slammed the phone down.

I forget how long I had been going round and round trying to get help. It must have been days. I even went to my GP, who had suggested the Health Council. She said there was nothing that she could do. My mind was now unable to think at all clearly. I was crying a lot and not sleeping much at all. Eventually, after I had contacted so many people, it was suggested that I contact the chief executive of the hospital trust. Why I had not done this earlier I do not know. I guess this shows the state of my mind. I was not in the habit of registering a complaint, and therefore, did not know of the procedures involved.

Eventually I reached the chief executive on the phone. She asked why I had not come to her before going to all of the other people. I tried to emphasise the urgency of the case. She said that she would set up an inquiry but that the NHS worked slowly and it would take a long time. When I shouted at her that my daughter was dying she replied, 'I think you are worrying unnecessarily. If that was to be the case there is an intensive care unit just across the way. I suggest you calm down and stop worrying.' I screamed back at her that I would take legal action if something was not done. Surprisingly she calmly replied' if that is what you feel you must do then I cannot do anything about it. I have been in the NHS for many years and experience has taught me that it takes a very long while for complaints to be looked into.' I begged of her again reiterating that my daughter was dying. There was no response.

Even at this late stage I was not being heard. When would someone acknowledge that Jan was dying before their eyes?

I knew in my heart of hearts that Jan had had some sort of stroke. Why else would she have paralysis down her right arm, be unable to speak properly and be sleeping most of the time, and say she could not concentrate and that half of her brain had gone? Also, why was she now so aggressive? This was very much out of character. She also became doubly incontinent and suggestions were made that she was doing this on purpose. One nurse told me over the phone that 'Jan has wet the bed again you know, and she knows what she is doing because when I wheeled her to the shower she wanted to know where I was taking her. When I told her and asked her whether she knew why, she replied that it was because she had wet the bed.'

I cried again. My girl was so meticulous in every way. She would never ever behave in this way.

It was while I was looking for help on the Internet that I came across The Brain & Spinal Foundation Helpline. I could not get onto them quickly enough. A lady named Angela answered the phone and I poured out my story. I was crying, in fact I could not stop crying. I knew that my daughter was slipping away from me and I was powerless to stop it. Angela told me to take my time. She let me get a little control, and as I took a deep breath she asked me to explain exactly what had happened and the symptoms that Jan was presenting with. After I had told her she said that it was imperative that we get the doctor to carry out a magnetic resonance imaging test, known as a MRI. Her tone of voice underlined my own concerns. At last I had someone who seemed to know what she was talking about and was trying to help me. She told me exactly what I must do and asked me to let her know how things went.

Angela was so helpful to me over the next months and supported my claims that Jan had serious brain problems which needed to be inquired into. She talked me through so many issues but I could not get my concerns across to the doctor and staff at the hospital. It seemed useless. I contacted Angela again and again. She always stressed the importance of a MRI. She was so supportive and I always felt better after talking with her; in fact I felt empowered that with her support I could persuade the psychiatrist to do what was necessary. My requests for a MRI were refused.

Immediately after putting the phone down from speaking to Angela the first time, I faxed the hospital asking them for a MRI to be carried out ASAP. This request was ignored. I repeated my request. A junior doctor rang me to talk about Jan. He said that they had to have a very good reason to perform a MRI and that they did not have the equipment there. I asked about Jan's hands and face being numb and her paralysis. He said it was thought it was a type of hysteria, which affected the body in this way. I said I did not want the consultant to treat Jan anymore and he responded by saying what a lovely person she was and what a wonderful sense of humour too. I was gobsmacked. This quite literally took my breath away and I could say no more. Did this type of comment bode well for my daughter?

Jan had said that not only half of her brain had died but that it felt as though all of her teeth had been pulled out because she could not feel them nor feel her mouth. She had asked for a MRI when she was more lucid, this was refused. Then Nick later asked for one. The psychiatrist asked for what reason. When Nick broached his concerns she refused his request.

On our next visit to the hospital, Jan was in a larger room to enable the nurses to get to her more easily. The walls were padded and she was still on the floor.

This time Jan was in a lighter sleep. I told her we had brought some food and she asked to sit up. But there was no support for her back. I pulled the pillows up against the wall and sat her up, but as I did so she screamed with pain and quickly slid down onto the mattress again, crying that her back hurt and to get help. In her struggle to lie down she had rolled off the mattress. I asked the nurse to help me and was surprised when she took hold of Jan by the ankles and pulled her onto the mattress. I commented about this and was told that the staff had been called to a meeting and told that on no account were they to lift her, as it was a "no lifting trust".

I managed to understand Jan's slurred speech as she said that she wanted someone to rub her back with cream. I first asked the nurse whether she could get some cream and was told it was not possible. Then I asked about a backrest. The nurse said she had no idea what we meant. Jan had returned to her original position, which obviously gave her some respite from the pain. Then she dropped back off to sleep after telling us that she could not concentrate on what we were saying. This had also caused us concern, because she had always enjoyed conversation and had a fine mind and memory. In fact, if we were given a telephone number and did not have anything to write it on we would tell Jan and she would recall that number at any time. Now she was unable to even listen or to comprehend what we were saying to her.

Later, the consultant psychiatrist rang me to ask me what sort of pain Janis was in. I was flabbergasted that she should be phoning me. I explained that it was of a burning stabbing type. She then said that they had blood tests back, which showed liver problems, and when I asked what that was all about she replied, 'I don't know, it's years since I did that type of thing. I leave that to the medics.' And she rang off.

At some point around this time I even contacted the Mental Health Commission and lodged a complaint. I was told that they would send an officer to the hospital to see first-hand what was happening. I had hope that this would resolve matters and necessary steps would be taken for Jan to receive the right treatment, or so I thought. I left it in their hands and sent them details in writing. However, some weeks passed and we heard nothing from them. I rang them, desperately needing their support. The answer shocked me. The man I had sent the details to had left his job and filed the paperwork away and nobody else knew anything about it.

I called on Moira, a family outreach manager at a branch of SENSE. She had known Jan for a number of years. I poured everything out to her. I was spent emotionally and could not contain my distress at all now. Moira was very concerned and rang Jan's social worker but could not get her. She then rang the hospital but was told that Jan was quite satisfactory. I pleaded with Moira to go and see for herself.

A few days later I collapsed again. I was in the kitchen making breakfast when I felt all of my strength leave me and I broke out in a cold sweat. I called for John and he helped me to bed and called our GP who diagnosed exhaustion. He wanted to know what was now happening, and when I told him he said that I must spend some days of complete rest and gave me a tranquilliser. But how could I rest when I was in total fear that Jan was near death and no one was taking a bit of notice?

I started taking phone calls in my bed. Moira phoned to say she had been to see Jan and that she was not eating and she wondered whether I could go and stay at the SENSE house and go in every day to give Jan some food. I told her it was out of the question. I longed to be able to do it, but I knew that it was physically impossible. I knew that I should be resting completely, but would my mind switch off? I needed to rest, but I also desperately needed to do more to get Jan out of that place.

I told Moira of my fears and about the funding for Jan's aftercare. She asked me whether I was serious about Jan dying, and I assured her that I was. She agreed with me that she was in a very bad way and suggested that I kept a log of all phone calls and correspondence. I told her that I had started one after the meeting in February. She did some research and then came up with a letter for me to send out to the local health trust and the social services. It basically informed them of Jan's deterioration and asked who was ultimately responsible for her aftercare. Within a short time we were told that funding to the tune of £182,000 per year was to be paid by Jan's local health care trust. This was now the level of care that Jan needed, with physiotherapists, speech therapists, twenty-four-hour care, walk-in bath, a special ripple bed and hoists and numerous other things. On top of this was the cost of the flat that SENSE was adapting.

The organising of everything would not be completed until the first of May and I hoped with all of my body and soul that Jan would make it. Still it seemed that Jan was being blamed for her state. She was now doubly incontinent, had liver problems, impacted bowels to the point of overflow at both ends, bed sores, could not feel any part of her body, was paralysed, and still it did not seem that her carers had any concerns. I was tormented by my impotence in stopping Jan's obvious decline.

I was a little recovered when we went to visit Jan in March sometime. She was deteriorating before our eyes. It seemed that she was unconscious most of the time, but we were always told that she was just sleeping. We could not rouse her at all. In our opinion she was not having essential medical nursing care and was still on a mattress on the floor in the mental health unit. We asked so many times for her to be transferred to a general medical ward. I asked that at least they could get a bed for her and was told that she would throw herself out. I suggested a cot but this was declined.

I asked to see the psychiatrist. I sat on the floor by Jan's side. She was not conscious. After some while the ward manager came to say that we could see the doctor now. As we entered her room I told the doctor that the funding had come through and she replied, 'Yes, we've heard. Isn't it wonderful? You will see a big improvement in your daughter when she is out of here. She's just not trying to get well as she is so unhappy here.'

The manager then asked us whether we were pleased with Jan's progress. I was incensed. The fact that she was now rarely awake (I thought she was slipping in and out of consciousness) was considered to be progress? The fact of the matter is that I just lost it.

I shouted at the doctor, 'Do you call this progress? My daughter is dying and you say she is unhappy. How long did you give her chlorpromazine and other drugs for?'

I shouted that I knew about the contra-indications of the drugs from my work with the GP clinic and I would prove that Jan had suffered a bad reaction. I wanted the names of all the drugs she has been given, the exact amounts and for how long. Her reply was, 'This is neither the time nor the place to be discussing this and I have to pick my daughter up.' She picked up Jan's medical folder and slammed it shut, then brushed past John and me and was gone.

I can't remember what ensued after that. My mind was all over the place trying to bring the right collection of ideas as to how we could take Jan away from this place. But she was sectioned and our hands were tied. I returned home and tried to contact the chief executive, but now I was transferred to her legal representative. I had to relay my case all over again from the very beginning. I never ever had a reply to my many letters of complaint apart from the initial one to say that the matter was being looked into. My faxes were never replied to either.

On one occasion I had written to the Chief Medical Officer and was told over the phone by the chief executive that he was going to hold a meeting and investigate my complaints. On the day of the proposed inquiry I waited and waited for the promised phone call. I was on edge all of the day hoping that at last he would see Jan's dilemma and act upon it. At five o'clock I rang the ward to ask for the results of the meeting. The response was, 'What meeting are you talking about?' I explained. My hopes evaporated. There had been no meeting at all and I never ever heard from the CMO.

Nick continued to visit every Saturday. On one of these visits he rang from where he was sitting on the floor at the side of Jan. He wept as he said that she now had clenched teeth and was rolling her head from side to side. She could not drink, except that he managed to squeeze between her teeth the straw from a drink he had taken in, and she had managed a little but it was all too much. She drooled and continued rolling her head.

At the end of March, Nick returned from his usual Saturday visit. He was very concerned and said that Jan had now developed new symptoms. She had facial grimacing. It was like a baby sucking a bottle, was the only way he could explain it. Also Jan seemed to be holding her breath a lot and seemed very breathless at other times. I commented that I had noticed this and that her pulse was racing (I had watched her neck pulse and it was going very fast). I told Nick that I had been to the staff office and was told that it was a hot day and that was the reason for her symptoms. He said he had tried to get her into the wheel chair and she could not help herself at all as she had no strength in her. He said she was like a rag doll. However, he did manage to take her for a little ride in his car.

I immediately rang to book the SENSE house for the Easter weekend in early April 1999.

No one, but no one could have prepared us for what lay ahead. We arrived at the hospital and it was unusually quiet with very few staff on duty owing to it being a bank holiday. The male staff nurse in charge of Jan's case said that she was doing OK. As we walked down the corridor with him we heard this terrific howl as if someone was in great pain.

'Who's that?' My heart was thumping.

'It's Jan,' was the reply 'The nurses are getting her dressed.' He showed little concern as he opened the door.

The level of deterioration was horrific. I gasped at how dreadfully ill she was. Jan lay on the mattress with her head flopped back over the edge and her mouth was wide open with her top lip curled under above her teeth, the whites of her eyes showing. I shouted at the nurse to get a doctor quick. He replied that there was no need. I tried to get Jan to know that we were there and she gradually moved her head and moaned what sounded like, 'Hello Bags.' I loved her and cried. She was so very thin and had no life in her. She lapsed into unconsciousness.

We left her with the nurse in charge, who sat in a chair reading and listening to the radio. We went to the office and the two staff nurses on duty came out of the staff room and into a visitors' room. I asked them to get a doctor. They just looked at me. I said that I had been in touch with the Queens' Square hospital in London and they were trying to get her a bed. I asked for help to get her there.

The male nurse said, 'You say that Jan has had a reaction to the drugs but that is not the case. There is nothing physically wrong with her.'

I begged them. I turned to the young female nurse and pleaded with her. 'I must say this,' I told her, 'if you do not act and do something now Jan is going to die and if she does you have the rest of your life to carry this on your conscience. You are young and I would not want that for you so please help me.' She just stared at the floor.

'Please I am begging of you both. Please help us to get her to London.' They both just sat and stared at the floor. There was nothing we could do and whatever we said had no impact.

I had contacted a couple who were trauma counsellors before I went to visit Jan and said that it was as though I was going out of my mind. No one at the hospital seemed to be listening to either of us, nor noticing the fact that our daughter was dying. Briefly I explained what had been going on. I told them we were going to see Jan on Easter Saturday. They asked whether they could meet us somewhere. I arranged a room at SENSE and they had agreed to meet us after our visit to the hospital.

If miracles happened, then perhaps they could help me to bring one about. I was clutching at any straw available. When the couple arrived I could not speak as the sobs were forcing the tears to pour. I knew that it was only a matter of a short time before Jan would die, and I desperately tried to push the thought away. The couple listened. They said little except that we needed to cry as much as possible. How much more could I do that and what good was it doing? The woman did say that I needed to write to a professor at the hospital who was the Chief Medical Officer of psychiatry. I said I had already done so but he never answered. In fact I eventually wrote several letters and I never received a reply.

John drove us back home in silence. As soon as we got into the house I was on the phone to the hospital. There were few staff on call. After several attempts to try and get a doctor to go to Jan I received a phone call from a link nurse who was on duty. I pleaded with her to help me save my daughter, I explained to her as best I could Jan's condition and she said that she would go and visit the unit and report back to me. At last there was a breath of hope. It was soon gone. She rang back to say that she had been over and talked with the duty staff and had been informed that there was no need to be concerned about Jan, that she was OK. I asked her whether she had been in to see her and she said she hadn't. I begged of her, saying, 'You would not keep an animal in the condition she is in, please go and look for yourself.'

She replied that she had done all that she could.

I was desperately exhausted, so John came and took over the phone. He began ringing many numbers but, again owing to the bank holiday, he had trouble making contact with anyone. Eventually John managed to speak with a director of maintenance. John poured out his story. He told him that I had managed to get the London hospital to take Jan but they had been waiting for some time for a letter of referral. The man replied that there was nothing he could do at the time but as soon as the holiday was over he would make sure that the letter was sent.

When would anyone take this matter as a case of urgency? I give credit because the letter did in fact go to London the following week.

What more could we do? Yes! I thought, I would get an ambulance and take her to London. Even though there is no bed at the moment surely they won't turn her away. I started ringing around. People were amazed at my story. It would be very costly, about £750, as they would have to supply a nurse and have oxygen and all first aid equipment on board. 'No matter' I said. 'I'll ring you back.'

I rang Nick and told him of our plans and he was all for it. Then I realised that there was no way that we could do this as Janis was being held under section III of The Mental Health Act which meant that she could only be removed on permission from a court. Once more my hands were tied.

Nick went to see Jan the following week. He lifted her and carried her to a wheelchair and managed to get her into his car. He went to get some throat lozenges as Jan had managed to tell him that her throat was very sore. He placed a lozenge in her mouth but she was unable to hold it there. She was drooling and the sweet kept coming out. Nick rang me on his mobile telling me how she was and that Jan wanted to speak to me. I listened and heard the most awful sound. It was my daughter, and yet all I could hear was this terrible drawled speech which I could not decipher at all. Nick came back on and I asked him to tell her that I loved her very much and was doing all in my power to get her out of the clinic.

As I placed the phone onto its cradle I yanked at my hair. Again I wanted to pull every thought out of my mind, all of the pain and horror of what was happening. My mind was shot to pieces. It raced and teemed in torrents of anguish, and images of the terrible state of Jan tormented me. We were all alone in our terrible dilemma. No one seemed to be taking a dammed bit of notice that our daughter was dying and that she was in agony and torment. I sought for answers, for some idea to penetrate in the hope that there might be something, someone, I had overlooked to help her. The hot tears coursed down my face and I sobbed uncontrollably. This was my child whom I adored and would die for, and yet all that I had done so far had proved useless.

My GP said that Jan should have been in a hospice receiving palliative care, but she was denied even that. They weren't even acknowledging that death was imminent so no-way would they transfer her to a hospice.

I rang the doctor that I had spoken to at the Queen's Hospital in London and told him of Jan's condition. He agreed that she was in a very bad way. I begged of him to admit her and he replied that there was no bed available but as soon as they had one she would be admitted without hesitation. I was crying to him, 'Please take her now she's dying.'

'I won't be emotionally blackmailed,' was his reply. 'I know how seriously ill she is, and she may well die, but so might we all. We do not have a bed so there is nothing that I can do at this moment.'

I replaced the phone and sat in stunned silence. My mind refused to comprehend what was happening. I was shocked. My last possible hope of saving my daughter had been snatched away. All I had now was that it might be possible for her to be admitted to Queen's Square, but I knew that time was not on our side. My only consolation was that at the very least she would have a proper bed and the medical care and attention that she needed. Dignity for her at the end of her life.

Even at this stage, neither the consultant nor any person on her team ever mentioned to us that Jan was in a very bad way. Never ever did anyone mention that she might die. Was I going mad?

Nick said that he would go again in the middle of the week and report to us. I also had people from SENSE going in to see her, but it was always the same – they said that she seemed to be unconscious most of the time.

When the phone rang I knew it was Nick but was not prepared for what he was going to say. He was crying like a child. He said that Jan was now in a very bad way. She was as a rag doll when he attempted to lift her and was desperately thin and lifeless.

I kept ringing the doctor or her staff several times a day and their attitude was still that she would improve when she made her mind up to do so. Then, late one afternoon, the consultant rang. She said that she thought that Jan had turned her face to the wall and was not trying to get better. The doctor was cheerful and had no concern in her voice at all as she went on to say that as soon as Jan was out of the unit we would see a vast improvement: 'It is wrong for her to be here because she is so unhappy.' Then she said the strangest thing. She asked me not to keep ringing her staff or sending faxes through, but to write to her personally. I screamed at her and put the phone down.

Next day I arranged for another bunch of flowers to be sent. I asked for these to be mostly freesias as they were Jan's favourite flower. She loved the gentle perfume. I rang the ward manager and asked whether they had arrived as I wanted them to be right close to Jan. Her reply was that Jan would not know they were there.

I asked 'Is it that bad? Is she too far gone?'

The ward manager replied that Jan was a very sick girl but did not add any more.

The next phone call shortly after this was from the junior doctor. He said that they were transferring Jan across to the general ward. This was in the same grounds but a short distance away. He said that her blood pressure was very high, her pulse 120 and her temperature 104 plus. I asked him for an explanation and he said that a CAT scan had been carried out and it had shown encephalitis of the brain. I asked what had caused that and he said that it was most likely the drugs she had been given.

I asked whether we should go straight over and he said that there was no urgency and that they would be transferring Jan by ambulance that night. He suggested we waited until the next day. Even at this stage I still had some trust left in me to suggest that the doctors must know what they were doing. If Jan was dying, surely they would have said so, and if death was imminent he would have said for us to go straight over. Although I had known for weeks that Jan was dying, I clung to any hope I could conjure up in my mind. Jan had now been in this unit for about 10 months.

The next morning, John and I went to the hospital. Nick was to follow. Jan had been placed in a side room on her own. As we entered the room I cried out, 'No! Oh No!' I dropped onto the bed next to her and placed my head into my hands. She was much worse than I had expected. I could not believe my eyes.

Jan was so very thin, her stomach swollen and her face contorted.

There were two nurses who had been sent from the mental health clinic to interpret for the medical staff if needed. They were just sitting at the foot of Jan's bed reading. I took her small hand and spoke to her. Then her dad spoke and she screwed up her nose in an attempt to smile. She groaned but I could not make out what she said. She had a drip-tube feeding her.

At that point, the staff nurse came in to change her nappy. I did not know that she was now in nappies. He asked me to tell her what he was going to do and asked me to help. As he rolled her over to one side, I cried. This was my beautiful talented daughter who had championed the disabled and fought against the tide all of her life, and she was reduced to this. The nurse made her comfortable. I asked what the blood was around her mouth, and he said that she had very bad mouth ulcers. He showed me how to moisten her lips with a little sponge on a stick that was resting in a jar of special pink solution on her locker. As I attempted to do this she was trying to bite on the sponge to get some fluid into her mouth, but began to cough as she did so. I panicked and lifted her forward to pat her back and was shocked when I realised that she did not have enough strength to support her head as it flopped onto her chest. I relaxed her back onto her pillow just as Nick arrived. Nick was not quite so shocked by what he saw because he had seen her just days before. I cried and John said, 'The bastards.'

I went out and met the nurse who had been sitting by Jan's bed and asked about Jan's bloodied mouth. She said, 'She was not like that before she came in here.' Even now there was denial. No-one could develop such ulcers overnight.

How much more could we take from these people.

The door to the room was open. As we all stood around Jan's cot the consultant walked past and she called out a cheery, 'Hi everyone.' I was astonished at her cheeriness. No attempt was made to come to us. I lifted my hand and motioned her to move on with a hatred I had never ever experienced before.

There was a visit from a dietician. She asked me what Jan's favourite food was. I told her that she liked most everything. She asked me to tell her of any particular food, and I asked her why she wanted to know. She told me that they needed to persuade Jan to eat. They were rehydrating her now and feeding her by tube. She explained that because Jan hadn't had solid food for a long time they had to feed her in this way first of all, then introduce solid food later. I thought they must be mad. There was no way that Jan could even try and eat in her condition. I was to learn later that she had been transferred for rehydration as a case of self-starvation.

Furthermore, it had been arranged for Jan to be seen by a speech therapist owing to our complaint that she could not now speak properly. This, to me, is proof that no one was accepting the situation as it really was. Here was a young woman who ten months earlier had been able to hold a conversation with a good command of grammar and beautiful expressiveness.

Around the time of Jan's admission to the medical hospital, the psychiatrist who had admitted Jan to the Mental Health Unit held a meeting with her staff to discuss Jan's discharge and whether, if she needed psychiatric care in the future, they would re-admit her to the unit. She said that she would most likely visit Jan at her new home at SENSE on an outpatient policy. There was no talk of Jan dying or being near to death at all.

John, then Nick and I, all tried to communicate with Jan but she was desperately ill. The male nurse came and said that the medical doctor who was now over Jan's care wanted to see us in his office. I then knew why the other doctor had gone past. This was not her neck of the woods. She had been summoned. I immediately asked whether she would be there and the nurse said that she would. I asked that we be seen without her being present, and he said it would not be possible.

In the room was the medical consultant, his junior houseman I think he was, a nursing sister and the consultant from the mental health unit. Their faces were grim.

The medical doctor began to say that Jan was now very ill. He said that they would do all that they could for her. I could tell by his tone and the fact that he had gathered other people to his room that it was very serious. I blurted out before he could go any further, 'So are you now telling us that Jan may die?'

'I'm afraid that is the case,' he replied. 'She has had a sudden deterioration in her CNS syndrome I'm afraid, but we will do all that we can.'

A *sudden* deterioration of her central nervous system syndrome? We had been saying for months that she was dying but now we were being told that it was sudden?

I can't remember exactly the order of things but I think I was the first to speak. I shouted at the consultant and asked her, 'Why did you give my daughter that medication when you knew that she was allergic to drugs?' Her reply still confounds me.

'You asked me to.'

'That is a lie. I have always asked you to refrain from giving her any drugs.'

At this stage I had no idea that the drug amitriptyline had been given in February and I later discovered that a nurse had rung through to Jan's neurologist a hundred miles away to discuss pain relief and he had suggested this. The consultant was in charge of Jan and had allowed this drug to be administered and at quite a high dose to begin with. Now she was saying I had requested it? This was preposterous and added to my opinion that she was wanting to shift the blame for what had happened to Jan onto someone else.

I know I shouted more. Then Nick said for me to be quiet so that he could speak. He also spoke his mind. Then John. After a while the male doctor said that they would leave us alone with the sister. They left the room and the psychiatric consultant never even offered a word of sympathy. In fact she did not look at us. The sister asked whether we would like a cup of tea. The rest of the time is a blur.

We had to say our good-byes to Jan and told her we would be back the next day. We needed to make arrangements so that we could stay close to the hospital.

I had been diagnosed as having a urine infection and was taking antibiotics. I knew that the infection was spreading to my kidneys as I was in so much pain, had a raging headache and high temperature. I also knew that the tablets would soon kick in. Unfortunately the next day I was worse. I was too ill to travel, but John assured me that it would be OK and for me to stay and try and get well for the next day. We had arranged to have the SENSE house again from the Monday and stay for as long as necessary. We regularly rang the hospital and were told that she was holding her own and stable. Even as I write I don't know why I didn't stay but I guess my mind did not grasp everything or did not want to. I was so exhausted and ill.

I asked John to take in a photograph of Jan and pin it above her bed. I wanted the nursing staff and doctors on the medical ward to realise that Jan was once a very capable girl, and for them to recognise that her behaviour and symptoms were not because she was deafblind. It was a picture of Jan with Sir Harry.

John came home looking much more relaxed. He said that Jan now looked much better. She was benefiting from the rehydration and was snuggled down in her bed and was in a very deep sleep while they were there. They did not disturb her. However, the male nurse had come into the ward and immediately spotted the photograph John had pinned up. He turned to John and said 'Who's that beautiful young woman with Harry Secombe?'

'You are nursing her now,' John replied.

'Never!' he exclaimed. 'Wherever did she come from in this condition?' John told him and he was not surprised but answered, 'No?'

This causes me great pain to write, but I was told that when she woke after John and Nick had left they told her she had had visitors. She managed to ask, 'And Mum?' then lapsed into unconsciousness.

Andrew had been to visit Jan before, but I am so glad he did not see her in this condition. It was enough that we had.

That night I was able to sleep like I had not slept for weeks. I thought that now that Jan was having proper nursing care she would rally round. I guess now, with the benefit of hindsight, that I was in denial really. I thought that maybe it would take a long time for her to get really well, but that she would pull through. I longed to go to her, and anxiously looked forward to seeing her on the Monday. Because it was the beginning of May and the package for her to be looked after by SENSE was to commence in May. The nursing staff from the mental health unit had withdrawn and members of SENSE had taken over. It was important for someone to be there at all times to interpret for Jan on her hands, and for the medical staff too.

We would be staying with her until she was well. I denied to myself that she was near death.

Chapter 29

That dreadful Sunday phone call had come a few days earlier and we were now, once again, in the Intensive Care Unit. It was very early in the day. We cleansed our hands and entered yet again, and as usual I immediately looked at the monitor to see whether her temperature had come down. I kissed her, gently took her hand and began to spell out on it. She looked so pretty and comfortable, and the nurses in ICU were very caring and looked after her so well.

The forty-eight-hour deadline was close, and still Jan had shown no improvement. When they told me that they were going to stop the sedative which had kept her deeply unconscious my hopes were raised. They wanted to see whether she would wake up. I was pleased to see that as she surfaced the facial grimacing had begun again. Her nose twitched and her tongue moved but she did not open her eyes. The next thing was that they needed to know whether she could breathe on her own without the aid of the life support. She could not.

We continued to go in every day and stay for some time before going to the hospital café for lunch. Then we would go in to see her again before going home. SENSE had now placed one of their team to be at Jan's bedside so that they could relay information onto Jan's hand.

On one occasion we were told by the staff nurse that they had washed out her lungs and there was a lot of horrid gunk at the bottom. Another day, a lovely junior nurse had managed to wash her hair. Jan took such pride in her hair but it had not been washed for a very long time. Now it shone its auburn colour and looked soft and silky.

The nurse said, 'I've tried to blow dry it into her usual style. I looked at some of the photos to see how she wears it.'

I gulped back the tears. I was so grateful. Then I ran my hands through Jan's hair and bent to take in her smell. The smell of a child that is unique to her mother.

On returning to our house we were asked whether we would like to go and see the flat that SENSE was preparing for Jan. They had asked us what her favourite colours were and the scent she loved most of pot-pourri; whether she had any particular likes and dislikes as far as furnishing went. But nothing prepared us for the amount of work and dedication that had gone into preparing the flat. It was all completely refurbished, and expensive furniture and fittings were in place. Even Jan's favourite plants had been chosen. The manager showed us around. It was beautiful. They had prepared a patio and were awaiting furniture and barbecue for this. The knobs on the kitchen utilities were all Brailled. The people here had been told that Jan would make a recovery and everything was planned for that time.

John and I stood in silence. I did not know what to say but in my heart I knew that Jan was not going to move here. The manager spoke in positive terms saying that they had ordered a special walk-in bath with hoist. A special ripple bed was to come. I looked at John and as our eyes met the tears just fell. Our hearts were breaking more each day. This package was to cost £182,000 per annum for Jan who had walked into the hospital with such capabilities, and no-one was asking why all of this was now necessary.

The next day, things had not changed. Now there was no information coming from the nurses at Jan's side. They just carried on with their routine nursing care but there was no mention of deadlines or of any improvement. Jan was now deeply unconscious.

I had contacted our friends Dave and Gaynor. They had lost a child after many years of hospitalisation, and I wanted someone to talk with who understood something of what we were going through. As soon as they heard our news they came rushing to the hospital. I took Gaynor to Jan's bed. David stayed with John in the waiting room, but as soon as I got to the bedside I knew. I really just knew.

I turned to Gaynor and said, 'She's gone.'

'What do you mean?'

'Gaynor, Jan has gone,' I repeated.

'No she hasn't Audrey. She's asleep,' Gaynor tried to comfort me.

The nurse then said, 'She feels cold because she's on a bed of ice. We still can't get her temperature down.'

But in my heart I knew that Jan's spirit had left her body. I cannot explain any more than that.

When we went in the next day the nurse in charge of Jan said that the doctor wanted to see us in his room, I knew what he was about to tell us. We followed the nurse as she led us to a room and asked us to take a seat and wait for the doctor.

A huge man came into the room. He appeared to be about 6'5" and was built like a haystack. A bushy beard covered his large face; his eyes were astonishingly kind. He took my hand and I felt his warmth of character as he gripped and then covered my hand with his other huge hand. He then turned and shook John's hand and settled into his seat looking down at his feet as he began to talk to us.

'I am so sorry but it is not good news,' he began. 'It is considered by several doctors that Janis is now brain stem dead. It is of course, very difficult for us to assess her owing to her lack of sight and hearing but a decision has been reached. I have to ask your permission for us to turn off the machine.' Tears were now flooding his eyes and beginning to trip over his eyelids.

I remarked that she was beginning to swell up and he confirmed this adding that it would be cruel to keep her alive on the machine.

'However, we have no idea why she has died and wondered whether you could throw any light on why this may have happened.'

How much more bizarre was all of this to become? Jan had been in hospital for ten months, transferred to the medical ward as a case of self-starvation, and now this doctor was asking me whether I knew what had caused her to die.

'She has pneumonia, we've been told,' my voice rushed out.

'Oh, that's nothing. We did a culture and she has been given the correct antibiotic. She is young and strong so pneumonia is no problem. She should have overcome that. Can you tell me anything more?' His face was creased with concern.

My mind flew all over the place. Here was a senior doctor in the ICU asking me why Janis had died. Then I had so many flashbacks pouring into my mind. All that had happened since she was admitted to the mental health unit 10 months ago. Was there a long silence? I am not sure, but I knew that I had to tell him what had happened and of our observations over the past 10 months.

I hesitated. I was worried that any accusation I made against any medical staff might be resented but I had to do what I had to do. I bent down to my handbag to get the photographs I had taken. I explained to him how Jan was when she was admitted and what had caused us to be very concerned. His face grimaced as he looked at the pictures. I began by saying that we thought that she had had a severe reaction to chlorpromazine and other drugs she had been given.

His expression changed and he sat forward in his seat. 'That explains a lot. There is such a thing as a toxic reaction to the drug Chlorpromazine. It affects the basal ganglion of the brain. There is treatment for this if it's given soon enough.'

My heart began to beat faster as my hopes rose. Was it possible that even now Janis might recover? I told the doctor that all of Jan's problems were indeed linked to the area of the brain that chlorpromazine affects.

'I'm so sorry,' he said, 'but it is too late for your daughter.'

My heart sank like a rock in water. The doctor went on: 'I must ask you, as a result of what you have just told me, whether you would give me permission to carry out a MRI.'

I told him that there had been at least three requests made over the previous months of her hospitalisation and it had been refused. I told him that Jan had even asked for this herself because she knew that something had caused problems with her brain, but this was refused too. Then I asked him why he needed our permission now. He explained that because a MRI was a magnetic imaging machine they could not put the life support system through and Jan would not breathe on her own. He went on to say that they could put extension tubes, etc., to try and keep her breathing, but there was a risk that this would not work.

I looked at John but there was no point in refusing. We both agreed that there was no option. We had been told that she was brain stem dead and that the machine should be switched off. All that was left was for us to notify Nick for his approval. He agreed that we had to let them go ahead.

The doctor began to rise to his feet and then hesitated to say, 'I'll leave it to you as to when we turn the machine off. There is no hurry. You decide when you are ready. I would say that it is not necessary for you to stay while it is switched off. Of course you can, but I must warn you that as the machine is switched off she may jerk. This is a natural reaction. You can go and see her and leave before we switch the machine off. It is entirely up to you. No one will think any the worse of you if you do not want to stay. I will be in theatre tomorrow but you must not worry. When you are ready, I will be notified and I will come to you no matter what.'

. His kindness was awesome. John and I thanked him as he left, suggesting that the sister fetch us a cup of tea.

The senior nurse returned with our tray of tea and took up her previous seat and asked if we were OK. I took the photographs and showed them to her, asking whether she had ever seen a patient admitted into hospital in this condition before. Her words were confirmation of my thoughts.

'I have seen many sick and very ill people, but I have never seen a patient in this condition at the point of admission, I am very sorry!'

We drank our hot tea and then went back to see Jan. I went behind the now pulled around curtains. She looked, as ever, beautiful and peaceful. The tubes that had administered food, drink and medicines were now discarded, and all that was there to show that she was desperately ill was the breathing tube in her mouth. Her chest rose and fell as before. She looked so normal and peaceful and yet she was considered to be dead. It was hard to accept and I did not want to. The nurse informed us that they would be taking her for a MRI in the afternoon and suggested that we went home and waited for news there.

'You can ring as often as you want to and it will be no trouble.' She asked whether we wanted to know anything else. We shook our heads and left for home.

The house was so peaceful. The sun was bright. I decided to go for a walk in the field at the rear of the property. I needed space and some fresh air, and time to gather my thoughts. Space to be and do what I needed to do without question. I walked in the beautiful spring sunshine in the field, which had far reaching views. Daffodils were heralding the birth of new life. I could hear children's voices and laughter wafting on the air. There was a large house in the far distance and a family gathered around a barbecue. It troubled my soul and more tears poured down my face. I walked slowly and limply. All strength was leaving my body. I wanted to flop to the ground. I could not speak or shout; I was totally spent. I returned to the house and John was slumped on the sofa lost in his thoughts.

I rang Nick and Andy to tell them the dreadful news and then made arrangements for them to come to the hospital the next day when the machine would be switched off. I asked Nick again about organ donation and it was agreed by all of us that if something positive was to come out of this then we should do it. I did not need persuading. I knew that Jan would have wanted to help as many people as she could and there were so many of her organs, or so I thought at the time, that could be used for the benefit of others.

I then rang the hospital to see whether the MRI had been carried out. The senior nurse told me to ring back later, as there was a problem. Immediately I thought that maybe Jan was not breathing and the end had come earlier than anyone expected. I pressed her to tell me what had happened but she repeated that I should ring later. When I eventually got through I was shocked at what I was being told. The nurse conveyed, as best she could, that the scan had shown that Jan was massively brain damaged 'from ear to ear' were her words. My voice caught in my throat as I asked what she meant.

'She is so badly brain damaged. The consultant couldn't read the scan. It has been decided that other experts should be called.'

I can't remember what I said, but I guess I thanked her as she said for me and John to try and get a good night's sleep before going to the hospital next day.

Sleep would not come. I wanted to ring the hospital but what was the point? Jan was now considered dead. My mind would not, did not, accept this. I thought that maybe she could be kept alive for as long as we wanted on the machine. We would look after her. There would be a miracle cure. So many thoughts and emotions flooded my tired brain. I did not want her to go.

Other thoughts penetrated my mind and I heard the doctor saying, 'It is cruel to keep her alive in this way.' Now we were being told that she was massively brain damaged. How would Jan ever cope with that if she was to wake up one day? My mind went over and over it, finding no resolution. It was all now a matter of trying to come to terms with the inevitable.

CHAPTER 30

Two ladies from the offices at SENSE, who had been looking after our welfare during our many stays at the house, offered to drive us to the hospital the next day, as John felt unable to concentrate. They offered to stay with us for as long as we wanted. They were so kind and did not intrude at all. They were just there for us, occasionally placing a hand on our shoulders as we wept. We went back and forth to see Jan. I told her over and over how much she meant to me and just how much I loved her. And yet my love was impotent.

All of my being wanted to do what a mother should do – to care and protect, to make better. I asked her for forgiveness. I begged of her to forgive me any mistakes I had made throughout her life. Then I promised her that I would do all that I possibly could to bring about justice and recognition of what had happened to her. That the denial to her of dignity and respect that I felt had taken place would be brought to light. She was even denied the rights of a dying person until she was admitted to the medical ward. She had been on the floor for months before that.

We returned again and again to the waiting room. Nick and Andy had been held up on the M6 as there had been a dreadful accident. I guess it was about lunchtime when they arrived. Nick looked very pale, and the strain of the driving and what lay ahead told on his face. He came into the room and wept. I tried to comfort him as best I could.

We all went into the ICU, going through the usual procedures. We arrived at Jan's bed. It was still curtained off and only one nurse was by her side now and there was no monitor blinking. There was no need for any further input. This struck me as I stood at Jan's side. Two weeks of fighting to save her and all had failed. Her cheeks were still pink and her hair shone. We took it in turns to speak to her. All of our inner private thoughts laid down on her tiny hand.

Then we were summoned into the room we had been taken to the day before. The same humble doctor came to us. He was dressed in his theatre gown and had a mask pulled down under his chin. He apologised for his manner of dress explaining that he had come straight from theatre. We assured him we were comfortable with that. He took a seat in front of the four of us. He addressed Andy and Nick this time, and went over the same information as the day before.

I do nott know when I mentioned the organ donation but his answer was that he would look into it for us. Eventually we all stood up and the huge doctor led the way back into the ICU ward. He stood a little way away from us.

I had decided that I could not bear to watch the switching off of the machine. I wanted to run out of the ward – out of the hospital and never have any of this to intrude into my mind ever again. I walked to where the curtains were drawn but instead of walking past I burst in to be with Jan for the last time. I could not leave her yet, although I must. I lifted her 'hearing hand' and kissed the palm, and placed it gently back at her side. Then I kissed her face many, many times and buried my own face in her thick hair and gulped down the scent of her for the final time. I never ever wanted to forget her scent, the scent which is unique to a mother.

Then John came to her side and I waited while he told her whatever was in his heart. Finally, we both turned and left her, never to see her again. My heart was now completely broken.

Nick and Andrew wanted to stay. John and I returned to the waiting room where the two ladies had been waiting for us. There was another couple in there too. I beckoned to the women so that we could go and find some other place of privacy but the couple, obviously seeing our distress, automatically got up and gestured for us to stay as they left the room.

It seemed an age and yet I guess it wasn't too long before Andrew came into the room, his eyes and face red from crying. Nick followed. His face was ashen. He said, 'It was very peaceful. The colour just drained from her face but she didn't move.'

Before we left I needed to see the doctor again. As I stepped out of the room he was looking for us. He apologised, and said that they could not use Jan's organs. I asked whether it was because of her rare syndrome and he nodded. I accepted that was the reason, but I was soon to find out that there was to be an autopsy and Jan's body was to undergo terrible invasion. Even in death she was not to be left in peace, it seemed.

It is all rather a blur, but I do know that after spending almost two weeks in the ICU we were to just walk out into the normal daily activities of the world. There was no one there to counsel or help us in any way. If there was we did not meet them. We made our way back to the house. The ladies had arranged for someone to set out another lovely lunch and there was a card and some flowers set on the table. We ate what we could. Then Nick and Andy drove back to Peterborough. We said we would stay and collect the death certificate and then go home.

But there was not only to be an autopsy to ascertain the cause of her death but an inquest as well. My immediate thought was that this would delay the funeral, but we were instructed that once they had finished all of the autopsy work we could have Jan home.

John and I returned to Peterborough, stopping on the way for me to buy a suit for the funeral. Why I needed to do so at that time I am not sure, but I was in a daze and on automatic pilot, it seemed. Everything and everyone around seemed to be as if in some terrible nightmare from which I could not wake.

Once home, we had to await further instructions and prepare for the funeral. A couple of days later we had a call from the coroner's office to ask whether we would give permission for Jan's brain to be taken. The coroner's assistant explained that it could not be ascertained what had caused the brain damage, and so it was necessary for the brain to be taken and sent to various scientists. To add to our pain, he said that the brain is like a jelly and it was necessary to take it out and allow it to set before they could begin work on it. I felt so ill. I am normally very squeamish anyway, but this was just so terrible. When the brain was out we could have the body. It was explained as coldly as that.

I wept again and pulled at my hair in the hope that I could pull out this entire dreadful traumatic ordeal forever.

My anger was so great and I needed for justice to be seen, and I started looking for ways to ensure it. I came across a woman who works for the BBC. She is an artist and draws the pictures that one sees when a huge court case is presented in the press. Her mother had died through medical neglect and she had set up a helpline. I contacted her. When I told her briefly what had happened, she was most helpful. She suggested that I might contact the police to see whether we had a case of involuntary manslaughter. She even mentioned corporate manslaughter, owing to the fact that we had contacted so many people at the health trust and had had negative responses to our continual persistence that Jan was dying. She also said that we must insist on a jury for the inquest.

I contacted our local police station and spoke with the chief inspector there. In turn he gave me the number of the chief inspector in whose district the hospital was. He was very sympathetic, but did say that I would have great difficulty as medical cases were always extremely hard to prove. As for corporate manslaughter, he said we would have an almost impossible fight on our hands and he drew my attention to the Hillsborough tragedy. However, he did go on to say that when we had the verdict of the inquest we should ring him again and he would take it from there. Nevertheless, he did stress that most inquests of this type were usually unsatisfactory in that they almost always returned a verdict of death from natural causes, or a verdict that relatives were usually very disappointed with, and not to build our hopes up.

Because there was some media coverage of Jan's death and impending inquest, several reporters were pestering me for a story. However, I was advised by the BBC woman that I must not tell them anything until after the inquest was finished as there would be an embargo on the case.

I will jump ahead a little further for now. The inquest had been officially opened and adjourned. Little did we know that it would take a further eighteen months or more before it was held. Expert witnesses were to be called and many investigations had to be undertaken. Nor did we realise that it would cover two days and that there would to be a jury. I wrote many letters to the coroner as thoughts came to mind. I did not want to leave a stone unturned in my endeavour to fulfil my promise to Jan.

On the day before the inquest the family stayed in the SENSE house. The staff at SENSE had kindly arranged for a taxi to collect us on both days to take us to the court. There were other family and friends waiting there to support us.

I wish to pay particular tribute to an organisation called ASSIST in Rugby. This is a helpline for trauma victims. I found the counsel of Barbara and her assistant Betty of immeasurable help after Jan died. I spoke on the phone to them over several months but did not meet them until the inquest. When we arrived at court both of them were there waiting to support us. They had travelled by train to be there and were with us throughout the whole two days, not interfering but standing by us in case we needed their help. Just the fact that they were there was a tremendous support for me, and the odd look across from the balcony where they sat to me lower down in the well of the court was encouraging. Thank you to both of you for your unswerving support.

Nothing can prepare any parent for any of this, but more was to come. To hear my child being discussed in such abstract terms was most dreadful, and when the pathologist began to say that he 'sliced into the brain' I cried out. Everyone was silent and my cries seemed to reverberate around the court. The coroner asked whether I wanted to stay or leave the court. If I stayed I would have to remain quiet. It was as cold as that.

Before this, though, I was surprised when the pathologist began his evidence by asking the coroner whether he could change his opinion of the cause of death. The coroner asked him why and approval was given. He changed the cause of death from cerebral damage and pneumonia to pneumonia and cerebral damage. This perplexed me fleetingly at the time, but later caused me to ask why was this necessary after eighteen months. What had caused him to change his mind? No one asked him and he never said, and I never did find out.

Several witnesses were called. Jan's brain had been sent to Edinburgh for examination for the human form of mad cow disease. It had also been sent to London, but none of the scientists were able to ascertain what caused the brain damage.

The solicitor we employed was hoping to show that it was the drugs that were the cause. However, the drugs expert stated that all of the drugs given were of the correct strength and that there was no evidence to show that this could be the case. There was no discussion about possible drug sensitivities.

We had paid for a psychoneurotoxicologist, a Dr Ray Singer in America to give his opinion on the case. I found him during my research on the effects of these drugs on the brain. I was recommended to approach him as he is an eminent doctor in this field. His web site ***www.neurotox.com*** shows the following:

<u>Expertise</u>: *Neuropsychology, nervous system effects of toxic substances (neurobehavioural toxicity, neurotoxicology), expert testimony, forensic services.*

<u>Description:</u> *Toxic chemicals can damage the nervous system and the brain. A person may or may not be aware of such damage when it occurs. Neurotixicity is the result of such damage. Symptoms may include problems with memory, concentration, reaction time, sleep, thinking, language, as well as depression, numbness of the hands and feet, confusion, and personality changes. Many types of nervous system disorders could be related with neurotoxicity, including numerous neurologic and psychiatric disorders. Legal problems may result from irrational, unusual or violent behaviour.*

As soon as I read this, it seemed as though he was discussing Janis. She had all of these symptoms. My heart was beating so quickly as I read. I was lost in the rush of adrenaline it caused and excitement grew until I came back to earth and realised that there was nothing that could be done for Janis now. But maybe for others?

Dr Singer's report to us as evidence was not used in court. I give more details of this report later.

When the consultant psychiatrist gave her evidence it was clear that at times she was lost for answers, and when our solicitor cross-questioned her she raised her hands to her head saying, 'I've lost it,' or words to that effect. The coroner asked her for her official diagnosis of Jan's illness and she said that in her opinion she was suffering an adjustment disorder (she wrote to my daughter's GP after she died saying she had been suffering a borderline personality disorder). I remember thinking, 'people don't die of adjustment disorders'!

The coroner asked one of the senior nurses how it was that Janis had sustained bangs to her head, a black eye and split lip, and she replied that she did not know. Later I was to discover, in her medical records, that Janis sustained many injuries owing to her being made to wash, shower and brush her teeth while standing. Unfortunately, unless nursing care can be suspected of contributing to the cause of death, an inquest is not really concerned with it and so this distressing aspect of Jan's treatment was not openly discussed to the extent that I believe it should have been.

The two days were intense and terribly draining. Half way through them, our solicitor said that we had a fifty-fifty chance of bringing a verdict of negligence, but added that often the verdict went the other way.

It was after lunch on the second day that the coroner began his summing up. Before he did so he asked whether anyone wanted to say anything more. I had asked our solicitor that we show the photographs,. showing Jan's state before she was taken to intensive care, to the jury. She had failed to do this. I had told the family that I was determined that the jury should see them and I would do whatever it took. Nick said he thought perhaps I shouldn't, but I think I persuaded him. So as the coroner invited any further comments my heart began pumping very hard and time ticked by. I was almost too late before my hand shot up in the air. The coroner said that I should speak through my attorney; she in turn stood and said that I wanted some photos to be shown.

The coroner did not hesitate but invited me to take the oath. He asked first of all that he see the photos, and then asked me whether I would like to say anything. I spoke loud and clear. In fact it seemed to me as though I was shouting. Every part of my body shook and tears choked me and poured down my face. In brief, I told the court about our previous experience of the affect of drugs on Jan and that she had almost died and the result on that occasion. I spoke about our observations on this occasion. But when I spoke about the doctor's attitude the coroner pulled me up by saying that this would not be allowed in court and that I must simply stick to the facts as I saw them.

Eventually the photos were shown and the jury asked whether they could take them out with them when they retired. I was pleased that I had had some of my say, but it had come out of me in a very unprepared fashion as I had previously been told that I would not be called into the witness box.

After I had finished I could hardly stand, and Nick quickly came to my aid and helped me back to my seat. Then the coroner turned to the jury and addressed them. He began by saying what a bonnie girl Jan was. But he then went on to say that we had heard an expert on drugs give his opinion, and we had also heard other people. The brain damage had never been ascertained. He went on a little more, but then to our surprise he said that they must sum up the proceedings and went through the possible causes set down. I am not sure of the exact wording but he added that a verdict of death from natural causes would be the correct one. He said that as far as the brain damage was concerned, 'In life she was a mystery and so in death.'

I was absolutely gobsmacked. We had had a two-day hearing and the jury had listened throughout, but now they were being more or less told what their verdict should be.

The jury was out for about forty minutes. They returned the verdict that Janis died from natural causes, these being bronchial pneumonia and cerebral damage. The court was dismissed. I was at least hoping that they would have added 'attributable to medical neglect'.

Chapter 31

My promise to Jan was now to begin. We had not been able to have her medical records, as the solicitor and the coroner held these, but now I asked to see them. I also asked the chief executive of the hospital for a full and proper inquiry. She said that I would have to go through the NHS complaint procedure. I did not have a clue as to what lay ahead but I met enormous amounts of bureaucracy and doors were slammed in my face time and time again.

I even got in touch with David Blunkett, who was stunned to hear of Jan's death. He wrote to say that he had passed my letter onto Alan Milburn, who in turn asked the appropriate Local Area Health Authority to carry out a full investigation. Over a period of two years I never ever heard from them, in spite of my many letters and faxes. My phone calls to them met with excuse after excuse as to why I could not speak to the appointed person. I was frequently told that he would ring me back but he never did. Months later our local paper took this up with the hospital trust and the LAHA. There was a double page spread of the facts of the case. The LAHA said that they had not conducted an investigation because I was taking the case to the NHS Ombudsman but at the time they were asked to make their inquiries we hadn't even got around to going to the Ombudsman.

I eventually received the medical records and began going through the nine box files of notes. I rose from my bed at 3 o'clock the next morning and continued ploughing through them. They were colossal and often difficult to read. Eventually, after almost nine hours of reading, I came across some vital information.

A gastrologist had been called to see Jan when the staff had told us that she had a tummy bug when she had diarrhoea shortly before she died. In the notes, the gastrologist had written that Jan's bowels were badly impacted and he had drawn a diagram of the bowels with an arrow pointing and the words 'ROCKS HERE!' He said that she needed high up enemas, and maybe surgical procedures might be necessary. The diarrhoea was overflow and it was coming from both ends.

I read on. The facial grimacing (which we had been told was Jan grinding her teeth) had become much worse and a neurologist had been called. This was indicative of encephalopathy (an inflammation of the brain) and he had initiated a CAT scan. He then wrote of the results, that Jan had brain atrophy beyond her years, that there was swelling and encephalopathy, which had been present for some time and which would account for her symptoms and had nothing to do with her syndrome which had changed little since the age of two. No one, not one person, had mentioned any of this to us. Furthermore, the appropriate drugs were not given to stop the swelling of the brain, and even worse she was referred to the general hospital as a case of self-starvation. Why was this knowledge kept secret even at the inquest? Then I discovered that there was an internal memo from the Chief Medical Officer thanking the consultant for her excellent report on the death of Jan and suggested that she should add that Jan was suffering from Refsum's disease and also Lupus. Jan did not have either of these conditions so why was it deemed appropriate to add this to the report?

My adrenaline was pumping and my anger raging. I knew that there was more to this than we had been told. Why was she allowed to go on for so long without proper intervention?

I pursued the NHS trust for an inquiry and it was refused every time. I wrote to David Blunkett as I have already mentioned, and the result of that was nothing. I wrote to the GMC and it was thrown out.

I again contacted the Mental Health Commission people and was told they would look into the case. Yet again we were thwarted. Their reply was shocking. Because there was a lapse of time between Jan being sectioned there was nothing that they could do. Was it possible that they thought that she could discharge herself at these times? If this is the case then they certainly need to look again. Janis was too ill to be moved.

Eventually I wrote to the NHS Ombudsman. They took up the case. I was told that only about 27% of all cases referred to them were taken on, so at last I felt that we had some hope of an explanation, and justice for Janis in her memory. But I have to say that even at this stage it would have saved a great deal of stress, and taxpayer's money, if the psychiatrist had had the guts to call at our home. If she had admitted that things had gone terribly wrong, said that she was dreadfully sorry, and looked into what they could all learn from this experience, I would most probably have invited her in and sat down with her and talked. We are all human and everyone makes mistakes, but this mistake was truly unforgivable in my eyes. Nonetheless an apology would have gone a long way to help me and the family in accepting what had happened.

At a time when my grief was such that I was tormented almost out of my mind, I received a booklet from someone on the subject of forgiveness. I tried, I really tried, but was not able to forgive on this occasion. All that had happened was beyond my ability to forgive this time. Then I read an article in the Daily Mail which said that to ask any parent to forgive the person who has killed their child is wrong.

I contacted Trisha Goddard, the TV host who is into mental health care issues. She rang me and gave me some people I might contact, but again this proved to be futile.

I was told that I had to go through the NHS procedures before the Ombudsman could intervene. These were very slow. I was now extremely exhausted and felt that I could not go on. Then I decided to phone the chief executive of Deafblind UK, Jackie Hicks. She had known Janis for a number of years. I explained my plight to her and told her that I had a great deal of evidence to support my case but could not continue on my own owing to my health not being good. She said that she would come out to see me.

After I had told her, briefly, what had happened, she asked whether she could take the records and all of my documentation away and she would come back to me with her decision. Within a few days she had decided from the evidence she had that she wanted to fight with me to bring resolution to the whole affair.

She attended the national health local resolution meeting with me and supported me throughout. In this meeting we were promised by the chief executive that she would make sure we would have an independent review of the whole case. This was ultimately refused.

However, Jackie was determined to help me to see this through and when I told her that I was referring it to the NHS Ombudsman she promised that she would draw up her report from the medical records in front of her. She worked solidly for several days, often going to her office hours before her usual time and working late. She provided a lengthy and factual report for the Ombudsman.

After more than two years and a great deal of correspondence and a visit from the case worker from The NHS Ombudsman's office, who interviewed us yet again in spite of all of the correspondence and phone calls, we were told that an expert witness was to be called.

During that time the expert witness travelled up from Cornwall to meet with the case worker at the hospital to interview the consultant concerned. I was advised of the date and I was on tenterhooks all day. The next day I could not hold back and rang to see how things had gone.

Perhaps I should not have been surprised but nonetheless I was when my case worker said that the consultant had not turned up. Apparently she had rung in sick the day before and they did not know. My case worker said that she would be made to attend and another date had been fixed. This went according to plan and I was told that now they had to wait for the expert's report.

I waited and I waited. After several weeks I rang to ask whether the report was finalised only to be told that the expert had had a heart attack and that the notes he had made were not decipherable so his secretary could not type up his report. Several months passed before his report was handed in.

Finally almost five years after Jan's death we had the report from the Ombudsman. In this, the neuropathologist(the expert witness) said that 'death was due to bronchial pneumonia and adult respiratory distress syndrome, and myocardial and cerebral hypoxia (lack of oxygen to the heart and brain). How these fit together in the light of clinical history is unclear'. The consultant neuropathologist considered the suggestion that medication had damaged Mrs. Cooper's brain, and while he said that it was conceivable that evidence of such had been destroyed by the severe terminal damage, he could not link any of the factors in the death to the therapeutic regime.

I further include some extracts from the report:

'No evidence of neuro-degenerative disorder or other pre-existing cerebral pathology was found, apart from optic atrophy. It is conceivable, however, that evidence of such a disorder was destroyed by the severe acute damage.

'In our opinion, the choice of drugs was appropriate, as was the dosage used. Although the possibility of an extremely rare, idiosyncratic adverse reaction cannot be absolutely excluded'.

The drugs used were thioridazine, then fluoxetine and zoplicone (at the same time as fluoxetine). Because there was no improvement and 'because Mrs. Cooper was more unhappy' she was given chlorpromazine. At this stage of the report, amitriptyline is not mentioned but discussed later. Also diazepam was used. These are the drugs mentioned in the report, but I do know that she was given a cocktail of painkilling drugs together with a antihistamine drug for several weeks, and this made her feel very ill.

The consultant also stated in the report that, after Jan's condition deteriorated, 'she had lain in a foetal position in an almost catatonic state and it was thought that she was suffering from a depressive illness'. Why did the psychiatrist not talk with Jan to ascertain whether she was depressed or whether there might be another cause? She prescribed a daily dose of 20 mgs fluoxetine (an anti-depressant) in early July, and this eventually rose to a dose of 30/40 mgs. The psychiatrist said that she would not usually prescribe more than 20 mgs of fluoxetine and took advice from the pharmacist. She was concerned that Mrs. Cooper was not eating or drinking and she did not want to use electroconvulsive therapy.

The psychiatrist had also stated during the investigation that I had asked for amitriptyline to be administered. Yet again, this doctor was stating that the mother of her patient had asked for this and that she had complied? Furthermore, lower down in the report it states:

A further letter to the neurologist from a Staff Nurse at (the clinic) dated January 20th 1999 included:

'(Mrs Cooper) has been complaining of moderate to severe pain in her right shoulder, lower back and both palms of her hands...

'I am writing to ask if you have any suggestions regarding...the treatment of her pain relief. We would be grateful if you could recommend any treatment...'

The neurologist replied on 23rd January. He wrote:

'...(this pain) sounds musculoskeletal in origin. It may be that her regular non-steroidal anti inflammatory agents such as Diclomax taken in conjunction with a tryciclic (an anti-depressant) such as amitriptyline 50 mg at night might help......'

This evidence in the report contradicted the accusation by the consultant that I had requested the use of amitriptyline, as stated in the same report and at the time when we were told Jan was dying. Why was the consultant so entrenched in her opinion? How could a professional report not see the fact that there were obvious inconsistencies?

The psychiatrist also stated in the report that Janis was well enough to go home at Christmas. This was another inaccuracy. Janis was terribly ill and never came home at or around that time. As I have already reported, Janis rang us from the clinic begging to be taken out of the place. She was in a very poor condition at this stage.

The consultant further stated, in the report, that after Christmas Janis deteriorated physically and went on a virtual hunger strike. Yet, there were no weight charts kept in the clinic or in her records.

This statement of a hunger strike is confirmation to me that throughout this time and the months that followed, Janis was blamed for not eating. In our frequent phone calls we continually heard it suggested that Janis was strong willed and determined and refusing to co-operate. In fact she could not feel her mouth, teeth, eventually had no control at all, her stomach was going into spasms and she was in and out of consciousness a great deal of the time.

The report went on:

'If the family had been warned some months ahead that death as well as improvement was a possible outcome, they would have had more time to begin to absorb the possibility, but none of the experts who saw Mrs. Cooper foresaw this possibility'.

'On 26th April Mrs. Cooper was seen by the Consultant Physician but he declined to admit her (to a medical ward). On 27th April, when she was clearly dehydrated, he admitted her but on condition that a bed at (the mental health unit) would be kept open.

'The assessors have commented that this appeared to be a somewhat harsh requirement from the Consultant Physician'.

'The psychiatrist did not expect Mrs. Cooper's condition to deteriorate as quickly as it did'.

In fact, the consultant psychiatrist had now given her opinion to the Ombudsman's enquiry that Jan's rare syndrome may have been the cause of her death. Yet, at the inquest, she had insisted that Jan merely had a behavioural problem and that her rapid deterioration came as a surprise. This more or less confirms, in my opinion, that the doctor did not see that Jan was dying, did not expect it to happen, and was not interested in investigating any other known potential causes of Jan's condition until it was too late. No medical notes suggest that the syndrome was taken into account in Jan's treatment, and the coroner would probably not have been called had the ICU staff been made aware of Jan's true situation.

There was nothing in the report about the nursing care provided in the clinic, nor about the terrible state Jan's body was in because of this, nor about her severely impacted bowels with overflow which was said by the nursing team to be due to a bug she had caught. The report never looked at the fact that treatment to a patient with encephalopathy should be to maintain a regular bowel movement possibly at least twice a day, nor that she could have received drug therapy to reduce the swelling of her brain or any of the other nursing concerns that we had. Neither did it mention the fact that she could not speak, was doubly incontinent, paralysed, then had to be catheterised because she could not pass water, and the many other matters I have discussed. She was in the most dreadful state, and in my opinion no one would keep an animal in a room on the floor in that state.

In conclusion, the complaint was not upheld.

I was incredulous. All of the self-evident grounds for finding unquestionable fault with Jan's treatment flowed through my mind, and my disbelieve turned to outrage at the way every official involved seemed to develop instant obtuseness. My response to the Ombudsman's report was acerbic and to the point.

> *I am absolutely alarmed by the statement (that an MRI would*
> *have made no difference) because had this been done then*
> *preventative steps could have been taken such as the administration*
> *of a drug such as mannitel, and probably intravenous steroids*
> *would have prevented the brain from swelling so alarmingly causing*

so much damage and terrible distress to Mrs Cooper. Furthermore, Mrs Cooper could and should have been given the respect and rights of a dying patient.

Not one of the experts named in the report was there at the time, and they had no first-hand evidence of what was happening. However, I have many witnesses and you have my records. I ask you to show me the documentation of records kept by Dr..... and her staff that suggests that Mrs Cooper was suffering a terminal illness and accepts the fact that she was dying. There is none. If there was, then nothing was produced in court as evidence, and nothing was said by Dr..... or her staff that this was so.

Dr..... had been at that unit for about five years. In that time, two young patients have died. The staff nurse at the ..... hospital told us, on the day of Mrs Cooper's transfer, how shocked he was at her condition, that they had admitted another patient from there, and that they had had others before her.

How long is it going to be before someone listens and takes note that this doctor is out of her depth and lies when it suits her to do so?

If it is considered acceptable for a patient to have:
- *impacted bowels to the point of overflow from both ends,*
- *an ulcerated and bleeding mouth,*
- *paralysis,*
- *liver problems,*
- *facial grimacing,*
- *gasping for breath,*
- *being unable to eat because of her stomach continually going into spasm,*
- *inability to feel where her mouth was and to contain food in her mouth because of lack of sensation, yet being accused of deliberately not eating,*
- *double incontinence but being accused of deliberately wetting the bed,*
- *to be diagnosed as having behavioural problems and of being deliberately responsible for all of her ailments until finally rushed to the ..... hosptal - but only as a case of self-starvation,*

then this is a clear indictment of the psychiatric profession and shows clearly how every event has been twisted.

The fact that evidence of drug misuse has, conveniently for the doctor, been destroyed by massive brain damage that was beyond the comprehension of many experts, does not detract from the fact *that excuses and assumptions have been made to cover up what was, in my estimation, gross negligence.*

In closing, I know without a shadow of a doubt that Dr..... consistently, and without for one moment hesitating in that opinion, held to her diagnosis of an adjustment disorder throughout Mrs Cooper's illness and later in court. Mrs Cooper was continually blamed for her own condition, and Dr..... was arrogant and dismissive of our concerns and observations.

God forbid that this should happen to another of her patients.

* * * * *

Now I will print the report that I received from Dr. Ray Singer and which was sent to the Ombudsman. I had supplied Dr. Singer with my notes and observations plus the medical reports and post mortem histology. His report reads as follows:

Comments regarding the Neurobehavioural 'Toxicology Assessment of the Death of Lauren Cooper'

My preliminary opinions

a. I did not have time to review all of the details of the medical records; however the following are my opinions to date.

b. It is likely that Lauren had a progressive neurological disorder that eventually affected her cognitive function.

c. It also appears likely that her neurological condition was missed by her treating physicians at..........................(the mental health unit). They treated her as if they could cure her by withholding 'reinforcement for disruptive behaviour, while in fact Lauren was distressed and required sympathetic, humanistic support.

d. The doctors treated her with lots of drugs. These drugs have significant side effects, some of which can hurt the nervous system. It appears likely that Lauren's nervous system was already compromised, prior to her treatment at the...............hospital. Adding drugs to Lauren's nervous system, which was already in a weakened state, may be adding insult to injury.

e. Without a more comprehensive review of the medical records, it is difficult for me to predict Lauren's death at age 34. If indeed this was predicted by her medical condition, then it should be in her medical record. If such a prediction is not in her medical records, it is possible that this prediction is a mere afterthought, and that Lauren's death was hastened by stressful psychiatric treatment, including excessive use of drugs.

f. With reservations as described above, it appears likely to me that Lauren's death was hastened by harsh psychiatric treatment, including excessive drugs.

g. Given more time for me to review materials, I reserve the possibility of altering or changing my opinion, depending upon the facts of the case.

When we received this we felt that we had enough evidence to support our claims of negligence and misdiagnosis. I contacted Dr. Singer again and he said he would prefer to do a fuller report but owing to lack of time with the impending inquest I asked him whether he would be prepared to attend the inquest if I could persuade the coroner to allow it. He agreed. The request was refused and our solicitor informed me that I could not decide which experts would be called. It was all in the hands of the coroner. Yet again my attempts to bring an expert to confirm what we already believed were thwarted.

* * * * *

The rejection by the Ombudsman of our complaint was the end of the line for us. Unless we could show new evidence to support a further inquiry the case was closed. Of course, we could take the case to The High Court of Justice and the Court of Human Rights. If ever there was a case to be heard on the human rights issue I truly felt this was one.

It was a very difficult decision for me. I wanted to fight on. I intractably believed that everything was obvious to the consultant and her staff but that they did not see. Could it be that things had gone too far and they could not by then admit to their failings?

The report was a terrible blow. I really held to the fact that the things that happened to Jan would be seen as a terrible indictment on our health care system. Now I had to concentrate on this book to inform people, and above all to restore the dignity to Janis that I believe was stripped from her in that mental health unit; to show just how incredible she was and how much tenacity and rarity of spirit she had. However, in the end she could not overcome. I hope above all else that I have done enough to bring to light all that I initially endeavoured to do.

In my research I discovered that a young man in the USA had died because of isolation and restraint whilst in a mental health hospital. He was also deafblind. People had fought for him and brought about changes in the law to outlaw isolation or restraint. And yet I saw first hand that this was used on my daughter. Isolated in her room until she stopped screaming, and restrained by injection. It was the most appalling time of her life and mine. In my opinion she died without dignity or respect. She lay for months like a wild animal on the floor in a padded room crying that she had had enough. In my opinion she was even denied the rights of a dying person.

Eventually I had to accept that I could not put myself through any more stress. My grief had been expressed and its progress halted. I needed to recover some strength and health. But I am still able to sit at my computer and write, and I need to tell people our story. If it saves anyone else from undergoing anything near what Jan sustained in those ten months, or maybe brings changes in our mental health system, all of my effort has been worthwhile.

I rang Angela on The Brain & Spinal Helpline to tell her the news. She had been a great support to me all the way through. When she heard the results of the report she was shocked. Again I asked her whether encephalopathy was an instant thing. Her reply was that it must have been there for a very long time. She is a wonderfully informed and kind person and I will be forever grateful to her for her ongoing support and counsel.

Ours was not an easy road to travel but we managed, even though it was often rocky. Would I have changed it for another? I would not have wanted to miss out on Janis – the whole person that she was – deaf and blind with physical problems, but first and foremost a wonderfully funny, loving and talented individual who brought so much joy into my life. I learnt so much along the way; I experienced so much joy and met some wonderful people too. I am reminded again that 'in the midst of great sorrow can be found depths of joy'.

CHAPTER 32

Andy phoned family and friends to tell them about Jan's death and the funeral arrangements. He did a splendid job. John and I were just too bereft to speak to anyone. Nick made arrangements for the hospitality and we all came together to discuss the finer details of the funeral ceremony. We decided that it was to be arranged as we thought Jan would have liked it.

It was a strange coincidence that during a family funeral a couple of years before, Jan had said to me that when she died she did not want sad hymns or prayers said. She wanted people to remember her sense of fun and love of music, and so this was arranged.

As we walked into the crematorium the song "My Love My Life", by Abba, was played. It was a favourite from Jan's Abba collection. The words snatched at my heart as we stood until the song finished. I could hold back my tears no longer and sobbed. Then we had a soloist from Peterborough Cathedral to sing Jan's favourite hymn "Make me an Instrument of Thy Peace". Rodney Clarke, the then Chief Executive of SENSE, gave the address and spoke of Jan's courage, sense of fun and her inspiring nature, also her love for life and her music. Then we had played a recording of "Salute to the Royal Children" played by HM Royal Marine Band, followed by another recording of Jan playing a composition on piano called "Benny's Song". She loved this. It was taken from the Crossroads programme on TV and I remembered how she had cried so much when Benny's girlfriend had died. There was a two minute silence. Finally another Abba tune, "Thank You for the Music".

The family sat at the front of the crematorium in silence and I looked again at the coffin with the flower arrangement formed in the shape of JAN. She was not here; the part that was Jan was somewhere all over the country being cut up and dissected. I reflected upon the time I stood by her bed with Gaynor and was aware that she was not in her body, that something – maybe her spirit – had gone. Her rare spirit which had enabled her to achieve, enjoy and do so much in her thirty-four years, in the end, unable to overcome. I hoped with all that was within me that that part of her which was so unique and incomparable was now free. Free to be whatever, or whomever. Finally free from any further assaults on her earthly body.

I longed to hold her once more and to smell her beauty. The wonderful scent that I will never ever lose. I wanted to nuzzle my face into her thick auburn hair.

The music stopped. We all sat in silence for a minute or two until the ushers came to lead us out of the chapel and into the grounds to where the many flowers had been laid. So many people, some of whom I had never met, filed past. They spoke their words of sympathy and love for Jan, and many spoke of the girl who had challenged and inspired them. Her tutors from college spoke of her fine mind and the joy they derived from teaching her.

A lady who had helped Jan in her home stopped to tell me how Janis had turned her life around. When I asked her how, she went on to explain that her son had killed himself just a year before she went to work for Jan. She was in torment of spirit herself and near to suicide, but on her first day in Jan's home she heard Janis playing "Nellie the Elephant" loudly on her organ. As she played she was beaming from ear to ear. The lady explained how it helped her to see that she must take each day for what it held, and on that day she had been moved to hear and see the joy that Jan had in her in spite of her disabilities. I thanked her.

It took a long while for everyone to pass by and give their condolences. Before I made my way to the funeral car I took a moment to glance through the cards attached to the flowers. My eyes rested on the one Andrew had attached. It simply read:

'Fly free Jan. Love, your brother xxxxxxxx'

My grief is boundless. It has neither height nor depth, it is all consuming. Every day without her is torment and I clasp tight to the memory of her rare and beautiful spirit which enables to me to go on.

TEAR
1981
By Janis Revell

It grieved alone, quietly, grey upon the chin,
A drop of something from the heart. From somewhere deep within.
A sign of something. Joy? No, sorrow:
It grieved not for itself alone, but for the tears to follow.

It hesitated on the chin, and whimpered a soft lament –
Afraid of falling feet below or wherever it was sent;
Alone it stayed, trembling, just beneath the cheek,
A herald of another; the herald of the weak?

It shimmered, shook and sighed, so loathe,
To leave its maker's sore
And bloodshot eyes and running nose,
To fall upon the floor.

But worse of all it feared to see
Another tear upon the shore.
For that would be too hard to bear –
It sighed and dripped onto the floor....

****

"This book is a gift to others. It is my greatest wish that it will speak to those that read it and hopefully prevent anything of this nature ever happening again.
Thank you for reading and travelling with me some way on my journey on a road much less travelled."

With love

Audrey Revell

ISBN 141209410-0